A PRACTICAL COURSE IN TERMINOLOGY PROCESSING

A PRACTICAL COURSE
IN TERMINOLOGY PROCESSING

JUAN C. SAGER

with a bibliography by
BLAISE NKWENTI-AZEH

JOHN BENJAMINS PUBLISHING COMPANY
AMSTERDAM/PHILADELPHIA

1990

Library of Congress Cataloging in Publication Data

Sager, Juan C.
A practical course in terminology processing / Juan C. Sager : with a bibliography by
Blaise Nkwenti-Azeh.
    p.   cm.
1. Terms and phrases. 2. Informations storge and retrieval systems -- Terms and
phrases. 3. Terms and phrases -- Data processing. I. Title.
P305.S24   1990
410'.285 -- dc20   90-1018
                                                          CIP

ISBN 90 272 2076 (hb) / 90 272 20778 (pb) (Eur., alk. paper)
ISBN 1-55619-112-X (hb) / 1-55619-113-8 (pb) (US, alk. paper)

ACKNOWLEDGEMENTS

This book is the result of many years of teaching terminology, of involvement in national and international standardisation committees, and of studies and design of termbanks. My experience in this field therefore has been acquired largely through interaction with many colleagues and students who will recognise their own contribution to my education and the presentation of the subject in the text.

I am particularly indebted to the late Eugen Wüster who started me thinking about terminology, Rod Johnson who helped me formulate a number of models, John McNaught who contributed to the term bank survey and design, Bruno de Bessé who has many years of theoretical and practical experience and especially Richard Candeland who designed the British Term Bank demonstrator model and the relational database model presented in chapter six.

I also want to thank my former students Mike Hann, Jeanette Pugh, Blaise Nkwenti Azeh, Colin Hope, Kyriaki Tsohatzi-Folina, Sam Massudi, Lisa Price, Catherine Yarker and many others who showed an interest in terminology and provided numerous examples, wrote outstanding dissertations and theses on specific issues summarised here and whose observations obliged me to think again on many topics.

CONTENTS

CHAPTER THREE: THE LINGUISTIC DIMENSION

CHAPTER FOUR: THE COMMUNICATIVE DIMENSION

CHAPTER FIVE: COMPILATION OF TERMINOLOGY

CHAPTER SIX: STORAGE OF TERMINOLOGY

CHAPTER SEVEN: RETRIEVAL OF TERMINOLOGY

CHAPTER EIGHT: USAGE OF TERMINOLOGY

Chapter One

INTRODUCTION
WHAT IS TERMINOLOGY?

1.1 A new field of enquiry and activity

Though concern with terminology can be traced back to the earliest semanticians, only in the twentieth century has a claim been made for terminology as an independent discipline. This claim rests on a dual foundation: the observation that an original theoretical framework has been developed to deal with the phenomena of designation in special languages, and the fact that in the field of communication terminology is considered a self-contained area of application.

This book denies the independent status of terminology as a discipline but affirms its value as a subject in almost every contemporary teaching programme. There is no substantial body of literature which could support the proclamation of terminology as a separate discipline and there is not likely to be. Everything of import that can be said about terminology is more appropriately said in the context of linguistics or information science or computational linguistics. We see terminology as a number of practices that have evolved around the creation of terms, their collection and explication and finally their presentation in various printed and electronic media. Practices, however well-established, do not constitute a discipline, but there is no denying a long history of methodologies which themselves require theoretical underpinnings to justify their distinctive nature. Disciplines establish knowledge about things and as such are justified in their own right; methodologies are only means to an end, in the case of terminology, how to do things.

The need for a methodology of terminological data processing has grown largely in response to the information explosion which led to increased concern with appropriate designations for the many new concepts created, especially in science and technology, and to a strong interest in effective international communication. After being the exclusive domain of a few theoreticians and diverse subject specialists for many decades, terminological practice was

forged into a coherent methodology with appropriate supporting theories by
the persistent efforts of a small group of academics and practitioners. Once
such a body of knowledge had been assembled which scholars could agree
upon to have its own theoretical foundation, objectives and methodology, it
could be described as a subject field and taught to postgraduate and undergraduate students. Courses in terminology are now being offered in a number
of European and American universities without, however, as yet the support
of adequate textbooks. The present volume proposes to fill this gap for the
English language.

1.2 Definition

Terminology has many ancestors, is related to many disciplines and is of practical concern to all students of special subjects and languages. It is, therefore,
appropriate at this stage of its emancipation as an independent practice and
field of study to delimit it and to relate it to the disciplines in which it finds
application.

Although essentially linguistic and semantic in its roots, terminology found
a more recent motivation in the broad field of communication studies, which
may be described as a modern extension of the mediaeval trivium of logic,
grammar and rhetoric. With this orientation terminology can claim to be truly
interdisciplinary. It is vital to the functioning of all sciences, it is concerned
with designations in all other subject fields, and it is closely related to a number
of specific disciplines, as already pointed out by its most distinguished modern
protagonist, E. Wüster. He called it an interdisciplinary field of study, relating
linguistics, logic, ontology and information science with the various subject
fields. The common element among these disciplines is that they are each
concerned, at least in part, with the formal organisation of the complex relationships between concepts and terms.

Since terminology is concerned with concepts, their definitions and names,
it is only appropriate to begin a discussion with a formal definition of the
subject.

Terminology is the study of and the field of activity concerned with the
collection, description, processing and presentation of terms, i.e. lexical items
belonging to specialised areas of usage of one or more languages. In its objectives it is akin to lexicography which combines the double aim of generally
collecting data about the lexicon of a language with providing an information,
and sometimes even an advisory, service to language users. The justification

of considering it a separate activity from lexicography lies in the different nature of the data traditionally assembled, the different background of the people involved in this work, and to some extent in the different methods used.

Etymologically speaking 'terminology' is a polysemous misnomer, i.e. a word with several senses, none of which correspond precisely to the analysis of the traditional meaning of its constituent elements.

By its etymology 'terminology' would mean 'the science/study/knowledge of terms' which would make it parallel to lexicology, the science/study/knowledge of the lexicon or lexical items; this interpretation is, however, rejected by most terminologists. Historically, the first usage of 'terminology' is recorded as referring to a technical vocabulary, i.e. a collection of terms, which has a certain coherence by the fact that the terms belong to a single subject area. It is now also used somewhat more narrowly to refer to an internally consistent and coherent set of terms belonging to a single subject field, as identified by the result of a particular terminological activity, e.g. the compilation of systematic glossaries. In contemporary usage it is necessary to distinguish three meanings of the word:

1. the activity defined in the first paragraph, i.e. the set of practices and methods used for the collection, description and presentation of terms;
2. a theory, i.e. the set of premises, arguments and conclusions required for explaining the relationships between concepts and terms which are fundamental for a coherent activity under 1;
3. a vocabulary of a special subject field.

In its first two meanings the word is a non-countable noun; in its third it is countable and can have a plural form.

1.3 Terminology and related disciplines

Like any other methodology, terminology is also influenced by the subject fields and areas of activity it serves; it has therefore been described as an interdisciplinary activity rather than a subject in its own right. It is distinct from general linguistics in that it has its own theories of the lexicon of a language and its particular methodology founded on these theories. (These are presented in chapters two and three of this book). These theories, like any other human experience, are influenced, however, by discoveries, views and developments that occur simultaneously in other areas of knowledge. Different compartmentalisations of knowledge also lead to shifts in the perception of terminology. Recently, for example, applied linguistics in its concern with the analysis and teaching of special subject languages—frequently called LSP— has laid claim to terminology as that part of linguistics which describes the lexicon of special languages. Because terminology has a need for a subject classification and has used the concept of thesaural structure it has been linked with information science. There is little to be gained from exploring such links and less in subsequent attribution of percentages of interdisciplinary connections. The concepts and methods terminology genuinely borrows from other subject fields and disciplines are of a rather general nature. From philosophy and epistemology it has taken theories about the structure of knowledge, concept formation, the nature of definitions, etc.; from psychology it has borrowed theories of perception, understanding and communication, etc.; from linguistics it has borrowed theories about the lexicon and its structure and formation; with lexicography, finally, it shares methods of structuring and describing words as well as experience about the presentation of information about words.

This wider connection of terminology is reflected in the definition given by the International Association of Terminology in 1982:

> 'Terminology is concerned with the study and use of the systems of symbols and linguistic signs employed for human communication in specialised areas of knowledge and activities. It is primarily a linguistic discipline—linguistics being interpreted here in its widest possible sense—with emphasis on semantics (systems of meanings and concepts) and pragmatics. It is inter-disciplinary in the sense that it also borrows concepts and methods from semiotics, epistemology, classification, etc. It is closely linked to the subject fields whose lexica it describes and for which it seeks to provide assistance in the ordering and use of designations. Although terminology has been in the past mostly concerned with the lexical aspects of specialised languages, its scope extends to syntax and phonology. In its applied aspect terminology is related to lexicography and uses techniques of information science and technology.'

This definition, though formulated comprehensively in order to reconcile the many diverse views on the subject, has nevertheless given rise to considerable discussion and controversy.

Terminology is now associated generally with the provision of information services which require the collection of information about terms in order to compile dictionaries and glossaries and more recently entries in term banks. In this sense terminology has undergone a radical change in recent years. Until database technology became available, dictionary and glossary production was like that of any other book production: pen and paper or typewriter and eventually printing. Now terminology collection and processing is a semi-automatic process, constantly responding to innovations borrowed from information technology, information science and computational linguistics. The principles and methods of terminology processing, therefore, must be understood as the current state of the art in this field; they do not claim a wider validity, even though some are likely to prove of a more permanent nature. Methods of work are also influenced by the special subject matter and the traditions and practices that exist in each area. The international nature of a great deal of biological and medical nomenclature, for example, has determined what type of terminology processing can usefully be undertaken.

There has also been a shift in the type of people working in terminology. Until recently terminology collection and processing was almost exclusively carried out by subject specialists working in their own fields and little contact existed between them. The development of term banks was accompanied by the creation of a substantial group of professionals who could be identified as practical terminologists. Once such a professional group is created there is then an incentive and an opportunity of harmonisation of procedures and techniques.

Lastly, considerable influence has been exercised by standardisation bodies who for several decades have been engaged in efforts to achieve the greatest possible agreement in matters of terminology processing. A number of countries, notably in Europe, have developed guidelines for the formation, definition and representation of technical concepts and some have even attempted to produce fundamental documents which set out the theoretical foundation of their work. This type of activity is, however, heavily language and culture dependent; it is, therefore, not surprising that little international progress has been made in developing standardised internationally applicable guidelines for the processing of terminology.

1.3.1 *Terminology and Information Science*

Terminology exhibits a number of striking similarities with information science, a subject of similar age, which has undergone a parallel process of searching for its identity.

Both can be called applicable sciences; the distinction between pure or theoretical and applied science we use for such disciplines as linguistics or physics, cannot be used here since in terminology as well as in information science theories are evolved with a view to applications only.

Both fields are relatively young and are still expanding their theoretical foundations and the scope of their application, notably within a common theory of communication, as evidenced by the regular colloquia on fundamental questions of terminology organised principally by Canada during the last decade.

Both initially took a pragmatic attitude to their work with a view to solving communication problems, in the one case by the content analysis of documents, and in the other by the description and standardisation of term formation processes. Both are, therefore, heavily dependent on empirical evidence such as usage, user needs and preferences, and are, therefore, responsive to the requirements of society. From a concern with communication in science and technology, they are now expanding into other fields, e.g. the social sciences, and other levels of communication.

Both serve the purpose of facilitating communication in special languages. The collection, structuring and organisation of information on the words, terms and expressions needed in special communication are merely the logical extension of the collection, structuring and organisation of entire texts or their bibliographic references by information scientists. Bibliographic databases are concerned with improving access to a regular flow of new information; terminological databases are concerned with improving the comprehension and expression of this information, i.e. with effective communication. They are thus necessary precursors of bibliographic databases, and, moreover, should exist alongside them in a supportive and complementary function.

There are obvious overlaps between the many professions concerned with collecting, analysing, supplying and mediating specialised information and the distinction may be said to lie between the macro or micro approach to texts: information science being concerned with texts and their constituents, terminology with concepts and their representation, the overlap occurring in such common tools as keywords, indexes and thesauri. Indexers and abstractors, for instance, use terminology in the same way as special lexicographers. Both groups of professionals are ultimately concerned with aids to communication and therefore provide services directly or indirectly to the scientific community. Information scientists are, however, frequently active in the mediating process itself, whereas in terminology the end user is expected to communicate on his own, and independently use the result of the work of the terminologists.

Even the approach to language exhibits clear similarities: terminologists and information scientists subject language to processes of regularisation, unification and standardisation in the interest of greater effectiveness of communication. In this process functionally restricted sub-languages may be created, either as information or documentation languages or as special languages of particular disciplines. The language of a classification scheme, though different in function and structure, exhibits similar characteristics as, for instance, the language of chemical formulae in that both are supranational, independent of any particular natural language, and artificial to the extent that they cannot be their own metalanguage.

Even with regard to the technical support needed there are close similarities. Only in recent years, with the availability of more flexible and cheaper computer power, have both fields been able to fully benefit from new information technology. Both need direct access to relatively large storage facilities and study data compaction for even greater efficiency. Database technology and networking are equally important to information science and terminology as are many software requirements and the demand for user-friendly storage and retrieval environments. It is in computational methods that both sciences are likely to benefit most directly from each other. Automatic keyword extraction is in principle the same process as automatic term recognition and many data handling routines in storage and retrieval have more common than divergent features, so that the intellectual effort spent on programming for one purpose can be utilised for the other. Terminology can thus benefit from advances in computer applications in information science and owes a particular debt of gratitude to Information Science for having initiated the formulation of an international standard concerned with an exchange format for terminological data. The considerable work involved in the construction of terminological thesauri can serve as preparatory work for the narrower conception of documentation thesauri, which, in fact, in-one of their functions, are translation dictionaries from the special language into the system-related information language.

Information Science and Terminology thus benefit from close collaboration as both pursue the same broad objectives and serve the same group of users. In general, a greater understanding of the paradigmatic units of special subject languages is of considerable advantage to information science. The practical objectives of terminology, i.e. to achieve greater unity, consistency and clarity of expression in special communication would greatly simplify the work of information scientists. Both are in their own way concerned with language planning; success in special language planning carried out by terminologists facilitates the work of indexers, abstractors, reviewers and translators and reduces the task of information language planning and the divergence of information languages from special subject languages.

1.4   Theoretical premises

The early stages of terminological theory in this century were dominated by engineers and scientists who felt a need to regulate the large quantity of new designations that accompanied the rapid evolution of science and technology. Institutionally this work was supported by associations of engineers and national standardisation organisations which wanted clear directions for the drafting of technical standards where diversity of terminology was undesirable. This work also coincided with the establishment of nomenclature commissions and the expansion of their activities in appropriate fields of the taxonomic sciences. The formulation of principles of naming technical concepts and similar work was furthermore only oriented towards the industrially advanced countries during the first half of the 20th century and their languages and assumed a target group of engineers and scientists who accepted Greek and Latin word elements as the most suitable means of developing systematic patterns of terminology. Since the purpose of a terminological theory was to justify the idealisation of linguistic facts and the prescription of 'good usage' in what amounted to an artificial language, it was consequently perceived as lying outside the concern of natural language and linguistics. This simplistic view is now challenged as a result of several independent developments:

– Linguistics itself has moved from a historical and prescriptive to a contemporary and descriptive approach. In the process the considerable diversity of designations and variants is being acknowledged and has to be accounted for.
– Linguistics has taken an interest in special language vocabulary and now claims terminology as simply another dimension of lexicology and lexicography.
– More recently, sociolinguistics and pragmatics have devoted attention to subsets of language and the conditions of their production and use and this has led to a more realistic appreciation of the diversity of linguistic forms.
– Non-European language communities challenge the European conceptions of term-formation patterns and resources and even of the Greek and Latin basis proposed for the unification of terminological forms.
– Large-scale language planning activities provide genuine experience which has to be accounted for in a theory of terminology.

At the same time the rapid evolution of natural language processing techniques has permitted the collection of experimental data which can be used to test, support or modify any theory of terminology.

1.5 Requirements of an applied field of study

In order to justify its independent nature as an applied field of study, terminology is conveniently approached from the point of view of its function, i.e. the provision of an information service. Seen from this angle, it is the users of terminological services who, to a large extent, determine the nature of the discipline by specifying what information about terms they want and the price they are willing to pay for it. From a needs analysis, the terminologist can then decide how to structure a database for his users, but he will also be influenced in his design by the nature of the data he has to collect and the methods by which they can be collected and represented. This approach characterises term banks which have evolved in response to particular user needs and which have been very eclectic in their resort to theory.

A totally different approach may be taken by language planners who have to construct new technical vocabularies. For such work the word-formation patterns of the general language, i.e. lexicological considerations, are of primary importance, because a properly integrated technical vocabulary uses the same resources as the general language but in different proportions and with different functions. Language planners are also interested in questions of efficiency of communication and can therefore look for support to psycholinguistics and communication theory. They may see a theory of terminology as being strongly influenced by pragmatics.

1.6 Conflicts between theory and practice

Theoretical considerations have in the past largely centred around the definition of concepts, relationships between concepts, their definitions and the appropriateness of designations. Differences arose according to whether a philosophical or a linguistic approach was chosen and secondly according to which linguistic theory was given preference. A great deal of attention has also been devoted to the structure of conceptual systems and the best way of representing them on paper. In this area in particular, conventional thinking is still largely dominated by pen and paper processing techniques and by the relatively simple relationships that suffice for structuring documentation thesauri and respond well to human attribution and processing.

Such topics, primarily of interest to theorists, have, however, found little echo in the discussion of the people directly concerned with terminology processing, notably in term banks. Here a totally different set of problems arises

—not without theoretical interest—that centres on the linguistic data with which term banks have to struggle every day. Here the problems of the distinction between variants, synonyms and quasi-synonyms loom large, and there is a major division between those who believe context to be relevant for the identification of usage and those who believe terms to be context independent. There is little, if any discussion of terminological relationships nor of their representation in term banks—such relationships are not yet widely introduced in large-scale working systems; instead there is concern about the absence of a generally acceptable subject classification scheme which theorists have so far failed to provide.

In recent years little new theoretical work is being produced that can be considered to be relevant to the applied nature of terminology. The major impetus in thinking is currently being provided by computational linguistics which is open to developments in theoretical linguistics, lexicography, computation and information science and can therefore stimulate progress in the applied field of terminology. The computational linguistic approach to language phenomena is currently producing a wide range of new linguistic theories which will have to be explored in due course for their value to terminology.

Besides, the theories underlying applied fields of study benefit from being application-driven rather than following separate paths as terminological theory has been doing in recent years. By adopting the engineering approach of identifying problems and seeking solutions, significant advances have been made which can then be examined for their model character for other problem situations. In this way theoretical insights can be gained from observation, modelling and generalisation which are more likely to be relevant to the applied nature of the subject.

1.7 The purpose and structure of this book

In its intended readership this book follows the two broad meanings commonly given to terminology.

Terminology as specialised vocabulary concerns every user of language and is part of our cognitive development. Particular terminologies are important to specialist education, and an understanding of the structure of terminologies and the relevant reference tools is important to people who are professionally concerned with communication, e.g. technical authors, editors, abstractors, information brokers, information scientists and librarians.

Processing of terminology is a specialist task in a wide range of occupations. Every specialist group concerned with the preservation of its language has its terminologists. In the past, keeping a wordstock for a specialist group of language users was an onerous task that few people had the ability or the dedication to pursue systematically. Since the advent of the computer, terminology management can be carried out by almost anyone who has learnt to use a microcomputer. The easier availability of terminology management tools has lead to a greater interest in systematic collection and consultation of terminology by both the general public and specialist mediators. At the same time the design and production of management programs for terminology has become a specialist aspect of computational linguistics.

Only a basic knowledge of linguistic theory, computational linguistics and information science is assumed of the reader.

The content of the book divides into eight chapters. After this introduction, chapter 2 presents the theoretical foundation of terminology in four sections. The first outlines a theory of reference which permits the distinction between terms and words, a division which is essential for separating terminology from lexicology. The other three sections present a theory of concepts, conceptual relationships and definitions. Mindful of the applied orientation of this book it does, however, examine these theoretical questions in the light of actual terminology processing.

Chapter 3 presents the specifically linguistic dimension of terminology. Its separate sections cover a theory of terms, term formation in theory and practice and the special cases of nomenclatures, which have their own motivation and rules of formation.

Chapter 4 places terminology firmly in the field of communication. A model of communication is developed which accounts for the use of terms. The next section examines approaches to terminology as an applied subject and especially the measurement of efficacy of terminology in communication. The last section deals with prescriptive aspects of terminology. It describes the many agencies and bodies, national and international, concerned with regulating usage of terminology and critically examines the merits and disadvantages of standardisation.

Chapters 5–7 link terminology with information science and computational linguistics. They represent the three phases of terminology processing: compilation in chapter 5, storage in chapter 6 and retrieval in chapter 7. It is firmly accepted that all terminology processing is now computer-based and there is, therefore, no reference to conventional methods.

Chapter 8 discusses the usage of terminology, attitudes and practices currently in existence, with particular attention to the growth and development of terminology and major terminology processing activities. This chapter must be considered open-ended since it is impossible to capture at any one moment the rapidly changing scene in terminology production and processing.

Chapter Two

THE COGNITIVE DIMENSION

Since it is semantically-based, terminology can be studied from three different points of view, i.e. from the point of view of the referent, from the point of view of the designation given the referent, and finally from the point of view of the use the equation of referent and designation can be put to. Consequently we identify three dimensions of a theory of terminology:

– a cognitive one which relates the linguistic forms to their conceptual content, i.e. the referents in the real world;
– a linguistic one which examines the existing and potential forms of the representation of terminologies;
– a communicative one which looks at the use of terminologies and has to justify the human activity of terminology compilation and processing.

In this chapter we consider the cognitive dimension.

Since terminology is concerned with the language used in special subject fields, this presupposes a division of language into as many special sublanguages as there are separate subject fields or areas of knowledge and activity in a given linguistic community. From the point of view of terminology, therefore, the lexicon of a language consists of the many separate subsystems representing the knowledge structure of each subject field or discipline. Each knowledge structure consists of variously interlinked concepts. Approaching the study of terminology from its cognitive dimension requires an understanding of the structure of knowledge in order to obtain as complete and coherent a picture of the nature, behaviour and interaction of concepts and their associated terms as possible.

Knowledge structures are not absolute entities but reflect the current state of knowledge of an individual or a group of specialists. In their effort of determining the terms relevant to a subject, terminologists start from the analysis of limited domains of knowledge and build up complex systems of concepts which eventually intersect and overlap. A characteristic feature of this work is the difficulty of fixing the structure of knowledge at any one time because conceptual systems are relatively fluid entities constantly undergoing change, especially in the research and development of innovative science and technology. Consequently the terminologist has to be a subject specialist himself or have very close contacts with subject specialists in order to keep track of innovation in concepts and terminology respectively.

Chapter 2 describes those elements which are considered essential to a cognitive foundation of terminology. It examines the case for a separate identity of terminology from lexicology and lexicography and describes the three fundamental notions of conventional terminological theory, concepts, definitions and the relationships between concepts and definitions.

2.1 A theory of reference

Concepts are elements of the structure of knowledge and as such have an important place in the philosophy of science and in theories of cognition. Terminology is concerned with concepts and hence knowledge structures only to the extent to which they are represented in the lexicon of a language. A theory of terminology is therefore primarily concerned with a referential system which relates knowledge structures to lexical structure and defines the constituent elements of each type of structure.

An important part of a theory of reference is a set of principles for classifying language items, not on the basis of their overt formal properties, as, for example, in an alphabetical dictionary, but according to the properties of the concepts to which they refer. Determination of the properties of these concepts by means of definitions and other techniques of classification is especially important in any overt effort at fixing the meanings of technical or scientific terms as, for example, in terminological standardisation. As Wüster (1955) pointed out 'it is impossible to standardize terms in any useful way without previously or at the same time having systematized all the relevant concepts'. This principle has also been acknowledged by the standardising organisations. BS 3669 (1963) paragraph 5a states: 'Before a technical term can be adopted it is necessary first to clarify and then to define the concept for which the term is to stand'. A similar principle is expressed in ISO Recommendation R 704:1968. Accordingly, the question of reference is approached by first proposing a model of knowledge which permits us to describe, relate and classify concepts.

2.1.1 *A model of knowledge*

The model of knowledge required for this purpose need only be concerned with knowledge designated by lexical means; in principle, therefore, this model need do no more than formalise some of the principles of conceptual organisation implicit in componential analysis, semantic field theory and lexical taxonomy. The model is conceived as a multidimensional space in which intersecting axes represent some kind of conceptual primitives or characteristics. They may also be seen as features or components. A concept, i.e. a unit of knowledge, can be represented and identified uniquely by references to its coordinates along each axis. Listing the values of a concept with respect to each axis, component or feature is equivalent to defining its position in the knowledge space. Alternatively it is possible to think in terms of fields or classes, with items belonging to the same class clustering together in the same subspace. The structure which we need to impose on the space in order to be able to represent areas of knowledge is generally acknowledged to be one of interdependence. We assume a certain degree of dependency between dimensions—e.g. the characteristic 'human' may limit our freedom of attribution of other primitive characteristics by precluding a simultaneous characteristic 'animal'. Some structures may be conceived as hierarchical, so that 'human' may imply 'living'. Consequently, there are likely to be considerably fewer degrees of freedom than primitives, so that the space will be inherently redundant. Since, however, this very redundancy is a consequence of the admission of structured concepts, it is easy to see that it becomes possible to represent taxonomies, intersections, relationships and dependencies between concepts and groups of concepts. The conventional tree model is in fact equivalent to an elementary subspace of this model. A further consequence of this type of model is that it allows us to handle the distribution of concepts along a continuum (or continua), as well as to represent variations in the conceptual 'distance' between items without affecting the relational structure (i.e. by changes of scale along one or more axes).

In general, each axis in the space represents a continuous valued feature and therefore defines an infinity of point values which the feature can assume. But if we allow each concept to occupy a single point in the space, we must allow for the existence of an infinite number of concepts, even in the most restricted subspace of knowledge. Since, however, most transmission of knowledge uses the discrete medium of language, we have become accustomed to accepting the constraints of approximation imposed by linguistic communication. We therefore postulate that the value of a concept with respect to a given axis is generally defined as a range and only exceptionally (as, for example, in the case of discrete valued features like 'quadruped') as a point. A concept must therefore normally be considered as occupying a region or a set of points in space and not a single point.

Changes in the structure of knowledge, may occur in one of two ways:

1. by augmentation: a new axis, defining either a new criterion for classification or a new feature, is added to the structure; all other existing concepts may then need to be redefined relative to the new axis; in a real sense, as it were, a new dimension is added to our thinking;
2. by modification: the dimensionality of the space is unaltered but we acquire a new way of 'looking at things' within the existing system, changing the relative configuration of items by increasing or decreasing the degree of available differentiation along a given axis or in some other way disturbing the spatial relationship of one concept to another.

2.1.2 *Subject disciplines*

In practice no individual or group of individuals possesses the whole structure of a community's knowledge; conventionally, we divide knowledge up into subject areas, or disciplines, which is equivalent to defining subspaces of the knowledge space.

Just as different disciplines overlap, so subject spaces intersect, although dimensionality and the relative configuration of items will vary from subspace to subspace. To cite a practical instance, the substance known as ferric chloride, $FeCl_3$, is represented by one concept in Electronics, where it is used for printed circuit boards, and by another concept in Textile Technology, where it is used as a mordant.

2.1.3 *The social norm*

All human beings possess the capacity for acquiring and using knowledge, a faculty comparable to the language competence of generative theory. In the framework of our model, human beings have the potential for enlarging the dimensionality of their knowledge and for modifying the configuration of elements within it. They are also aware, to a greater or lesser degree, of the configurational properties of a number of disciplinary subspaces, up to the limiting case of the leading experts in a discipline who, by their research, may themselves contribute to the determination of the boundaries and internal structure of the corresponding subspace.

Given the principle of continuous axes, expressed above, it is unlikely that any two individuals, though their states of knowledge might be said to be comparable, will assign precisely the same configuration of knowledge space to the 'same' concept. The fact that people do, or seem to, agree on designation must be attributed to the existence of an idealised and pragmatic knowledge structure pertaining to the community and to its specialist disciplines. This idealised knowledge structure is determined by the social norm, to which all individual knowledge tends. The norm represents a synthesis of the collective view of the community, tacitly endorsed by its members, and determines, on a supraindividual level, not only the region occupied by any given concept but also the bounds of disciplinary subspaces and the configuration of concepts within a discipline. The chances that the knowledge structure of any individual will actually correspond exactly to the social norm—or to that of any other individual for that matter—are very small. In extreme cases, when a configuration of concepts within a subspace in the knowledge of an individual differs radically from the norm, we can say that that section of the individual's knowledge is false or unorthodox with respect to the rest of the community.

2.1.4 *Knowledge and reference*

Knowledge can only be transmitted by physical communication and the primary medium of communication is language. Given that the number of elements in the lexicon of a given language must be denumerable, language manifests itself as a sequence of discrete segments, in contrast to the structure of concepts which is conceived as essentially continuous. Reference is thus, in the proposed model of knowledge, a function which maps a discrete and denumerable repertory of symbols, the lexicon, into the continuous knowledge space. The reference of each lexical item then has as its image a region of knowledge space whose bounds may vary between individuals although the range of possible variation may be to a greater or lesser extent restricted by the social norm. As a result, any internal structure which may exist over the knowledge space is automatically transferred to the lexicon, but only by virtue of the relationship which holds between each single discrete lexical entry and the totality of points which constitute the corresponding region of knowledge. It is important not to confuse lexical form with lexical substance; substance may have an intrinsic structure, for instance, the conventional ordering of letters of the alphabet in graphic substance, but its relationship to the structure of knowledge is in general quite arbitrary. Linguistic symbols are not items of knowledge, except in the trivial sense that we are able to memorise their form; they are merely labels through which we can refer to knowledge.

Since lexical items are discrete entities, it is relatively simple to agree on a fixed form for any one item; it is far more difficult to specify its substance, i.e. the bounds of the region to which it refers. To exemplify this point, the distinction between form and substance is also important on the level of linguistic realisation: only the 'written form' of a lexical item can be fixed; its phonic substance is realised in a continuum. Whilst the social norm represents a tacit agreement on the bounds of a concept, the individual is nonetheless free to interpret the social norm in the light of the structure of the totality of his own beliefs. Perhaps in consequence of this, a greater or lesser degree of flexibility may attach to the determination of bounds under the social norm, depending on the extent to which empirical evidence is generally available or brought to bear, to support a convergence of opinion within the community. This flexibility which permits individual variation has important consequences for communication, since the participants involved may each use the same lexical item, fixed in form by the social norm, but with reference to subtly different regions of their own knowledge space, each of which may individually represent only partially the reference sanctioned by the social norm. In semantic theory these distinctions are discussed under the notions of intended, effective and conventional meaning.

2.1.5 *Special subject languages*

Within any given language, a wide range of phonological, grammatical and lexical variation is available, but, within the range of possible variation, the social norm operates to determine criteria for the selection of codes, whose phonological, grammatical and lexical properties may be functions of the situation in which communication takes place. In general, diversification at the levels of phonology and grammar is most evident in regional and social variation and is therefore of marginal interest for terminology. Variation on the lexical level is most characteristic of special subject languages, the linguistic subsystem selected by an individual whose discourse is to be centred on a particular subject field.

Within a subject field, some or all of the included dimensions may assume increased importance, with a greater need for distinction between a larger number of concepts along a given axis: at the same time, the necessity to avoid overlap between concepts, i.e. intersecting regions, will tend to reduce the degree of flexibility admissible in the delimitation of the bounds of any given concept. There is thus a difference of degree between the intradisciplinary structure of concepts in the bounded subspace of a special subject or discipline and the less well-defined, less 'disciplined' structure of 'general knowledge'. This does not mean that general knowledge cannot contain well-defined facts; but only that disciplines have a greater need for more rigorous constraints on the overall delineation of items of knowledge. The referential function at the extremes of this distinction is classified as 'special reference' and 'general reference' respectively.

2.1.6 *Words, terms and standardised terms*

The lexicon of a special subject language reflects the organisational characteristics of the discipline by tending to provide as many lexical units as there are concepts conventionally established in the subspace and by restricting the reference of each such lexical unit to a well-defined region. Beside containing a large number of items which are endowed with the property of special reference the lexicon of a special language also contains items of general reference which do not usually seem to be specific to any discipline or disciplines and whose referential properties are uniformly vague or generalised. The items which are characterised by special reference within a discipline are the 'terms' of that discipline, and collectively they form its 'terminology'; those which function in general reference over a variety of sublanguages are simply called 'words', and their totality the 'vocabulary'.

Since the number of lexical elements in a language is finite, some items may have to do double duty, so that words may be pressed into service as terms in particular special languages (e.g. 'noise' in communication theory). Although such items may be indistinguishable in their substantive realisation, so that 'noise' the term and 'noise' the word look and sound the same, it might turn out to be convenient to classify them as distinct forms. For example, the general reference of the word 'lion' may involve the attributes 'fierce, proud, aggressive, majestic, heraldic', etc., but in special language the 'lion' is, for example, either heraldic or a genus of the species felis, but not both. The same item, e.g. 'entropy' may function as a different term in different languages. In general reference, if a particular attribute is to be emphasised, the emphasis must be achieved by contextual contiguity, syntactic devices, additional reference, etc., but in special language the emphasis is already present through prior delineation of the subspace, which effectively excludes all attributes (dimensions) which are not assigned by the social norm to the discipline. While we can specify 'gale force 9' it is impossible to qualify this further by saying, e.g. 'strong gale force 9'.

Terms can, of course, only be used as such if the user already possesses the configuration of knowledge which determines the role of the term in a structured system. The limiting case of this restriction is the requirement that a new term be learned contemporaneously with new knowledge, e.g. through text books; a term acquired without awareness of the conventional configuration of knowledge to which it relates is communicatively useless. On the other hand, by the nature of disciplines, the number of individuals in possession of the requisite knowledge is relatively small, so that consensus on the specification of bounds for concepts is relatively easy to achieve. In particular, it is sometimes possible to codify very strict specifications together with a recommended term, and to seek to achieve agreement on the part of all users to use that term with the specified fixed reference. In this case, the social norm is refined down to the norm of a small group, which can then make a deliberate attempt to impose uniformity of usage, by publicly fixing the relationship between the term and the associated concept and proposing the term as a standard.

We are accustomed to think of standards as strictly inflexible, with absolute uniformity of reference from term to concept. In effect, absolute uniformity is not always feasible, and its achievement can depend as much on the conceptual properties of the discipline as on the goodwill and good intentions of users. A standard is by definition published and publicly available, and for the codification of standards we must rely largely on language. But a standardised term, even more than a term, only has validity if both aspects of reference, the term and the concept, are both specifiable and specified. The problem arises as soon as it becomes necessary to specify the bounds of a concept through language; absolute specification is then only possible through use of other standard terms which themselves have already been specified absolutely. Ultimately, the only specification which is not language-dependent has to be made through direct empirical observation, i.e. through diagrams, photographs or the use of objective measuring instruments calibrated to a suitably fine degree of approximation. We should therefore distinguish between two types of standard: pure standards, which refer to concepts ultimately describable through actual non-linguist experience and observation; and pseudo-standards, which refer to concepts which are only describable in language, implying ultimate circularity of reference. That the distinction is felt to be present is clear from examination of published standards, among which terms from the physical sciences and technologies, codifiable as pure standards, predominate.

2.2 A theory of concepts

Because of its applied orientation terminology is not concerned with the philosophical or psychological aspects of concepts. A theory of concepts for terminology in essence only has to provide an adequate explanation for cognitive motivations in term formation and to provide the basis for structuring vocabularies in a more effective way than is offered by alphabetical ordering. The theoretical basis outlined in this section is therefore highly selective and claims validity only to the extent that it satisfactorily explains phenomena and patterns of terms as seen from the focus of terminological practice.

A theory of terminology is usually considered as having three basic tasks: it has to account for sets of concepts as discrete entities of the knowledge structure; it has to account for sets of interrelated linguistic entities which are somehow associated with concepts grouped and structured according to cognitive principles; it has, lastly, to establish a link between concepts and terms, which is traditionally done by definitions.

Through the activity of definition we fix the precise reference of a term to a concept, albeit by linguistic means only; at the same time it creates and thereby declares relationships to other concepts inside a knowledge structure. By means of the linguistic form of the terms we operate with concepts both for communicating with others and for formulating our own thoughts, an activity frequently referred to as the ideational function of language. We expand the knowledge structure of a subject field by the addition of new concepts for which we have to create linguistic forms before they can be used in special subject discourse.

Seen from an applied point of view these three tasks are also required in the normal exploration of a subject field for the purpose of teaching and learning or indeed for the compilation of such teaching and learning aids as dictionaries. The concept has to be placed into its knowledge structure which delimits and confines it, it has to be named so that we can clearly refer to it, and it has to be defined as an act of clarification, confirmation or fixation of an item of knowledge. For practical applications we are again faced with these three approaches. The terminologist describes the concepts of any one discipline in three ways: by definition, by their relationship to other concepts— as expressed by the conceptual structure and realised in linguistic forms—and by the linguistic forms themselves, the terms, phrases or expressions chosen for their realisation in any one language.

2.2.1 *Concepts: definition*

The primary objects of terminology, the terms, are perceived as symbols which represent concepts. Concepts must therefore be created and come to exist before terms can be formed to represent them. In fact, the naming of a concept may be considered the first step in the consolidation of a concept as a socially useful or usable entity.

Our first approximation to a definition of 'concept' is indirect. By examining what we do with a concept, and the environment in which we use it, we arrive at a justification of its existence and its relative position to other concepts. In this way we gather information which can be used in the defining statement.

Concept formation is a process of variously grouping and ordering the material and immaterial objects which we sense, perceive or imagine into abstract categories. In a first stage of observation of our environment we identify a number of individual objects as having certain properties or characteristics in common. From the individual objects we have identified as having certain common features, we abstract some of these properties in order to arrive at types of objects; for example, we identify certain animals as having a number of common features which we group under the concept label 'cats', or we observe mechanisms which tell the time and find it convenient to group some of them under the label of 'clocks' and others under the label 'watches'. In a further stage of ordering, we may then group the already abstract types of objects into broader classes, e.g. group cats with dogs as animals, set up separate categories for domestic and wild animals, divide material objects into animate and inanimate ones, or combine hour-glasses, watches and clocks into timepieces. An important distinction is thus created between the individual objects of our sensation, perception and imagination and the abstract categories, i.e. the concepts which represent them. We therefore define concepts provisionally as 'constructs of human cognition processes which assist in the classification of objects by way of systematic or arbitrary abstraction'.

We can contrast this definition with various others formulated over the years by several committees concerned with standardisation of terminology and which therefore have a need and a desire for clear and unambiguous description of the basic components with which they operate.

– Concepts are mental constructs, abstractions which may be used in classifying the individual objects of the inner and outer world. (British Standard Recommendation for the selection, formation and definition of technical terms, BS.3669:1963)
– The objects of all fields of knowledge and human activity, such as things, their properties, qualities, phenomena, etc., are represented by concepts. (a UK proposal for the revision of ISO document R 704)
– A concept is a mental construct for classifying individual objects of the outer and inner world by means of a more or less arbitrary abstraction. (1968 draft version of ISO Standard 704)
– A concept is a unit of thought, produced by grouping of individual objects related by common characteristics. (draft of a German DIN document)
– A concept is a coherent group of judgements concerning an object whose nucleus is made up of those judgements which reflect the inherent characteristics of the object. (a Soviet-Union proposal for the revision of ISO document R 704)
– A concept is any unit of thought.

Notes:

1. A concept is used to structure the knowledge and perception of the surrounding world and need not be expressed.
2. Different schools of thought have different definitions of the concept 'concept'. (Final version of the Draft International Standard ISO/DIS 704, 1985.)

These definitions make explicit reference to mental activities either as a result or as a process and are therefore clearly mentalist in outlook, except for the ambiguously worded 'judgement' of the definition proposed by the Soviet Union. From this great diversity of definitions formulated with the same intention and purpose it is obvious that there is considerable divergence of opinion on the matter. In order to escape this initial difficulty we propose that for the applied purposes of terminology as conceived in this book, 'concept' be considered another axiomatic primitive, like 'word' or 'sentence', conveniently left undefined.

2.2.2 Characteristics

In the process of concept formation we group the data of our perception and experience according to common elements which are usually called characteristics. For example: the concept 'table' requires that we identify such characteristics as 'horizontal', 'flat surface', 'within a certain range of dimensions and proportions of dimensions', 'raised above the ground in a certain range of height which does not exceed approx. 1 meter'; these are necessary but not sufficient characteristics to distinguish what we understand to be 'tables' from e.g. 'chairs'. It is therefore necessary to add another characteristic which separates the concept of 'tables' from the concept of 'chairs' or any other which has the characteristics listed above. A functional characteristic will serve in this case, e.g. 'used for placing objects on, to perform work on, etc'.

The sufficient and necessary characteristics for identifying a concept are also called essential, in contrast to inessential ones which are observable in the individual object, e.g. the colour, material, number of legs of tables. Inessential characteristics in one scheme of concept creation may, however, become essential for the creation of other concepts. For example, the concepts 'side-table', 'coffee-table', 'dining table' are differentiated by more detailed characteristics of height and size than were relevant for the broader concept of 'table'; they are necessary, however, for a furniture catalogue.

Any observable or imaginable feature may be used as a characteristic. Very broad concepts, e.g. 'liquid', 'animal', 'vehicle', have relatively few characteristics and always fewer than the narrower concepts in the same group, e.g. 'milk', 'poodle', 'motor car', which are characterised by the fact that they are particular types of 'liquid', 'animal' or 'vehicle'. The sum of characteristics which constitute a concept are called its intension, i.e. a unique grouping of characteristics different from the nearest concept by at least one such characteristic. Concepts identified by many characteristics are said to have a narrow intension, i.e. their possibility of reference is limited to a small number of objects in the real world. In the extreme case a narrow intension identifies an individual and unique object.

The range of objects a concept refers to are called its extension. We speak of a broad concept as having a wide extension because it encompasses many types of objects in its scope of meaning. There is, however, still a difference between broad special subject concepts and general concepts without particular subject affiliation.

The scientific process provides a systematic approach to the selection of characteristics and concept formation. In chemistry, for example, new entities are named according to their constituent substances which are also the differentiating criteria for the characteristics. In engineering, products may be differentiated by sizes and shapes, e.g. 'screws'. The choice of characteristics for concepts of special subjects expressed as terms differs quantitatively and qualitatively from that made for general reference concepts.

Characteristics can be expressed as properties of the concept; they can also be expressed as relations to other concepts. The concepts belonging to the field of family relations, for example, can only be expressed by means of the relationships identified among the members of this group, e.g. 'cousin' or 'uncle'. In fact it can be argued that every characteristic refers to the class of concepts that possesses this characteristic, and which is a class by virtue of this common characteristic. For example, the characteristic of roundness places a ball and a balloon into the same class of round objects.

In the practice of creating conceptual fields, however, we rely on characteristics chosen for a particular systematic order. For example, the class of red objects is irrelevant in a conceptual system that associates 'letter boxes' (incidentally red in the UK) to other types of street furniture. Characteristics, such as being a product of a particular process, or being the raw material for a particular manufacturing process, are more commonly expressed as relationships between concepts; these are discussed in section 2.2.4.

2.2.3 *Types of concepts*

The conceptual structures of special subject fields are distinguished not only by special reference, as described in section 2.1, but also by the nature of the concepts which predominate in particular subjects. Just as material objects are ordered into classes for the formation of concepts, concepts themselves are ordered into classes such as physical entities (e.g. plants, minerals, chemical substances), scientific methods of analysis and description (e.g. the inductive method, the analytical method), properties relevant to established scientific and technological processes (e.g. measurements), and the many other concepts representing concrete or abstract entities, manufactured products, industrial processes and relevant properties which rely on a broad consensus among users for their definition. Some concepts have a very limited scope of application, e.g. a product definition in a list for custom tariffs. Normally a definition of such concepts can never be exhaustive but must be seen as being applicable to a concept in the specific field in which it has been identified. In other cases concepts have a wide area of application, to the extent that they are the object of different definitions in different branches of science.

There are four main methods by which concepts are structured:
– Concepts can be attributed to a class so that types of concepts are identified, e.g. 'Venus' is attributed to the class of planets; 'wisdom' is attributed to the class of virtues.

– Concepts can be grouped into categories as established by distinctive features of classes and groups of classes, e.g. according to common properties, as in 'quadrupeds = animals having four legs'; quadrupeds can be divided by the distinctive feature of 'being tamed for human use' into domestic and wild animals.

– Concepts and groups of concepts can be differentiated by a process of discrimination between categories and the establishment of relationships between them, e.g. tables, chairs, cupboards etc. are grouped together as 'furniture' but differentiated into 'household furniture', 'office furniture' etc.

– The interaction of categories of concepts can be effected at the level of functions, in order to relate states to changes of states; e.g.

> input – storage – retrieval
> process – product of process
> chemical reaction – chemical compound

By these methods we obtain concepts for classes, properties, relations and functions which vary from subject to subject and situation to situation, e.g.

> class concepts   : fastener, container, vehicle
> property concepts: strength, albino, visual
> relation concepts : sister, more, parallel
> function concepts: operate–operation, rub, friction

Because of the strong interdependence between language and concept formation it is usual to associate word classes with concept classes and speak of noun-concepts, adjectival concepts and verb-concepts. Alternatively it is common to consider all concepts to be conveniently represented by a single class, that of nouns, and to ignore the linguistic form at this level of analysis. In such a case the linguistic realisation of the concept is considered a function of its use. For example, such a view would permit the concept 'WHITE', which would then be linguistically realised as 'white', 'whiteness' and 'whiten'. This approach may be favoured by language groups that do not clearly distinguish word categories at the formal level, e.g. English, where a single linguistic form may function as noun, adjective or verb, e.g. the English, the English language, to English. It is however difficult not to be influenced by linguistic form altogether.

On the broadest of levels we can distinguish between such concept groups as

(a) ENTITIES, which we derive by abstraction from material or abstract objects;

(b) processes, operations and actions, here called ACTIVITIES, performed with, by or for entities;

(c) properties, dispositions, grouped under the name of QUALITIES, with which we differentiate among entities;

(d) RELATIONS that we wish to establish between any of the other three types of concepts. Relations are therefore themselves concepts.

There are various studies of a typology of concepts based on their linguistic forms, but since they are mainly concerned with general language, they are of little use for terminology. For the purposes of this textbook we can adopt the system of conceptual reference classes which systematically covers a wide range of concepts developed by Pugh (1984). Even though this system was originally conceived with specific reference to noun-compounds in the field of data-processing, it is of wider interest and application. The diagram below presents a structure of the entity concepts of the field of data processing. The first level of analysis appears to be of general validity; the second level, however, makes a subject-specific distinction which is confirmed by the definitions provided for each category. We conclude that at a more detailed level of analysis, different subject fields may require different types of substructures in order to account fully for the diversity of types of concepts with which they operate.

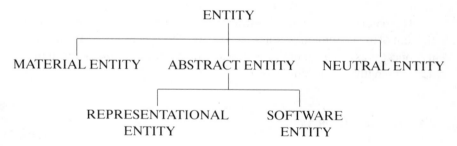

Definitions:

– MATERIAL ENTITY = an entity considered to have physical properties.
– NEUTRAL ENTITY = an isolable entity which is considered to be neutral with regard to the specific classes of material and abstract entity, e.g. unit, set, assembly, group.
– ABSTRACT ENTITY = a class of entities considered not to have physical properties.
– REPRESENTATIONAL ENTITY = an entity which represents information in a formalised, conventional manner and/or is used for the organisation or control of such formalised information, e.g. data, symbol, character.

– SOFTWARE ENTITY = an entity considered to pertain to software, e.g.
program, pause, instruction.

The definitions of the other types of concepts identified by Pugh appear to
have also a broader validity.

– ACTIVITY = an event or individual action or a set of actions regarded as
a repeatable collective activity, the performance of which requires time and
can be carried out by man and/or machine, e.g. data processing, corrective
maintenance, programming.
– QUALITY = a quality, property, condition or disposition attributable and/
or attributed to one or more concepts, which is not quantified in 'data processing'. Note the particular restriction which indicates that quantity concepts in one subject field may not have any validity or relevance in another,
e.g. stable state, flexible disk.
– QUANTITY = a measurable quantity or a quality, property, condition or
disposition which is quantifiable and which is not a predefined relational
value.
– RELATION = a predefined relational value, i.e. a fixed value expressing
the relation between at least two concepts which is measurable in quantified
units.
    The category of 'relation' distinguishes between the measurement and
the unit of measurement; in this case, e.g. the difference between such quantity concepts as 'time', 'length', 'width' and the measurable units 'rerun time',
'record length' or 'packing density'.

2.2.4 *Structures of concepts*

In terminological theory it is accepted that concepts should be ordered according to some conceptual classification scheme and presented in a systematic
structure. In order to do this concepts are characterised by the relationships
they form with neighbouring concepts. It is also recognised that new concepts
can be generated by combining others. The declaration of relationships of a
genetic, generic and compositional nature is in fact overtly and systematically
carried out in many designations in the fields of chemistry, biology, mineralogy etc. However, while we readily perceive a great number of relationships
between terms, very few are reflected in the structure of glossaries.
    To date there is no single generally accepted or acceptable classification
for concepts which goes beyond relatively small and well established subject

areas. While this is no problem for isolated terminological collections, it is a serious problem for term banks.

2.2.4.1. *Relationships*

The relationships between objects of the real world are diverse and manifold. Part of the process of forming concepts lies in the selection of particular relationships between characteristics of concepts and therefore indirectly also between concepts and even objects. The relationships between concepts we select and declare relevant for a particular purpose of ordering, are therefore a subset of possible relationships.

In a knowledge structure divided into special subject fields, groups of concepts are more or less closely related to each other whether they belong to the same or to different subsets. Inside subject fields concepts are also related either by their nature or by the real-life connections of the objects they represent. As in real life between objects, the kinds of relationships which exist between concepts are numerous and varied.

While there is no doubt about the desirability of using conceptual relationships, there is no consensus about the importance of conceptual relationships in the clarification of the concept–term equation, independent of or supplementary to definitions. It is widely accepted that they are needed for determining conceptual fields but it is not established how much useful supplementary information they can provide. The fact, however, that we can now model relatively complex systems and their internal relationships on the computer has influenced theory to the extent that the number of relationships between concepts admitted as being useful for structuring conceptual fields has increased considerably. The simplistic view of the past that concepts are adequately represented by three types of relationships (generic, partitive, other) has been generally abandoned.

It is now recognised that for practical applications, virtually any number and type of conceptual relationship can be established and declared as required by a particular need; e.g. an object can be related to its geographical origin, its material substance, its method of production, its use and function, etc. The size of conceptual fields and the complexity of the relationships to be declared within it, is a matter of the practical assessment of the purpose for which the conceptual analysis is undertaken; in other words, terminology relates terms to concepts (and not vice versa) and is therefore not concerned with absolute conceptual systems but only with systems created for the specific purpose of assisting communication.

The following relationships are frequently used in terminology:

Generic relationship. The generic relationship establishes a hierarchical order; it identifies concepts as belonging to the same category in which there is a broader (generic) concept which is said to be superordinate to the narrower (specific), subordinated concept or concepts. The generic relationship is the most common type of relationship and underlies the taxonomies of e.g. biology and geology.

The *generic relationship* can be expressed by the formulas:

      X is a type of A.
or   X, Y and Z are types of A.
or   A has the specific concepts X, Y and Z.
or   A has the subtype X.

Example: Newsletter, Journal and Magazine are types of *periodic publications*.

In this type of relationship, all objects which have the characteristics of the superordinate concept—i.e. all objects which in our example can be called 'periodic publications'—include the subordinate concepts, in our example 'newsletter', 'journal' and 'magazine'. The relationship between the superordinate concept and the subordinate concepts is not reversible. While all that can be said of the generic concept can also be said of the specific concept, there is more to be said about the subordinate concept which does not apply to the superordinate concept. Or expressed differently: all newsletters, journals etc. are periodic publications, but the concept of periodic publication is not exhausted by the concepts of newsletters, journals and magazines. Firstly, because there are other types of periodic publications. Secondly, because subordinate concepts contain all the characteristics of the superordinate concept as well as at least one differentiating characteristic. Only those features which the subordinate concepts, e.g. journals and newsletters, have in common are covered by the concept 'periodic publication'; those which separate them, in this case the range of readership and the nature of the information contained, are particular to the subordinate concept only.

    The generic relationship entails both a vertical and a horizontal relationship, and can also have several layers which can be represented by a tree structure.

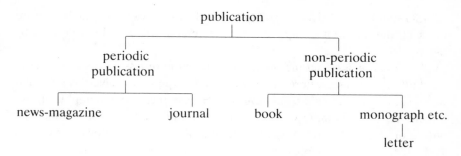

At each lower level, the degree of specificity becomes higher and, hence, the intension of the concept becomes narrower.

Declaring a generic relationship may not be a sufficient criterion for identifying subordinate concepts in a particular set. For example both 'rollerbearings' and 'single-row anti-friction bearings' are types of bearings, but we should not attribute them to the same generic class of concepts. In such a case it is convenient to indicate the criterion by which types have been declared, e.g. 'by types of rolling bodies' or 'by number of rows of rolling bodies', as in the case of the example below. Such type-indicators are also known in information science where they are called 'facets'.

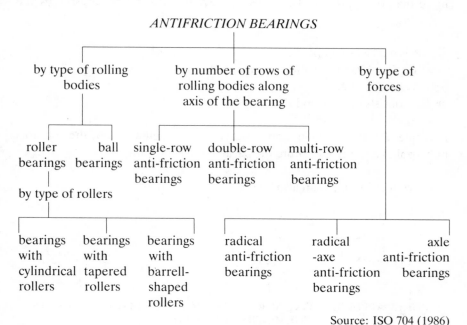

Source: ISO 704 (1986)

ISO standard 704 gives an example of such a complex conceptual structure in which the different groups of subordinate concepts are differentiated by facets.

A distinction is sometimes made between more or less permanent generic attributions. In cases where the attribution of type is conceived as less solid we speak of *quasi-generic relationships*. For example, a 'dandelion' is always a member of the botanical class of Taraxacum of the family of Compositae but according to use it is a weed, a medicinal plant, a wildflower or even a vegetable.

The nature of the relationship can be tested by a simple method:
– In a generic relationship we can say:
  All dandelions are members of the family of Compositae.
  Some members of the family of Compositae are dandelions.
– In a quasi-generic relationship we can only say:
  Some people consider that dandelions are vegetables.
  Some vegetables are dandelions.

Partitive relationships. These relationships are also called 'whole–part' relationships and serve to indicate the connection between concepts consisting of more than one part and their constituent parts. It can be expressed by the formula:

	X is a constituent part of Y
or	X , Y and Z are constituent parts of A
or	A consists of X
or	A consists of X, Y and Z.

Example: A wheel is composed of a hub, spokes and a rim, or the concepts hub, spokes and rim constitute the parts of the concept wheel.

Partitive relationships can also be represented by trees.

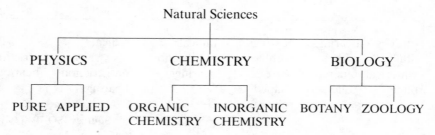

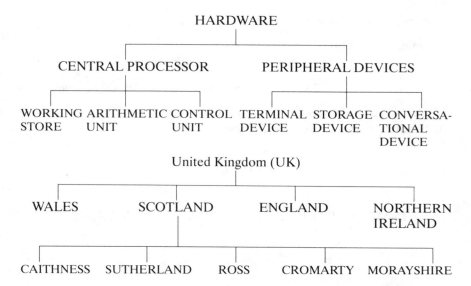

Several subtypes of partitive relationships have been identified by Hann (1978), according to the number and types of the parts.

1) The parts are atomic constituents of the whole, i.e. the whole consists solely of many of the same parts; e.g. the units of a scale, the characters in a character set.

2) The parts are a finite numbered set; e.g. the 52 cards of a deck of cards.

3) The whole consists of various groups of numbered and unnumbered parts; e.g. the individual values of a deck of cards; a print unit has only one hammer mechanism.

4) The part or parts are an optional constituent of the whole ; e.g. a car radio is an optional part of a motor car.

5) The part is a constituent and sometimes the whole; e.g. a page feed is part of a form feed, if the form feed also contains such parts as a page throw and a page eject; but if the page feed is the only facility of the form feed it constitutes the entirety of the form feed.

6) The part or parts are alternatives; e.g. a ribbon feed mechanism has either a ribbon spool OR a ribbon roll, but cannot have both.

Polyvalent relationships. When considering the place of a concept in a conceptual system, it is necessary to evaluate possible alternative attributions. All the relationships of a concept with other concepts need to be considered in detail and it should not be assumed sufficient to have found a single place for it.

A part may have a different place in different types of assembly, e.g.

    lamination – part of a binding process
               – part of book preservation processes

                    Source: BS 5408:1976 (Glossary of Documentation Terms)

Polyhierarchical relationships occur when a concept is placed in more than one hierarchy within a given subject field; e.g.

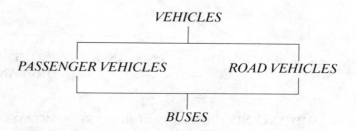

This figure indicates that 'buses' have been classed both as 'road vehicles' and as 'passenger vehicles'.

2.2.4.2. *Complex relationships*

Concepts are often seen as being inter-related in a complex manner which cannot be conveniently captured by straightforward generic and partitive structures. The following relationships may be considered equally important and more revealing about the nature of the concepts.

TYPE OF RELATION

FALLOUT	is *caused by*	NUCLEAR EXPLOSION
PAPER	is *a product of*	WOOD PULP
COMPRESSIBILITY	is *a property of*	GAS
PETROL	is *a product of*	OIL-REFINING
TEMPERATURE	is *a quantitive measure of*	HEAT
COMPUTER	is *an instrument for*	DATA PROCESSING
INSECTICIDE	is *a counteragent of*	INSECTS
TOOL BOX	is *a container for*	TOOLS
DIAMOND DRILLING	is *a method of*	DRILLING
IRON	is *a material for*	BRIDGE BUILDING
COAL-MINE	is *a place for*	COAL-MINING

The list of possible relationships is very large:

RELATIONSHIPS:			EXAMPLES:		
cause	–	effect	explosion	–	fall-out
material	–	product	steel	–	girder
material	–	property	glass	–	brittle
material	–	state	iron	–	corrosion
process	–	product	weaving	–	cloth
process	–	instrument	incision	–	scalpel
process	–	method	storage	–	freeze-dry
process	–	patient	dying	–	textile
phenomenon	–	measurement	light	–	Watt
object	–	counteragent	poison	–	antidote
object	–	container	tool	–	tool box
object	–	material	bridge	–	iron
object	–	quality	petrol	–	high octane
object	–	operation	drill bit	–	drilling
object	–	characteristic	fuel	–	smokeless
object	–	form	book	–	paperback
activity	–	place	coalmining	–	coalmine

Subsets of these relationships can be created by placing concepts into conceptual reference classes such as 'objects', 'methods', 'properties', 'qualities', 'states' and 'processes', or into the classes described in 2.2.3. The number of conceptual classes may be increased and made more specific.

The relationship between two concepts is bound by the conceptual class of each. For example, relationships of product or material can only exist between material entities; in this way a pattern emerges which shows restrictions on the nature of the relationships between concepts by virtue of their categories. Examining concepts in this way may lead to greater insight into ways of establishing conceptual relationships.

It is also possible to combine the generic relationship with an indication of the nature of the type of subdivision employed. For example, 'laser printer', 'daisy-wheel printer' and 'dot-matrix printer' are all types of printer distinguished by the mode of operation of the print mechanisms.

This kind of subdivision of a concept made on the basis of a particular characteristic is called a facetted classification, in analogy to the same device used in subject field subdivision in information science. Facets are frequently used in documentation thesauri where a subject area contains groups of terms associated with a common area of knowledge. There is also a growing tendency to use such divisions in systematically structured glossaries where terms are grouped together because they share a characteristic of division of the broader genus.

The following are examples of divisions using facets:

(a) by parts: LITHOGRAPHY

                             CHROMO-LITHOGRAPHY
                             OFFSET LITHOGRAPHY

          INKING SYSTEMS

                             DUCT ADJUSTING SCREW
                             DUCT BLADE
                             INK DRUM
                             INK DUCT
                             INKING ROLLER

(b) by process: PRINTING

                             INTAGLIO PRINTING
                             PLANOGRAPHIC PRINTING
                             POROUS PRINTING

(c) by method: INTAGLIO PRINTING

                             PHOTO GRAVURE
                             STEEL-ENGRAVING PROCESS

(d) by function: AIRCRAFT

                             PASSENGER AIRCRAFT
                             FREIGHT AIRCRAFT
                             MILITARY AIRCRAFT
                             CIVIL AIRCRAFT

(e) The same concept can be subdivided according to different facets, e.g.
FLANGES

(by property)	(by method of connection)
DETACHABLE FLANGES	CONNECTING FLANGES
ROTATING FLANGES	SCREWED FLANGES
LOOSE FLANGES	WELDED FLANGES

(by flange face configuration)	(by shape)
FLAT-FACED FLANGES	BOSSED FLANGES
RAISED-FACE FLANGES	WELDED FLANGES
FULL-FACED FLANGES	

Source: BS ROOT Thesaurus, 1981

Facet subdivisions can be made to various levels of specificity as can be seen by the example of 'flanges' where 'flanges', instead of being subdivided by undifferentiated types, have been divided by characteristics such as 'property', 'method of connection' and 'flange face configuration'. The information provided is definition-like in its completeness and usefulness. Facets also avoid the difficulty of polyhierarchies and leave it open whether categories are exclusive or inclusive. The total number of possible concept divisions and, hence, possible facets is given by the diversity of subjects in existence. As well as being as broad or as specific as required, facets can also be subject-oriented (e.g. 'by flange face configuration') and tailored to very narrow and specific subject areas.

2.2.5 *Subject classification*

Besides relating concepts to each other, there is a need for larger groupings of areas of concepts within subject fields. We therefore speak of two approaches to conceptual structures: the 'bottom-up' approach, which proceeds from the individual concepts and builds larger structures of association according to the perception of the microcosm under analysis; and the 'top-down' approach which divides knowledge into subject fields or disciplines, subject fields into special subjects, special subjects into areas of specialisation etc., until it arrives at the smallest number of terms which can be grouped under a common descriptive label.

Classification is a well-known ordering device, probably best known for its wide use in information and library science. Detailed classification schemes like the Universal Decimal Classification or the Dewey Decimal Classification provide for many small subsets of knowledge in hierarchical order which have been used by various authors for arranging terms in systematic order. The structures that can be obtained in this way represent a great improvement on the alphabetical order of traditional dictionaries and glossaries, but they are limited by the fact that they cannot reflect the relationships that pertain between individual terms.

A compromise solution and a meeting point between classification and conceptual relationships is provided in the thesaurus. In documentation thesauri, subject fields are often divided into sub-categories via subject class headings. In the Root Thesaurus, the MECHANICAL ENGINEERING class is divided into HEAT ENGINEERING, FLUID ENGINEERING, VACUUM ENGINEERING and more specific sub-categories PRIME MOVERS and MECHANICAL SYSTEMS. The hierarchical structure may be quite deep and reach seven and more levels of subdivision. At the end, however, we are left with categories of topics or subject areas and not concepts of separate entities, activities, properties and relations. In thesauri sub-categories can also be created and specified further by facet labels, so that in some cases the 'top-down' subject classification would appear to reach the same degree of detail and diversification as the 'bottom-up' approach. Theoretically this is possible only if the 'top-down' analysis is fully exhaustive, i.e. if it reaches the lowest level of conceptual analysis. In practice this is, however, not achievable because classification schemes do not pursue conceptual analysis to the level of the individual; terminological analysis, on the other hand, which is identified with the 'bottom-up' approach, starts with the individual term for a concept and creates structures only to the extent that this activity is considered helpful for the identification and explication of the concept. In the end, therefore, there is no conflict between subject classification and terminological analysis: both complement each other with priority on one or the other aspect according to the specific objectives pursued by each type of ordering. Subject classification may be helpful in the structuring and selection of entries for a specialised dictionary. Brinkmann and Schmidt's Dictionary of Data Systems Terms (1974), for example, divides the field of Data Systems into 59 subfields, each of the terms being assigned to a single subfield classification label. Having at the outset subdivided the field of concepts, it is, hence, easier to test comprehensiveness and to provide an internally consistent set of definitions and other explanations based on the relationships among terms.

The appeal of using hierarchies provided by subject classification schemes as a framework for building terminological systems diminishes as one examines the practical problems this imposes. Not all subject areas are equally suited to hierarchical analysis and representation. A hierarchical superstructure may be quite helpful in a subject field which concentrates exclusively on concrete entities, their parts and types (machinery, types of machinery and constituents parts, for example). For most other subject fields, particularly those which cover a significant number of abstract entities, one may observe the contrary. In mathematics the rigidity of a structure based on hierarchical relationships would be an unsuitable means of representing a conceptual structure. The concept VARIABLE, for example, occurs in Propositional Calculus, Predicate Calculus, Statistics, Basic Algebra and Differential Calculus, in each case with a different application. In this case a General category has to be created to deal with the various concepts that overlap several subject areas. Links to other concepts can then be provided by extensive cross-referencing; in this process a systematic hierarchically-based structure of concepts becomes redundant.

In conclusion we can state that subject classification can at best provide a broad outline structure for terminology collection. The restrictions imposed by hierarchical ordering, even when mitigated by facetted classification, are too severe to be acceptable as a general pattern for terminology representation. Classifications offer a convenient starting point, but beyond this they have to be supplemented by a more complex set of relationships.

2.3 Definitions and alternatives

2.3.1 *Definition of 'definition' in terminology*

Defining is generally understood to be the process of explaining the meaning of linguistically expressed symbols and, in this sense, it is possible to define both 'unicorns' which do not exist and 'spanners' which do, both 'regular dodecahedron' which is a possible geometrical form and 'regular decahedron' which is not. As a product the definition is a linguistic description of a concept, based on the listing of a number of characteristics, which conveys the meaning of the concept. It takes the form of a simple predication about a word or expression and has also been described as an equation of an unknown term and the sum of its constituent meaning elements. General or encyclopaedic definitions describe a concept in a generally comprehensible way by giving all its functions etc. in the respective subject fields in which it occurs. Specialised definitions describe a concept within a special subject field.

Definitions provide the link between concepts and terms by means of an equation in which the definiendum is the term. A terminological definition provides a unique identification of a concept only with reference to the conceptual system of which it forms part and classifies the concept within that system. In this way we separate the necessary and sufficient definition of terminology, which is required for the identification of the concept–term equation, from the many other definitions which explain a concept to all manner of dictionary and database users ranging from children and laymen to specialists.

In terminology it is customary to restrict the use of 'definition' to the explanation of the accepted specialised meanings of lexical items the occurrence of which can be documented in a variety of sources. It therefore excludes consideration of other types and functions of definition, e.g. the very important stipulative definition by which individuals in discourse redesignate the function and meaning of lexical items for a specific purpose.

The definition fixes the intension, i.e. the reference of a term; in precision it varies from the extreme rigour of definition of the taxonomies and other highly restricted languages to the flexible definition in innovative technologies where functional defining characteristics are more often used than formal or material ones. Definitions presuppose the existence of a defining vocabulary the meanings of which are taken as axiomatic, not requiring any further explanation. This raises the problem of the levels of understanding and education that can be expected of the reader of the definition.

2.3.1.1 *Scope of definitions*

The difference between the so-called lexicographic and encyclopaedic definition is one of method rather than purpose. In both cases the purpose is to explicate the meaning of lexical items of a language by relating them to other items evocative of entities of the real world for which they are symbolic representations. Both are therefore nominal definitions of the classical word–thing type of philosophy. The word–word definition can be said to exist in bilingual dictionaries in which equivalences are established between the lexical items of two languages, i.e. two symbol systems.

In general language dictionaries definitions serve the specific purpose of differentiating between homonyms and polysemous words and of explaining the meaning and use of less common words. Therefore not every word in a general dictionary is accompanied by a definition. In such dictionaries words are usually explained by means of other words the understanding of which is taken for granted. Because of the polysemous nature of many words and the overlapping of types of meaning, general language words are often defined by listing of synonyms so that the meaning of the item to be defined can be interpreted as the common features of all the synonyms given. Thus, an impression may be gained that general language definitions are confined to giving sense relations only; this would permit a distinction to be made between the 'linguistic' nature of many lexicographic definitions in contrast to 'terminological' definitions.

The difference between the lexicographic and encyclopaedic method of definitions in the field of terminology lies in the nature of special languages. As items of natural language discourse, terms are elements of language and could in principle be described purely linguistically by means of the sense relations they form in discourse. Their meaning would thus, with Wittgenstein, reside exclusively in their use in the context of other words. But in a theory of terminology, the nature of the special reference, described above, leads to a different approach in the method of definition. By convention special lexical items are considered to be devoid of other than referential meaning within their area of usage, i.e. special subject communication. Because they occur in a limited range of collocations only, for the purpose of definition terms are also considered to be context-free. Though synonyms do exist, they have the same reference, assume the same types of meaning and their use is on the whole controlled by clearly defined areas of usage (levels).

Inasmuch as the terms of a particular subject field represent the currently accepted knowledge structure of that field, we can define a concept of a particular subject by delimiting its position with respect to all the other concepts in the field of knowledge to which it belongs known at that time.

The difference between general language definition by synonyms and special language definitions can be represented diagrammatically as follows. A word can be defined by its synonyms or by words with various overlapping meanings so that a word may be adequately defined by the sum of the common features among all the synonyms listed.

A word surrounded by its synonyms:

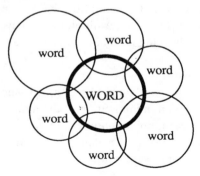

A concept cannot be defined by synonyms of a term as this would be tautologous. It can however be defined by all the concepts surrounding it in the special field of reference in which it occurs.

A term in its subject field:

		TERM		TERM
		TERM	TERM	TERM
TERM	TERM	**TERM**	TERM	TERM
	TERM	TERM		

2.3.2 *Methods of definition*

Terminological theory can recognise only one type of definition: the analytical definition which fully and systematically identifies a concept with respect to all others in the particular subject field. Terminological practice is, however, faced with the problem of which definition among various existing alternatives it should give preference to, or whether it should restrict itself to a purpose-specific 'terminological' definition.

In this section, definition is understood as the process of referring someone from a term to the concept which is the meaning of this term so that he can connect the symbol with the concept. It is primarily a verbal activity but also includes non-verbal means, i.e. the ostensive definition.

There are various methods of defining concepts, which are used according to the nature of the concept to be defined and the particular purpose of definition, which ranges from the precise delimitation of the knowledge space occupied by a concept to an aide-memoire; from the need of a translator to check the equivalence of a term to the subject specialist who has to identify a new process or product.

Traditionally the theoretical position concerning definitions was that the proper way of defining was given by the classical pattern of 'genus et differentiae'. In fact, however, very few definitions have ever followed this strict pattern. A more relevant theory of terminology will have to admit the full range of definitions currently being used both in lexicography and terminology.

1. *Definition by analysis* (genus et differentia):
    pneumonia   = an inflammation of lung tissue
    stomatitis   = an inflammation of the mouth
    gingivitis   = an inflammation of the gums
    oblique plane   = (Bot.) any plane of a flower other than the medium
                         and lateral planes.

2. *Definition by synonyms*:
    software   = logiciel
    daisy   = bellis perennis

3. *Definition by paraphrase*:

whiteness	= the state of being white
flotation	= the action of making something float
lengthen	= the process of making something longer

4. *Definition by synthesis* (by identifying relations, by description):

metatarsalgia = a painful neuralgic condition of the foot, felt in the ball of the foot and often spreading thence up the leg.

5. *Definition by implication* (by using the word in an explicative context):

dial = a clock or watch has a dial divided into segments for hours and minutes over which the hands move.

diagnosis = we make a diagnosis when we identify certain symptoms as characteristic of specific conditions.

6. *Definition by denotation* (by listing examples, by extension):

dog = dogs are spaniels, poodles, pekinese, alsatians and similar animals.

ocean = oceans are the Atlantic, the Pacific and the Indian Ocean.

7. *Definition by demonstration* (ostensive definition):

e.g. drawings, photographs,
  pointing to an object ('This is a fly-over'),
  situational reference ('This diagram here...')

Many definitions are mixed:

by analysis and description:

oak (timber) = a strong, tough and heavy hardwood, very durable in exposed positions. Commonly used in constructional work for timber bridges, dock gates, heavy framing, piles as well as for joinery.

by synonym and description:

obliterating paint = a special dense flatting used over a primary coat to give a ground for a final coat of glossy paint or enamel.

by synonym and analysis:

| oblong | = elliptical, blunt at each end, having nearly parallel sides, and two to four time as long as broad. |

2.3.2.1. *Rules of definition*

There are traditional rules of definition—usually derived from Aristotle's Topics—many of which have found their way into standardisation and even theories of terminology. Some of these are restrictive with regard to method, usually giving preference to the analytic approach. Others are concerned with expression, e.g. that a definition should not be expressed negatively or by means of obscure or figurative language.

The rule most difficult to interpret requires that a definition must give the essential characteristics of a concept. In practice this means listing the features which distinguish or differentiate a concept from its immediate hyperonym and co-hyponyms. A strict interpretation of this rule would require a redefinition every time the terminological system is altered, however slightly.

2.3.3 *Definitions in context*

In terminology definitions do not occur in isolation; they must be considered as part of the total information gathered on terms in a term record. The definition is therefore only part of the semantic specification which can itself be complemented by morphological, syntactic and at times pragmatic specifications.

2.3.3.1. *Definition as part of the semantic specification*

The semantic specification of the term is documented through reference to sources which give evidence of the use of the term, and can thus be kept up to date. The various data categories in this group, i.e. the data fields: subject classification, definition, relationships to other terms (equivalence, partial equivalence, hierarchical, antonymic, associative), context, and usage note are documented by reference to up-to-date publications and complement each other.

There can, for instance, be a close relationship between the subject classification and the usage note whereby the former provides a broad indication of area of use and the latter identifies levels of discourse within this area. Definitions are usually complemented by a subject classification so that a particular definition is applicable to one subject field only and can therefore be as narrow as indicated in the subject field. Definitions can be related to the context in that the context may contain terms or expressions which occur in the definition, or indeed provide a definition by implication or example.

It is generally maintained that the definition serves to explain the intension of a term and that the terminological relations establish the extension of a term. The complementarity between definition and relation goes, however, much deeper.

Most definitions refer to other terms, usually described as BROAD TERM, NARROW TERM, RELATED TERM where these relationships are declared within the subject classification chosen for the particular area of knowledge. An analytic definition always relates a term to its superordinate and may also include coordinate terms. A synthetic definition identifies the place of a concept in a system of relations and mentions the subordinate terms. A denotative definition simply lists all the subordinate terms, thus covering the extension of a term.

Certain types of definition therefore do no more that list data which may otherwise already be present on a term record and for this reason definitions in terminology are usually not of the denotative, contextual or demonstrative type. Nor is there much scope for the definition by synonyms, partly because of the nature of synonyms in special languages, partly because some users require more detail than such a definition can provide.

We conclude that in terminology a definition is only a part of the semantic specification contained in a term record and that there is therefore no need for it to be exhaustive and self-contained. In addition separate term records complement each other via the terminological relationships and the terms in definitions which are defined in other records.

2.3.4 *The purpose of definitions in terminology*

In order to determine the need for definitions we have to examine two aspects: user requirements and the nature of the concepts to be defined.

There are three basic needs for definition:
a) the initial fixation of the term–concept equation;
b) the identification of a term via the verification of the existence of an independent definition;
c) the explanation of the meaning of a concept for specialist users of term banks such as translators and subject specialists and possibly also laymen.

In the first case we have the fundamental process of concept formation which proceeds independently and prior to the work of terminologists in creating reference tools. Scientists and technologists regularly form new concepts and name them according to whatever criteria have been evolved by convention or habit. This act is sometimes accompanied by a formal act of definition; in other cases definitions are written for the purpose of patenting an idea, method, process or object, for textbooks or other instructional material, or even for catalogues and other listings. This objective lies outside the concern of terminologists. The terminologist must, however, examine to what extent these definitions, written for other purpose and contexts, can be used for the other two needs.

In the second case we are concerned with definitions as they occur in all manner of documents as well as with the definitions constructed by terminologists for the purpose of all manner of reference tools. The question that arises here is to what extent the definition constructed for the new electronic reference tools should differ from the type of definition users are familiar with in other contexts.

In the third case we are dealing with definitions especially constructed for term banks, though it is likely to be difficult to satisfy both the layman and the specialist with a single definition.

The needs of the dictionary user and the terminologist who produces a definition coincide in a number of respects. We can therefore first analyse the role of definitions in the lexicographers' or terminologists' work.

The identification of a term is made first contrastively, in texts, by delimiting lexical units. In this way we isolate uniterms, compound terms and terminological syntagmas which have to be confirmed as to their terminological or lexical status. This confirmation is a semantic process which is carried out by checking the knowledge structure of the terminological field for the place of the term in the system. If the lexical entity meets the requirements of precisely and uniquely naming a particular entity, process, property, etc. of the field in question we can declare it to be a term. We achieve certainty in this process by reference to existing definitions. By contrasting procedures we can also test the position of a term relative to other terms in the immediate field and we can record a number of these relationships in more or less detail. So far there is no need for a terminologist to construct his own definition and the terminologist who builds up a terminology in this way does not require it.

If the terminologist is, however, asked to propose a translation equivalent for a term in another language he will want to verify the terminological status and position of the foreign language term in exactly the same way. If there is no definition in the target language which matches a definition in the source language, he will have a reasonable certainty that he will have to create a translation equivalent. He can then propose a name which fits in with the surrounding terms in the target language and the requirements of this adjustment override any additional information he may gather from a definition in the source language. In order to explain the new term it may be desirable to define it, but this cannot be done automatically by a translation of the source language definition as the respective conceptual fields in the two language communities may not be the same. Coincidence of conceptual fields is likely to exist in the taxonomic sciences, and in other sciences in which there has been a considerable amount of knowledge transfer and linguistic borrowing so that the two conceptual fields show a great similarity. A definition should then also clearly differentiate the new term from its surrounding terms especially its co-terms whether they be generically, partitively or otherwise related.

The definition could then be analytical and descriptive according to certain fixed patterns, e.g.

x is a type of y, differentiated from the other co-types r and q by ...
a is a part of b, differentiated from the other parts c, d and e by...

Such a definition presupposes that the user is familiar with the subject field as the terms used in the definition are of the same order of specialisation as the term defined.

The translator as end user approaches the term bank in a slightly different way. He has a source language text in which he has to verify the identity of terms. In case of doubt he interrogates the term bank to ascertain that a particular lexical unit is a term. The reply can contain the target language term he is to use. Provided he fully understands the text he may obtain sufficient information by seeing immediately related terms with or without their translation equivalent. (He may, of course, require information on the usage of the target language term and this is provided in the term bank by the usage note, by grammatical specifications, by a context or quality codes, etc.) Information on related terms may be presented in list form, as a graphic display of a tree structure, or it may be in the form of the fixed pattern of definition, exemplified above, which contains additional information on the type of relationship and the distinguishing features from co-terms.

If he requires yet more information in order to understand the text, he may need what amounts to textbook, or encyclopaedia-type information. Definitions which provide this type of explanation require a different level of language not usually found in the specialised dictionary or a term bank. Future lexical data banks may therefore be provided with several levels of specialisation of definitions to meet different user needs.

In between these two positions of minimal definition which reinforces and clarifies the relational position of terms and the general language definition of terms, there is the specialised definition as we know it from e.g. Chambers' Technical Dictionary. Like so many reference works which have become institutions in their own right these dictionaries and encyclopaedias fulfill many functions simultaneously but unfortunately not systematically. As forerunners of term banks they are useful but inconsistent. Besides giving synonyms and abbreviations (of full forms and v.v.) they sometimes have full descriptive articles and sometimes only highly specialised analyses. Modern techniques of data storage and retrieval permit the segmentation and staggered provision of information so that the multifunctionality of technical dictionaries can be broken down into information units suitable for different types of users.

2.3.4.1. *Functional types of definitions*

The justification for the inclusion of definitions in dictionaries, term banks and other similar reference works resides in three broad objectives which give rise to three types of definitions.

1. The definition is needed for placing the term in its position in the appropriate knowledge structure. Since this is a purely terminological activity, we call this process 'terminological definition'. It presupposes an understanding of the intension of the term which is gained from existing definitions, from contexts, from consultation with specialists and through subject knowledge. It serves to single out the essential characteristics of the intension and to delineate the extension by reference to other terms.

2. The definition is needed for fixing the specialised meaning of the term. This is the 'intensional' definition used by subject specialists for determining the precise reference of a term. It has to be flexible and will be less rigorous in certain areas of knowledge, e.g. in innovative technologies where it can also have varying degrees of stipulative functions. Small variations in design or performance are often added to the intension of a term without leading to redefinition or redesignation. (For example, telephones or direction indicators on motor cars have changed almost beyond recognition since their invention, but are still called by the same name). In other areas of knowledge, e.g. the taxonomies, the intension is rigidly fixed and the terms used for describing a plant or stone may themselves belong to closed systems of reference. This type of definition moves on the same level of

discourse as the defined term, i.e. most of the terms used in the definition may be defined elsewhere in the subject field.

3. The definition is needed for giving the non-specialist some degree of understanding of the term, and this type can be called 'encyclopaedic'. This type frequently uses the synthesis method combined with some synonymy, as appropriate and possible when general language words are used to paraphrase an item of special reference. This type must then indicate the areas of special knowledge involved, as e.g.

Phosphorescence = (chem.) The greenish glow observed during the slow oxidation of white phosphorus in the air.

(phys.) A glow emitted by certain substances after having been illuminated by visible or ultraviolet rays. It may be regarded as fluorescence which persists after the exciting radiation has ceased.

(zool.) Luminosity; production of light usually (in animals) with little production of heat; as glow-worms.

Source: Chambers Technical Dictionary

2.3.4.2. *Needs analyses*

Summing up this section we can say:

The terminologist needs a definition in context for compiling terminologies and for proposing new terms. Such an 'external' definition does not necessarily fit the requirements of a term bank as it may be too specific to match the subject classification, too specialised in language or too general for the consistency of level of expression aimed at in the term bank. He may therefore in appropriate cases have to construct his own 'terminological definition'.

The specialised translator should not need a definition for understanding the source text as he works from a context. He needs a definition of a target language equivalent only if he cannot trust the reference tool he uses. Beside a definition he may need the confirmation of a detailed subject code and a usage note to guide him.

The subject specialist knows the concept he wants to use and only needs reminding of the existing terminological structure of his subject both for verification and creation of terms. Both their needs may be met by a 'terminological definition'.

The non-specialist needs an explanation in the form of an encyclopaedic definition as he would not benefit from any other type.

2.3.5 *Use of existing definitions*

We can now turn our attention to a practical matter, i.e. the question of whether existing definitions can be used and the need for new definition for the construction of term banks and other terminological information services.

In order to decide which terms in a term bank have to be defined, we must establish what definitions exist elsewhere.

1. Terms referring to observable physical entities such as chemical substances, plants, minerals, etc. are well known and defined in the specialised literature and do not require new definition in term banks. These entities may also have various functions in different subject fields where they could be defined differently.

2. Terms referring to various forms of scientific methods of analysis or description do not require definition in a term bank as they are well known and are rarely the cause of misunderstanding or the object of redesignation.

3. Terms referring to properties relevant to established scientific and technological processes are usually adequately defined, e.g. measurements.

4. Terms which are standardised are already defined and in most cases also classified as to their position in the terminological structure, because standardised glossaries are usually systematically ordered.

All these terms can be considered as points of reference necessary for fixing the reference of other terms. Their definitions have a high status and are therefore usually more reliable than dictionary definitions.

5. This leaves the large number of terms designating other entities, concrete or abstract, manufactured products, industrial processes and perceived properties which are less rigidly fixed in the knowledge structure and which rely on a broad consensus among users for the confines of special reference associated with them. Some of these have a very limited reference in a small area of usage, e.g. product definitions in lists for customs tariffs. Definitions of these terms are often inconsistent, widely scattered and therefore unreliable and difficult to access. They can only be taken over together with an indication of their area of applicability. In such a case it is important to indicate this clearly and it may be advisable to choose a listing method of the features of reference which are considered to be essential for location of the term in its environment.

Such a process of listing essential features of a concept would be supplementary to that of fixing the term in relation to others in the immediate field and could adopt some of the techniques developed in information science for identification of descriptors, such as factoring, scope notes, qualification, and facets. The method would be essentially analytic to which would be added a synthesis approach. Its purpose would be clearly signified by calling it 'terminological'. This would mean that the present known field of reference is that indicated on the terminological record without any prejudice to a widening, narrowing or shifting of meaning within the knowledge area so signalled. It is also clear that such a method would not be suitable for the four other categories of terms listed above.

2.3.5.1. *The need for terminological definitions*
We can conclude that terminological definitions may be conveniently applied to those terms which are not already clearly defined and which are therefore likely to require further specification in addition to the declaration of terminological relationships.

It does not appear to be necessary nor useful to define every term specifically for a term bank:
a) many terms are already adequately defined elsewhere and such definitions should be taken over if the term bank aims at supplanting existing sources of information. Reformulation of existing authoritative definitions may lead to misunderstanding;
b) many terms are clearly understood and require no definition;
c) many terms are clearly identified by the relationships they form with other terms and thus require no further identification or explanation.

Many other terms, however, require terminological definition in the form of an extended analysis of relationships which, in addition to declaring the conventional relationships to other terms and naming the immediately adjacent terms in the knowledge structure, also elicit the differentiating or distinguishing criteria, especially of any horizontally and diagonally related terms.

2.4 Terminological definitions and relationships

It is now recognised that the definition is not alone in providing a link between term and concept but is supported by the declaration of a sufficient and appropriate set of conceptual relationships. The definition can therefore concentrate on the essential characteristics a concept has in common with others and which differentiate it from other concepts; by contrast the relationships indicate the type of link a concept has to other concepts in the system. These two complementary types of information assist in the identification of equivalent terms of the same or other languages and can also be used in case the meaning of a concept is to be restricted with a view to its use in a standardised form.

This dual identification of concepts may in future be formalised so that the natural language formulation of the conventional definition can be replaced by a listing of characteristics only.

THE INTERACTION OF RELATIONSHIPS AND DEFINITIONS

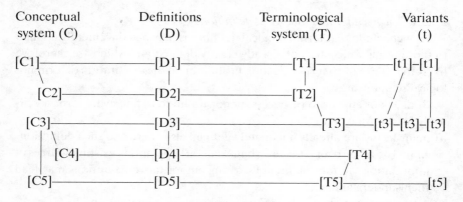

The definition links concepts to terms (expressed horizontally in the diagram), but concepts and terms are themselves linked to each other (expressed by vertical and diagonal lines in the diagram). Terms are further linked to their variants and variants themselves may be linked through their form.

Terms can be classified and presented in a thesaural structure. The flexibility of data selection and presentation in term banks permits displays of terms surrounded by their broader, narrower and related terms. The usefulness of this type of display has been demonstrated in documentation thesauri but also in such pioneering lexicographical works as Wüster's Machine Tool Dictionary (1968). There is also a tendency to construct documentation thesauri so as to permit consultation for terminological purposes, e.g. the new ROOT Thesaurus of BSI (1980) and the Construction Industry Thesaurus (1976).

The relationships among terms contain elements of definition as shown by such simple statements as the following which underlie the symbolic representation of Broad Term, Narrow Term and Related Term.

x is a type of Y
x is a part of Y
x is related to Y

Such statements can be generated automatically by the computer which converts this kind of information into a simple definition. It is equally possible to generate automatically expanded defining statements such as:

x is a type of y together with z and q
x is a part of y; other parts are z and q
x is related to y and so are z and q

Moving further up, down or diagonally across the relationships expanded statements, giving, e.g. the top or bottom terms of a hierarchy, are equally possible.

Partitive and generic relationships are not the only types of relationships and others, such as the causal or genetic, can be added, thus diversifying and adding to the basic information required in definitions. Property terms can be associated with the entity terms they qualify, process terms can be associated with the products which are involved. In this way differentiating characteristics between generically related terms can be associated with the narrower specific term.

If systematically pursued such more detailed terminological identification corresponds to the requirements of the terminological definition described in the previous section.

A close link can thus be established between definition and placing a term in its environment, and defining a term can be considered to be synonymous with fixing its identity in relation to other terms.

The practical adoption of such new types of information categories in term banks would, however, require clarification of a number of issues currently insufficiently researched. They are here expressed as a number of questions to which answers would have to be given before progress can be made with new information types.

1. The nature and types of terminological relationships.
   – Beside the well-known relationships are there others common to all subject fields?
   – Are there relationships particular to certain subject fields?
   – How can the relationship between horizontally related term be specified?

2. The identification of terminological relationships.
   – Can simple techniques be devised for accurately identifying relationships?

- How many different relationships can a terminologist be expected to identify accurately?
- How can one achieve consistency of attribution among different terminologists?
- What computational techniques can assist in this task?
- How can the computer be employed to control consistency of work?
- What is the minimal information required for the computer to generate a full representation?

3. The presentation of relationships to users.
   - Which defining patterns can provide the maximum amount of relevant information to all specialised users?

2.4.1 *Complementarity of definition and relationships*

The process of defining as performed by terminologists is conveniently seen as an extension of the work involved in establishing relationships among terms. The equation of these two operations has a number of theoretical and practical advantages. On the practical side it maintains the unity and consistency of the identification of a term within the knowledge structure where it is used.

On the theoretical side it represents an acknowledgement of the fact that many terms, in particular those for which no definitive external definition exists, undergo small variations of meaning which impinge on the intension of other terms and would thus invalidate a highly restrictive definition.

It is the recognition of varying degrees of elasticity of the knowledge spaces occupied by some types of terms which suggests that the static approach of definition is unsuitable as it tends to ignore the dynamics of the segmentation of the whole knowledge structure.

It is therefore the type of term which determines the need and the type of definition required. Definitions should never be allowed to restrict the flexibility of natural language and seeing terms as variously strictly defined allows for the innovative use of language in harmony and not in conflict with the control mechanisms inherent in term banks and dictionaries.

Chapter Three

THE LINGUISTIC DIMENSION

This chapter deals with terms as isolated linguistic items as they occur in the metalinguistic discourse of dictionaries and glossaries. Their origins in texts of genuine natural language must, however, never be forgotten because terminologists use texts as their basic material and the dictionary tools they develop are intended to explicate natural language items or advise on the usage of terms in natural language contexts.

3.1 A theory of terms

A theory of terms is, in principle, part of a theory of lexicology. In accordance with the practical objectives of this book, however, this theoretical introduction is concerned only with those aspects of lexicology which are directly relevant to the dual function of terminologists as producers of tools in the form of automated dictionaries and glossaries and as advisors on usage in special subject designation.

3.1.1 *The onomasiological approach*

One of the fundamental differences between lexicography and terminology lies in the attitude to the lexicon, the raw material to be collected and processed. The lexicographer in principle collects 'all' the words of a language in order to sort them in various ways. Once he has collected his words, he proceeds to differentiate them by their meanings. His ideal dictionary covers all the words and all their meanings, even though in practice he will produce various types of subsets for diverse uses. The terminologist starts out from a much narrower position; he is only interested in subsets of the lexicon, which constitute the vocabulary (or lexicon) of special languages. In order to arrive at these subsets he needs a structure of knowledge, which justifies the existence and the boundaries of special languages, so that he can attribute words to separate areas of this structure. Since a word can belong to more than one area of knowledge—the well-known phenomenon of homonymy—the terminologist has to distinguish meanings before he distinguishes words.

Traditional terminological theory therefore identifies its approach as 'onomasiological', i.e. a 'naming' approach, because in principle it starts from concepts and looks for the names of these concepts. By contrast the lexicographical approach is called 'semasiological', i.e. a 'meaning' approach, because it starts from words and looks for their meaning. In reality the onomasiological approach only characterises the scientist who has to find a name for a new concept (an invention, a new tool, measurement etc); the terminologist, like the lexicographer, usually has an existing body of terms to start with. Only rarely is a terminologist involved in the process of naming an original concept—as distinct from secondary term formation in translation. What is distinctive in his work is the fact that he orders the terms he has discovered by reference to a conceptual system which he may have to draw up himself in consultation with a subject specialist. He also needs the conceptual system in order to determine the completeness of his terminological collection because the subset of the lexicon he is working with at any one time can only be delimited in connection with a special subject field. Once a conceptual system has been defined, the terminologist is more certain that he can exhaustively cover the vocabulary of the particular subject field he is describing at any one time.

The onomasiological approach avoids the occurrence of homonyms, both in theory and largely in practice. In theory, because each concept has its own name or, expressed from the opposite point of view, each separate meaning of a term is represented by a separate concept and the entries in a terminological glossary are of separate concepts; in practice, because the subject field structure of the data separates homonyms belonging to different subject fields. In this way terminological dictionaries largely avoid the problem of establishing separate senses of words and numbering and ordering them in a single entry.

The onomasiological approach is most clearly in evidence in bilingual technical dictionaries and glossaries. Since the dictionary entry corresponds to a concept which is fixed by the definition given in the source language, a matching target language term can only be considered a suitable translation equivalent and not the linguistic representation of a matching concept. The conceptual, onomasiological approach also raises the question of the word categories that can suitably represent the concept, whether, e.g., activity concepts are to be expressed by nouns, verbs or both and if the latter, how the entry is to be structured.

3.1.2 *Terms and their forms*

Terms are the linguistic representation of concepts. Unlike in general language, where the arbitrariness of the sign is accepted, special languages strive to systematise principles of designation and to name concepts according to pre-specified rules or general principles. General language fully exploits polysemy, metaphor, and adjectival determination; genuine word creation is relatively rare. Where it occurs it is based on the experiences of every-day life and thus represents a prescientific approach to knowledge. The process of scientific observation and description includes designation of concepts and this in turn involves re-examining the meaning of words, changing designations and coining new ones. This concern with manipulating lexical forms leads to an attempt of reflecting elements of thought and perception in language. Designation in special languages, therefore, aims at transparency and consistency; often attempts are made to make designations reflect in their structure major conceptual features or characteristics of the concepts they represent. Parallel forms of designation are aimed at in related terms, e.g.

tape select switch	record muting button
band select switch	tape transport direction button
interference suppress switch	

Both synthetic and analytic means of term formation are used extensively in English terminology. Analytic methods of designation combine independent lexical units into larger units, as, for example, in compounding. Synthetic methods modify lexical items by means of affixes. Affixes are lexically meaningful items which in English cannot stand on their own. Their function in their language of origin is in this case irrelevant for their role in English, e.g.

ante	cosm	graphy	heter	mono	ocul	odont
ops	opt	oro	orth	pedia	pre	tele

Sometimes they have no meaning of their own but acquire one of several possible meanings in combination with a stem, e.g.

-a-	-age	amphi-	-ana-	im-	ne-

The distinction between analytic and synthetic methods is relevant for English because it also has affixes which historically had meanings of their own, e.g. '-dom', '-hood', '-ship', or have meanings of their own in other languages from which they are borrowed, e.g. Greek and Latin numerals, or are abbreviations of independent words, e.g. 'al' (alcohol).

Modern terminological theory accepts the occurrence of synonymic expressions and variants of terms and rejects the narrowly prescriptive attitude of the past which associated one concept with only one term. It is recognised that one concept can have as many linguistic representations as there are distinct communicative situations which require different linguistic forms. Terminology now adopts a corpus-based approach to lexical data collection. By being studied in the context of communicative situations, terms are no longer seen as separate items in dictionaries or part of a semi-artificial language deliberately devoid of any of the functions of other lexical items. The increasing tendency to analyse terminology in its communicative, i.e. linguistic context, leads to a number of new theoretical assumptions and also to new methods of compilation and representation.

3.1.2.1. *Terms in dictionaries*

Concepts represented in terminological dictionaries are predominantly expressed by the linguistic form of nouns; concepts which are linguistically expressed as adjectives and verbs in technical languages are frequently found only in the corresponding noun form and some theorists deny the existence of adjective and verb concepts.

Since terminological dictionaries only contain nouns and selected verbs and adjectives, dictionary entries are relatively uniform and largely concentrate on semantic and increasingly also pragmatic information. Graphic information is, of course, always present but phonetic and phonological information is seldom given. Morphological information is rarely required since there are few irregular forms; grammatical information, such as part of speech, is only useful in languages with a weak system of word category affixes and inflections.

Detailed attention must instead be given to variant designations for the concept to be described. Acronyms and other abbreviated forms have to be identified and particular attention has to be devoted to contextual variation which is frequent with complex lexical forms. Multiple compound nouns, for instance, occur in truncated form in running text and may therefore be identical in form to their hyponyms which represent other, superordinated concepts.

3.1.2.2. *Homonyms, synonyms and variants*

The recognition that terms occur in various linguistic contexts and that they have variants which are frequently context-conditioned shatters the idealised view that there can or should be only one designation for a concept and vice versa. In order to account for different meanings of the same term as they occur in texts (homonymy), it had always been accepted that a term form could belong to more than one subject field, where it would be differently defined. Thus the division into separate vocabularies according to subject fields was a necessary pre-condition for the terminological theory that excluded the natural existence of homonyms. As soon as the one-to-one correspondence is broken in the other direction, i.e. as soon as we accept that there can be several synonyms (contextual or other) for one concept, it becomes necessary to establish criteria for identifying the one regular and proper name for a concept to which the others are variants, or alternatively to define the context in which the regular paradigm of the term occurs. For the semasiological approach this is a theoretical rather than a practical problem because in the practice of an automated dictionary, there are simply several addresses or term entry points to the same file. In the onomasiological approach and in the search for translation equivalents, however, the choice between forms must be made via contextual examples which are translated into rules of usage. In this way terminological theory gains a practical dimension. (See also section 8.2.2.2.)

3.1.2.3. *Status of terms*

Terms can have a variable pragmatic status, which is usually associated with their age, or more precisely, with their acceptability, exclusiveness of existence, and spread of use. The observation of the usage conditions of terminological innovation and of the immediate capture of new term creations in term banks or glossaries indicates that new terms undergo various changes in status until they become fully established. Most monolingual neologisms are initially provisional, linked to a provisional concept by a stipulative definition, until the equation TERM–DEFINITION–CONCEPT becomes widely accepted and so incorporated into the lexicon of a particular special language. At this stage one of a number of rival terms gains a higher status and the rivals will gradually loose ground or become confined to a small area of usage. A similar phenomenon occurs when a term has to be provided with a foreign language equivalent, e.g. in the translation of a manual or a textbook, and there is no foreign language term which corresponds to the definition. In this case a translation equivalent is created whose validity is restricted to the context in which it has been created unless it becomes accepted as a full term with its own definition, which means that it has become associated to a concept in a conceptual system that is expressed in the foreign language. This phenomenon is well-known in translation theory; in terminological description it is hidden behind what is usually called a quality label.

3.1.3 *Processes of terminologisation*

In both his roles as recorder of new terms and advisor on designation, the terminologist must also be aware of the gradual evolution of terms.

The evolution of concepts is accompanied by stages of naming, a process which is called terminologisation. In the development of knowledge the concepts of science and technology like those of other disciplines undergo changes; accordingly their linguistic forms are flexible until a concept is fully formed and incorporated in the knowledge structure. The designation can, therefore, oscillate between the absolute fixation of reference of standards and the flexibility of notions. Innovation in science is dependent upon our ability to question the validity of certain concepts while keeping others fixed. Consequently, we have to accept not only a different relationship between term and concept from the one we are accustomed to between word and notion, but degrees of special reference and hence a different semantic force attached to a term according to the text in which a particular designation is encountered.

The question of terminologisation is fundamental to the description of special languages. A particular grouping of lexical items, e.g. 'delayed action', 'relay-race', 'flat belt', which in general communication may be analysed either as free collocations or compounds without much effect on the communicative intention, must be clearly assigned to one or the other category in special communication as it can change confirmation into addition of knowledge, a retrospective speech act into a progressive one and so considerably unbalance the information load of an utterance. Idioms like 'small talk' or 'fine art' are either understood or not and may in some cases be analysed and thus understood—with more or less success—in the speech act; as used by specialists an expression like 'delayed action' is terminologised; it is a term of a particular special language, whereas in general language it may or it may not be seen as lexicalised.

Lexicographers and terminologists are faced with different problems. The lexicographer has to distinguish between the inherent and the collocational meaning of a lexical item. He retains what he considers to have become lexicalised into a unit, e.g. 'out of breath', 'by hook or by crook'. Separately written units, e.g. 'front door', 'tool box', are usually entered under the nucleus or headword of the compound. The terminologist decides on his entries according to the conceptual framework in which he is working at the time. He establishes terminological units such as 'laterally reversed' or 'multiple-start screw thread' for one subject field without claiming lexicalisation of this unit in another or in general language. Such units are then also treated as separate entries in the dictionary. For example, the following sequence is appropriate for clearly separate concepts: 'bend testing – Brinell hardness testing – hardness testing – tensile testing'.

In practice terminologists face difficulties with the recognition of terminological units in running text, which can generally only be resolved by general or special subject knowledge. Even without the assistance of capital letters a compound term like e.g. 'Great Dane' must be recognised as referring to a separate breed of dog whereas a 'great bulldog' simply refers to the size of a particular animal. Such entities are often acknowledged because they exist in opposition to other terms, e.g.

dedicated computer	–	general purpose computer
compression moulding	–	injection moulding
infinitely variable speed transmission	–	step-by-step variable (speed) transmission

Whereas lexicalisation in general language is often accompanied by some form of external characteristic like graphemic signs such as hyphenation, writing together, capitalisation, or even omission of articles, terminologisation is much less dependent on such devices. The special language user is expected to know the appropriate concepts, but it must also be recognised that many new terminological units are of relatively recent date and therefore have not had the time to develop special forms.

3.2 Term formation: theory and practice

Unlike words, whose origin is rarely traceable, terms are the result of more or less conscious creation. In a number of well-defined areas and subject fields, e.g. in Botany or Chemistry, term creation occurs according to some specific plan and it is this which gives rise to theoretical speculation. If we can discover a greater number of regularities in the naming patterns of textually related lexical items, it is assumed that we shall be able to:
(a) construe the rules of naming applicable to a subject field,
(b) establish rules for future rule-governed designation,
(c) possibly even relate the motivation of naming patterns to the more elusive motivation of concept creation.
Furthermore, if it can be shown that naming patterns, as reflected in complex terms, by means of such devices as determination, derivation, etc., are developed on the basis of the systematic selection of certain properties and

characteristics for overt inclusion in the form of a term, then we may actually gain some insight into the mental processes involved in concept formation and association.

The possibilities offered by computational analysis of large quantities of linguistic data are considerable and far from being even theoretically mapped out. Significant insights are expected to be gained both in respect of the naming techniques and comprehension of complex terminological units and in respect of the way we represent knowledge by linguistic means. Statistical data are available on the vocabularies of distinct special subject fields and parsing and term recognition techniques are currently being perfected that should permit the accumulation of representative samples of terminology for analysis.

Any attempt to discover regularities in term formation must, however, be fully aware of the limited usefulness of this enterprise and of the circumstances in which term formation occurs. Most new terms are formed as and when new concepts are created in such instances as new discoveries, restructuring of existing knowledge, incidental observations or planned industrial developments. In each of these cases the new concept to be named is seen in a particular light in relation to other concepts around it. It is therefore not surprising that the linguistic sign for a concept can be quite arbitrarily chosen and often is. Quite regular sequences of terms can be broken by irregular formations which may be historically explicable but which clearly disrupt what would otherwise appear to be a highly efficient set of terms. For example, in a sequence of types of characters we find a long list of compounds with 'character' but also one type called 'format effector', the subtypes of which are, however, again called according to the main pattern, e.g.

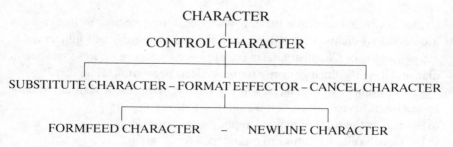

It would also appear to be the case that the effort spent on appropriate term formation is essentially justified by the need of the creator rather than by the need of an interlocutor or future listener. Scientists sometimes take considerable trouble over naming a concept in a consistent and transparent manner, by choosing determiners or qualifiers for nouns which express the characteristics of a concept they consider to be relevant. There is, however, no evidence that, in the effort of comprehension, we decompose a terminological unit into constituent parts in order to understand it better. We do not, for example, decompose the meaning of 'modem' in order to understand the meaning of this name for a transformer of computer signals into telephone signals. The case of abbreviations, acronyms and other forms of shortening clearly confirms this paradox.

3.2.1 *Motivation for designation*

The objects and methods of enquiry of each special subject determine the concepts with which it operates and the designations required for these concepts. In general language, using general reference, we have names for some parts of some systems but not necessarily for all parts, e.g. we have the general name 'elbow', 'knee', 'flower' but do not have separate popular names for all the constituents of these complex entities. In fact, in general reference we do not normally consider or acknowledge the elbow, the knee and flowers to have separately named constituent parts. In general reference we also group together similar objects, e.g. books (as distinct from documents, in general), or plants (as distinct from trees), which in special reference do not represent distinct and independent classes. In Information Science, however, books are types of document, and in Botany trees are a subtype of plant.

In special reference the classificatory use of language is exploited for designation and this leads to a certain consistency of choice of naming technique and order of elements of term formation. Processes and methods are usually named as nouns which have a higher classificatory value than the corresponding verbal form. This need accounts for such verbal nouns as 'milling', 'slicing', 'pulping' and derived nouns such as 'emulsification', 'saponification', 'esterification', 'evaporation' in special reference.

Properties, qualities and states, which in general reference are usually expressed only by means of adjectives, also acquire nominal forms in order to fit the requirements of systematic categories for special reference. Some properties are exclusive to special reference and do not then have adjectives at all, e.g.

| property terms | – | elasticity, toxicity, viscosity, conductivity, density, corrosibility. |
| states | – | severity, abnormality, animation, suspension, corrosion, mobility. |

Concepts indicating measurable properties of entities, processes or states, require a double name for the quantity measured and the unit of measurement. The processes involved in measurements and the associated instruments create complete sets of terms to permit the expression of detailed, verifiable and repeatable quantification which distinguishes the exact sciences.

The systematic method of designation is based on consistency in the creation of terms by choosing qualifiers indicative of some property or other essential characteristic of a concept. Regular patterns of compound terms could in theory be developed with one, two, three and more elements to indicate hierarchical dependencies. Such patterns rarely succeed beyond minimal sets in the applied sciences. For example, in the language of civil engineering the terms 'bascule bridge', 'swing bridge', 'folding bridge', 'lift bridge' are seen to be related by the fact that the determiner indicates a mode of movement of the bridge. It would be reasonable to expect 'bridge' to be the superordinate term: in fact it is not, but all these types of bridges are types of draw bridges, a term which by its linguistic form is indistinguishable from the other four terms. Another difficulty arises from the fact that some terms are mutually exclusive and others are partly intersecting in reference. For example, 'isolated footing' and 'combined footing' are mutually exclusive terms in the field of civil engineering, but 'cantilever footing' overlaps with 'combined footing'.

In practice purely logical principles of naming do not succeed and are overtaken by the conventions developed in each subject field. There are conventions for naming parts of engines and there are rules for naming organisms. In English compound nouns the determiner more frequently indicates a type of the object named by the nucleus than anything else. Plant names are based on genetic types, chemical compound names on constituent parts. Otherwise parts are traditionally rarely identified as belonging to a whole. For example, most parts of the body have unique names. Designations of parts may, however, reflect their similarity horizontally, e.g. 'to input–to output'. In the following example we observe both horizontal and vertical regularities of naming:

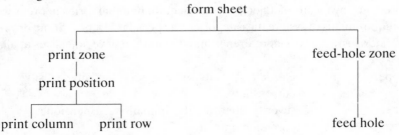

Many special terms are created by identifying the particular function of an object which is essential for the new concept, e.g.

OBJECT	FUNCTION	NEW TERM
hammer	locking	hammerlock
ribbon	shifting	ribbonshift
forms	stacking	form stacker
forms	feeding	form feed
carriage	control	carriage control

Further specification can then produce more complex entities like e.g. 'automatic carriage control', or 'continuous form feed'.

The specification can use various criteria, e.g.

TYPE OF SPECIFICATION		EXAMPLE
functional:	a box for tools, mail	toolbox, mailbox
material :	a box made of steel	steel box
place :	a box for under a window	window box

Certain types of determination abound in connection with certain concepts. There are, for example, many more compounds with 'box' based on function or use than of any other type, e.g.

callbox	signal box	money box	letter box
horse box	flower box	witness box	sentry box
lunchbox	jurybox	gearbox	

Consecutive stages of determination produce sequences of terms in hierarchy, e.g.

GENERIC HIERARCHY

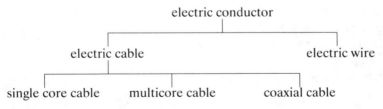

PARTITIVE HIERARCHY

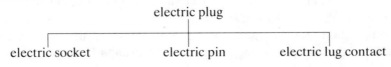

Determination can be expressed both by compound and derived nouns and any word class can be used as determiner. In each case the new term is considered a more specific term in intension.

Examples:

DERIVATION			COMPOUNDING		
charge	–	supercharge	retrieval	–	fact retrieval
natal	–	antenatal	translation	–	machine translation
heading	–	subheading	test	–	test sample
arm	–	forearm	iron	–	T-iron
melted	–	pre-melted	feed	–	fast feed

In English compounding is much more widely used for this purpose.

Determination can be introduced progressively. An originally free collocation, e.g. a box for tools, can be reduced step by step to its shortest form, e.g. tool box, tool-box, toolbox. Not all these stages are systematically gone through, nor do all compounds eventually end up as single orthographical words. This type of reduction to simple juxtaposition of nouns, while being brief, looses its transparency for comprehension; e.g. 'diamond drilling' signifies drilling by means of diamond drill bits, whereas 'concrete drilling' signifies drilling into concrete.

Difficulties of interpretation occur when the determiner does not precede the concept determined or modified. In some cases ambiguity can be avoided by means of hyphens, e.g.

open-ended, wide-angle lens, high-tension wire.

There is a tendency to reduce longer compounds to their shortest possible form, e.g.

holding down clamp ⇒ hold down
magazine feeding attachment ⇒ magazine feed ⇒ magazine
power-operated feed ⇒ power feed
oil bath lubrication ⇒ bath lubrication

Much less frequent techniques of term formation are conjunction and disjunction.

Conjunction is the process by which two concepts are combined as equals in a new concept and this fact is reflected in the term. The most common form of conjunction occurs in numerals, e.g. 'three hundred and sixty-five', which combines the use of conjunction and simple juxtaposition, with or without hyphenation or truncation. The expression form can then signal the equal standing of the joined elements by any of these devices, as e.g. in

Anglo-French, socio-economic, socio-cultural
black-and-white (as an antonym to colour[film])
modem
condenser–receiver
gas and air mixture
dot and dash system
lifting and forcing pump
climbing–falling film evaporator

Many names for chemical compounds are formed on the basis of conjunction, e.g.

glyceryl monostearate
ethylenediamine tetraacetic acid

The use of conjunction is common in geographical names which express the unity of previously separate entities, e.g.

Mersey–Trent Valley Water Authority
Czechoslovakia
Swiss–German

It also occurs in expressions of complex measurements, as, e.g. 'meters per second', 'man-year'.

Disjunction is the process by which the extensions of two or more concepts are combined into a new superordinated concept. It presents two alternatives as a single concept and is therefore an either/or relationship, as it occurs in the syntagm 'either direction working of lines' which is not fully terminologised. 'Left–right indicator' is a clear example of a disjunctively formed term. Other such terms are, e.g.

glide–sail parachute
on/off valve
drive-on/drive-off ferry

3.2.1.1. *Names and proper nouns*
An understanding of the issues related to naming of individual objects as distinct from concepts or general notions contributes to our full use of the methods of naming in terminology. The rules of naming developed for particular

sets of vocabulary have been derived from interpretations of cases of spontaneous naming. These rules attempt to achieve simultaneously maximal efficiency of naming for the purpose of comprehension and optimal linguistic forms for ease of communication. A critical analysis of these very conscious efforts of systematising natural language processes permits us to draw valuable conclusions about our own perceptions of the functions and operations of natural and artificial languages.

Names, in the sense of proper names, are quite distinct entities and differ from common nouns in many respects. They have reference but no sense, i.e. their meaning cannot be decomposed into constituent elements. 'Boy' can be defined by the words 'young', 'male' and 'human' and is understood to refer to a member of a class. By contrast we have established the convention that proper names are seen as representatives of more or less unique entities; 'George', for example, refers to an individual, but cannot be endowed with sense as it could possibly refer to a boy, a man, a girl, a woman, a town, etc. Names cannot be used predicatively; e.g. I can say 'he is a boy' but I cannot say *'he is a George'. The individual referred to by a name can be described but not defined: all the statements we can make about a person called 'George' reinforce the individuality of this person, whereas a definition of 'boy' permits us to identify the many individuals who can be referred to by this word. Proper names have definite reference only; we cannot say *'have you ever seen an Eiffel tower' and it is only under exceptional circumstances that we can say 'do you know a George Evans?' which means in effect 'do you know an individual person called George Evans?'.

In general usage proper names of persons have two functions: a referential function like common nouns and a vocative function. This function is apparent with names of persons which are used as forms of address, but this function is by no means exclusive, because titles are also used as forms of address, e.g. 'your worship'.

In his description of the ontogenesis of reference, Quine (1960) deals with naming and proper names. He identifies four phases of development. In the first phase of the development of the classificatory function of language all words used refer to unique or uniquely perceived items or phenomena; in the second phase a distinction is learnt and made between individuals and categories or classes of individuals which is linguistically reflected in the distinction between proper names and common nouns. The third phase is of less interest here and concerns the ability to distinguish between membership of classes and temporary attributes, i.e. nouns and adjective + noun constructions, e.g. 'books + a blue book + a book with a broken spine'. The fourth phase identifies the ability to make comparisons between individuals and classes, e.g. not only 'John is taller than Mary' but also 'John is taller than the average man'.

The transition from the first to the second stage is the starting point for the later development of special reference and terms. In child language acquisition the important breakthrough occurs when a child learns the distinction between what society sees as an individual and what it sees as member of a class. This distinction is further reinforced through the naming techniques available. There is on the whole a much greater freedom of choice hence arbitrariness in the naming of individuals than there is in the naming of classes. The learner takes over the conventional designations for classes of objects in existence, and even names 'new' ones by analogy. The child learns very soon that names of individuals, especially persons are both freely and arbitrarily bestowed, e.g. nicknames, petnames, endearments, and also governed by certain rules which distinguish between first name and surname etc. The important aspect, however, is that names are more strongly conditioned by the social norm than by the linguistic norms of any one language as can be readily demonstrated by examining patterns of naming persons and geographical objects.

Proper names are subject to change under pressure from society. Names of streets and towns are regularly changed for political reasons. Border changes can affect the names of an entire geographical region and the former names can then acquire particular connotations, e.g. the use of 'Danzig' when referring to the now Polish city of Gdansk.

Proper names do not necessarily belong to any one language, which can be seen by the fact that only very few proper names have translation equivalents. The English name for the Italian town of Livorno is Leghorn, and clearly both refer to the same geographical place, but the English name would not necessarily be used in all English texts because it has particular historical and literary associations. Very common placenames have language-specific orthographic variants, e.g. Geneva, Geneve, Ginebra, Genf; Praga, Prague, Prag, Praha. It is a commonplace that we do not translate the names of persons, i.e. we do not say Joseph Green for the Italian composer Guiseppe Verdi.

Names of persons are usually structured into individual and group/family association; in some cases change in social status, e.g. marriage, leads to a change in name (e.g. Adela Josefina Hernandez Garcia de Castro). A number of surnames have arisen from first names, e.g. the many surnames in '-son' or 'O'-'.

Even proper names do, however, take on classificatory attributes or require further specification by class association. In some geographical names there is a need to identify the class of objects to which the individual belongs, e.g. Mount Everest, Botany Bay, River Thames, Scilly Isles.

In special languages there appears to be a particular need for combining the individualising value of proper names with the classificatory function of common names. Industrial products are given what can only be described as class names. To call a motor car a 'Valiant', a 'Polo', a 'Rover', are attempts to provide a suitable individualising or even personalising designation for a product beside the technical names of the models in question which are usually the name of the manufacturing firm followed by a serial number, e.g. Rover 2000 GL, Volkswagen Polo GX. Product names are sometimes changed in order to follow fashion, but this tendency may enter into conflict with the necessity of maintaining clear reference within a classification. This conflict can be demonstrated in the case of colours of paints. In order to maintain clear reference to colours, professional painters identify colours by reference to a standardised classification, based on a numbered system of colours, which is ultimately supported by a national standard specifying the exact chemical composition of colours used for paint. In this way the market is left free to invent the names it believes to be most successful for selling the product, e.g. 'tangerine, salmon, apple-blossom'. These colour names can only be understood if they can be related to a steady set of designations and a supporting classificatory scheme; the professional painter translates the fashion names into the numbers of the preestablished classification scheme.

The strongest example of individualising tendencies in naming comes from botany and horticulture where many plants are named after the person who identified or classified them. New varieties are then also given individualising names, e.g. 'Aster Esther' which is a hybrid from 'Aster ericoides' and 'Aster novii-belgii', the latter of which itself has the varieties of 'Ada Ballard', 'Lady Frances', 'Mistress Quickly', 'Percy Thrower' and 'Raspberry Ripple'.

A further extension of the use of proper names occurs when they are used to refer to a wider set of objects. This is a common occurrence with some geographical names used for the typical produce of the place, e.g. 'burgundy, champagne, sherry (Jerez), gouda, cheddar, edam.' With names of persons the first step is to associate a person with a product, e.g. a Biro pen, a Mae West jacket (inflated life-jacket). The next step is to name a product directly after the inventor, e.g. 'macadam, mansarde, macintosh'. A further stage is the generalisation of a proper name into a class name. This occurs with the use of trade names such as Biro, Hoover, Kleenex for all makes of ballpoint pens, vacuum cleaners and paper handkerchiefs respectively. These names do not normally have a long life as products change characteristics and advertising ensures the use of other names.

3.2.2 *Patterns of term formation*

The objects and methods of enquiry of each special subject determine the concepts with which it operates and the designations required for these concepts. For all sciences and technologies new terms are regularly required for new objects, parts of objects and new processes.

We distinguish three major approaches to the creation of new designations:
1. the use of existing resources,
2. the modification of existing resources,
3. the creation of new linguistic entities.

3.2.2.1. *Use of existing resources*

In this approach it is common to extend the meaning of an existing term to embrace that of a new concept, e.g. 'spaceship' or 'aircraft' even 'car' now refer to objects which were not imagined when the words were first created. New names may be given in analogy with existing designations and meaning may be transferred by such rhetorical figures as metaphor.

The most common way of new designation is the use of simile, i.e. the naming of a concept in analogy to another, familiar one, e.g. 'a rock-like substance', 'an L-shaped room'. After reflection, an initial similarity may often prove to be irrelevant or even misleading. It may, therefore, later be found to be an inadequate motivation for naming. Simile can also be considered as a preliminary to term-formation which assists in the fixation of a concept by some easy means of comparison. Comparisons using simile are particularly useful in textbooks or other introductory material to a subject, e.g.

'Concrete is "as" durable "as" any material known to man and is capable of supporting enormous loads. It can be poured into forms and it hardens in place so that the whole structure is "like" one massive stone.'

'Though brick is not quite "so" enduring "as" stone, it is fireproof which wood is not.'

Simile can be overtly expressed by the use of such qualifying expressions as '-style', '-like', or '-type', as exemplified in the following compounds:

modern-style building	plate-like frames	track-type bulldozer
tooth-like projection	arch-gravity type dam	wheel-type bulldozer

Another technique of using existing resources is to explore the polysemic nature of general language designations. Instead of saying that something is like something else we call it by the thing it most resembles. This produces metaphorical combined names the motivation for which can be found in similarities of form, function and position, e.g.:

mushroom ceiling	insulation blanket	trunk of a column	bedrock
umbrella cupola	ball hinges	ribbed floor	pile-head
barrel vault	pin hinges	river bed	pile-foot
shell of the house	wing walls	canal bed	

Parts of the human body and the particular shapes of animals provide many metaphoric expressions.

In some cases the metaphor is complete and stands on its own. In terms like 'furring', 'anchor', 'apron', 'bleeding', 'pocket', we cannot distinguish between the general language form and the special reference given to these terms in the field of civil engineering.

A special designation in one field can also be re-used in another field for a different concept. This produces homonyms as in the following examples:

'hardware'   – in the language of computers and in general usage;
'plumbing'   – in the language of surveying and in hydraulic works;
'piping'   – in the language of soil mechanics, in hydraulic work and sewing;
'alinement'   – in the language of surveying and in road construction.

3.2.2.2. *Modification of existing resources*

The most common method of designation of new concepts is the modification of existing ones by means of

1) derivation or affixation, which is the addition of affixes;
2) compounding, which is the combination of existing words into new ones;
3) conversion, which is neither affixation nor compounding, but a syntagmatically varied use of the same form, e.g. a noun used as a verb, an adjective used as a noun. This form is strongly expressed in general English, but is also common in technical English;
4) compression, which is any form of shortening of an expression form by means of abbreviation, clipping, acronyms, etc.

In special reference, conversion is largely used for creating the noun concepts associated to verbal ones that are required by the classificatory function of language. Compression has the dual function of providing shorter expression forms for frequently used terms and new exclusive names for long forms which might not be understood as terminological units.

Functionally, derivation and compounding serve the purpose of closer determination of a concept—narrowing its intension—while at the same time showing the relationship that exists between the new concept and its origin. In this way determination can make transparent a particular dimension of the conceptual structure. This is both its strength and its weakness: by expressing one relationship, it is silent on others which conceptually may be considered more significant. One of the most frequent modes of determination is to relate an object to its particular function or use in the special subject field, e.g.

design drawing	fire resistant material	drainage ditch
design chart	rock tunnelling machine	field work
traffic-bearing lane		

The technique of determination as a word formation device probably originates in syntagmatic determination. We may assume an evolution from a longer syntagm as e.g. in 'a post which is built to support a beam' where the relative clause determines 'post' by its function, or 'girders cast prior to construction'. There are then various grammatical possibilities of closer specification of which one, usually the shortest becomes generally accepted, e.g. 'beam support post', or 'pre-cast girders'. In other cases a more complex compound may be created, e.g. 'bridges which have members that are joined by pins' which becomes 'bridges with pin-joined members'.

Determination can affect any word category, e.g.

NOUNS:	bolted connection	round channel
	covering material	wind load
	groundwater pressure	masonry structure
VERBS:	pre-fabricate	pre-build
	prestress	pre-cast
ADJECTIVES:	v-shaped	inlaid

The determining modifier usually precedes the concept modified. Difficulties of interpretation occur when a concept is determined by more than one modifier, e.g.

water supply systems	minimum safe distance
road building material	site-assembled acoustical materials

In case of difficulty of interpretation or ambiguity it is possible to indicate the closer relationship between two of three items by means of hyphens. Hyphenation then offers some help in overtly explicating the relationships of the parts, e.g.

sound-proof construction	loosely-packed	rock-type soils
soil-moisture conditions	high-tension wire	anti-freeze agent

Compounds of phrases containing prepositions, articles, conjunctions and adverbs are more often hyphenated than noun compounds, e.g.:

simply-supported beams	cast-in-place	stick-and-rag work
well-packed earth subgrade	tile-and-a-half-tile	right-of-way

Affixation. Affixation takes several forms and has several functions. By form it can be pre-, in-, or suf-fixation; by function it can serve for determination and for changing word categories. In practice most suffixes serve to determine change of word category and prefixes serve for determination.

Changing word categories (suffixation). In many cases the change of word category is accompanied by some type of determination, e.g. to indicate a specific process associated with a more general verbal action.

VERBS ⇒ NOUNS

Verb + -ing

plan	–	planning	load	– loading
break	–	breaking	cover	– covering
loose	–	loosening	mould	– moulding
fill	–	filling	plumb	– plumbing
grade	–	grading	tunnel	– tunnelling

> NOTE: Verbs forming nouns in -ing, can also indicate either the process or an entity associated with the process.

Verb + -ion

found	–	foundation	transit	– transition
elevate	–	elevation	install	– installation
project	–	projection	circulate	– circulation
erode	–	erosion	intersect	– intersection
expand	–	expansion	compress	– compression

Verb + -ation

accumulate	–	accumulation	irrigate	–	irrigation
stabilise	–	stabilisation	excavate	–	excavation
pulverise	–	pulverisation	elevate	–	elevation

NOTE: Verbs ending in '-ize', '-ise', or '-ate' usually indicate processes.

Others:

| reinforce | – | reinforcement | shrink | – | shrinkage |
| treat | – | treatment | press | – | pressure |

NOUN ⇒ ADJECTIVE

| angle | – | angular | horizon | – | horizontal |

ADJECTIVE ⇒ NOUN

elastic	–	elasticity	moist	–	moisture
grave	–	gravity	humid	–	humidity
intense	–	intensity	able	–	ability
stable	–	stability	viscous	–	viscosity
flexible	–	flexibility	fixed	–	fixity

NOTE: In engineering the suffix '-ity' usually describes a property.

CONCRETE NOUN ⇒ ABSTRACT NOUN

| drain | – | drainage | tunnel | – | tunnelling |
| excavator | – | excavation | | | |

COUNTABLE NOUN ⇒ MASS NOUN

SINGULAR	PLURAL	MASS NOUN
sheet	sheets	sheeting
scaffold	scaffolds	scaffolding
pile	piles	piling
panel	panels	panelling
brace	braces	bracing

Determination (prefixation). The number of affixes in special English is very large because English has borrowed or adapted many Latin and Greeks words, word elements and affixes. In general, English freely admits and assimilates word elements and words from other languages and in science and technology, particularly, draws continuously and heavily on Greek and Latin for prefixes, suffixes and stems, e.g.

PREFIXES	STEMS	SUFFIXES
superelevation	intersect	anhydrous
transitional	centerline	adhesive
superstructure	interpose	corrosion
hydrodynamic	homogeneous	deposit
reinforcement	rheology	compaction

Prefixes can assist considerably in the systematic structuring of special vocabularies by the creation of term pairs, e.g.

upstream   –   midstream   –   downstream
stabilise   –   destabilise
overpass   –   underpass

Opposite terms can be created easily by the negatives 'un-', 'dis-', 'a-', 'de-', 'in-', e.g.

| unbalance | unstable | displacement | anhydrous | inefficient |
| unload | disconnect | decompose | inconsistent | |

Noun Compounds. A compound is a combination of two or more words into a new syntagmatic unit with a new meaning independent of the constituent parts. In terminology we add the requirement that the new entity created must represent a concept.

When there are two elements in a compound the first element usually determines the second which is called the nucleus, e.g.

| water load | rock floor | damp course |
| canal bed | masonry structure | sight width |

Compounds themselves can enter into combinations for new compounds as either nucleus or determinant, e.g.

rock-typesoil   weather-resisting feature
foundation soil failure   vibration-proof construction

When there are three elements two patterns are possible.

(A + B) + C   e.g.   simply-supported beams
A + (B + C)   e.g.   overload relief valve

More complex patterns occur and are usually understood only in the framework of a special subject. In the following examples the structure is indicated by brackets:

> (bending-moment) diagram
> (extra-rapid-hardening) cement
> advanced (waste water) treatment
> minimum (strain energy) (twisted-folded) energy
> (data control) (block fill-in) process
> (reinforced concrete) (underwater construction)
> (simply-supported) (steel beams)

Eponymic compounds with proper nouns, names of persons or places are frequent. They are used to designate substances, materials, objects, instruments, methods, processes and measurements. They have the advantage of unique differentiation but lack systematic import, e.g.

Warren truss	Ohio cofferdam	Eddy's theorem
French drain	Portland cement	Pratt truss
Portland stone	Poole's tiles	

Noun compounds contribute to the building of terminological systems. The nucleus of the compound, usually the last element, can then indicate the category to which the concept belongs and the determinant indicates the criterion for the subdivision of the category, e.g.

wind load	riveted connection	canal tunnel
ice load	bolted connection	pedestrian tunnel
snow load	glued connection	vehicle tunnel
water load	screwed connection	subway tunnel
	dowelled connection	railway tunnel
marble structure	nailed connection	traffic tunnel
metal structure		underwater tunnel
masonry structure		underground tunnel
		mountain tunnel

According to the nature of the nucleus it is possible to distinguish between types of compounds, which designate:

a. Objects

concrete breaker	concrete placer	concrete pile
concrete mixer	concrete roof	concrete pump
concrete paver	concrete pipe	

b. Properties
   concrete strength   concrete stability

c. Processes and Operations
   concrete slump test   concrete casting

Depending on the nature of the nucleus, the determinant can specify in greater detail, indicate a purpose, the means by which an operation is carried out, the object to which a process is applied, or the time, place or other circumstances which, in this way, become an integral distinctive feature of the new concept.

The determinant may specify the material of which the nucleus is made in order to differentiate it from similar objects made from other materials, e.g.

wooden post	steel post
concrete post	stone post

The determinant may express an inherent property of the new concept which is not inherent in the nucleus, e.g.

waste deposit	granular material	wind pressure
volume computation	rock floor	pneumatic caisson
retaining wall	power shovel	

The determinant may specify the regular use of the nucleus, e.g.

insulating material	freezing-point depressant
anti-freeze agent	rock-tunnelling machine
sound absorbing units	weather-resistant feature

The determinant may specify the object of the verbal noun, e.g.

site paving	earth moving	rock clearing
site clearing	soil testing	plan drawing

Compound adjectives serve to describe processes of production, to typify and specify operations and to identify new entities, e.g.

light sensitive	sound-insulating
heat resistant	air-entraining

Compound verbs are usually formed with particles and are in practice indistinguishable from general language verbs, e.g.

outfall	overload	overflow
underpin	overlie	underplant

Conversion. Conversion is the change of word category without morphological alteration of the word inflection. In practice, however, it cannot always be determined clearly whether a noun is converted to a verb or vice versa, e.g.:

mould	supply	tread	load	sound
pile	site	span	design	frame
form	strip	incline	wire	crane
fill	support	slope	force	finish

Compression. Special languages can also create new forms by various forms of compression of existing expression forms. The most common form is that of acronyms formed from initial letters of longer words, e.g.

FM, AC, TNT, DDT; A (Amp), V (Volt)

The names of many institutions are abbreviations, some of which have taken over so completely that the full form is practically never used, e.g. 'Unesco', 'Nato', which have evolved to such an extent that they have become letter words, i.e. their pronunciation is like that of any other word.

Another frequent and highly productive method is clipping or shortening in which syllables or letters are omitted from any part of the word, e.g. 'maths', 'lab', 'vet', 'intercom', 'vertijet'. A particular case is that of compounding and simultaneous clipping as, e.g.

stagnation + inflation   = stagflation
biological + electronic = bionic

3.2.2.3. *Creation of new lexical entities (neologisms)*
Neologisms in science and technology result from the need for the unique naming of new concepts. Regarding their form neologisms are essentially of two types; either they are totally new creations or they are borrowings from other languages. English relies heavily on borrowing elements from Greek and Latin which are variously anglicised. After Greek and Latin English borrows from French, though with such a long tradition of borrowing from all three languages it is not always clear whether a word has come into English via French or whether it has been taken directly from one of the classical languages. Since Greek, Latin and even French words and word elements (e.g. 'caisson', 'manoeuvre', 'reservoir') are such an integral part of the English language, it is at times difficult to distinguish between genuine neologisms and the re-use or modification of existing elements. There is consequently uncertainty in attribution between the processes of derivation with the aid of

Latin or Greek word elements and that of borrowing. The word 'television', while obviously a new form can be said to have been produced by derivation, because it has not been borrowed as a whole and with its current meaning. Only the taking over of Greek and Latin concepts and their designation would, therefore, be properly described as borrowing, e.g. the geometrical concepts of 'diameter', 'tangent', 'spiral', and 'circular'. On the other hand, the use of Greek and Latin expression forms for new concepts produces neologisms, e.g. 'excavator', 'telemeter', 'pylon'.

3.2.3 *Pragmatic aspects of term formation*

Term formation always occurs in a particular environment, e.g. in a research laboratory, a design office, a workshop or in any other situation where people have need for new expression forms. A major distinction is being recognised between terminology creation which accompanies scientific and technological innovation in any one linguistic community and that which accompanies the transfer of scientific and technological knowledge from one linguistic community to another. While the former is spontaneous, the latter can be designed and engineered. It is now realised that term formation is and can be influenced according to the subject area in which it occurs, the nature of the people involved and the origin of the stimulus for term formation.

With regard to the circumstances of creation, two major types are therefore distinguished: primary and secondary term formation.

Primary term formation accompanies concept formation and is therefore monolingual; it may be provisional, i.e. accompanied by a stipulative or otherwise temporary definition or it may be seen as definitive. Secondary term formation occurs when a new term is created for a known concept and happens in two distinct situations:

(1) as a result of monolingual revision of a terminology, e.g. for the purpose of producing a standards document, or
(2) as a result of knowledge transfer to another linguistic community which is carried out by means of term creation.

Primary and secondary term formation are ruled by different motivations and influences. The fundamental difference between the two methods lies in the fact that in primary term formation there is no linguistic precedent, though there may be more or less strict rules for the formation of appropriate terms, whereas in secondary term formation there always is the precedent of an existent term with its own motivation. The new term to be created must then be justified in some way and this justification may include reference to the form of existent terms. Secondary term formation is more often subject to guidelines than primary term formation and it may, therefore, be said that it is the proper concern of terminologists to provide such guidelines on the basis of the term and word formation patterns of the subject field and natural language in question.

Primary term formation resulting from new concept formation in scientific disciplines is externally uncontrolled and uncontrollable, though it is, of course, influenced by existing patterns of terms already created—at its most notable in the nomenclatures of the taxonomic sciences. New scientific terms created by one linguistic community spread quickly to the international scientific community by means of conferences, articles in journals, and now also databases. The still growing tendency of this community to choose from a small number of vehicular languages, i.e. English, French, Japanese, Russian, means that it may take a considerable time before new scientific terms find equivalents in other languages. Since the scientific community which genuinely deals with the creation of new concepts is relatively small and educationally homogeneous, communication, which is largely internal to the group, is not seriously impeded by the absence of other language versions. Nor is the arbitrary creation of equivalents, which sometimes co-exist for years with the original term, a serious obstacle to communication under these circumstances. Difficulties occur and have been identified when the scientific community addresses other groups. It is then that accusations of 'jargon' are levelled. The need for an intermediate language, possibly also with an intermediate vocabulary, between scientific and general has been recognised.

In technology and in industrial applications a much larger and more heterogeneous population is involved and the terminology used also occurs in general speech situations. This community takes over some terminology created by science and creates its own voluminous terminology with distinctive characteristics determined by the diversified communicative situations of this community in contact with others.

The technological vocabulary is partially controllable and controlled. Like all linguistic phenomena it cannot be strictly separated from the scientific vocabulary on the one hand and from the general language vocabulary on the other. Some of it shares characteristics with scientific terminology and some comes close to general language. It may be defined as that vocabulary which is the result of conscious creation as a result of industrial/technological innovation and which is susceptible to planning—in the way that some scientific terminology and general language vocabulary are not.

Both primary and secondary term formation in this area are subject to heavy synonym formation which is either accidental—possibly caused by parallel industrial developments—or deliberate—possibly in response to the need for popular versions of scientific terms and product differentiation. The formation of synonyms is further characterised by the creation of hybrids in the form of term/names (e.g. a Ford Fiesta). This latter development is influenced by publicity criteria, i.e. the emotive use of language, which is normally considered to be absent in terminology.

The terminology of technology, unlike that of science which, once it has been created, is likely to stay unchanged (at least in the original language), is volatile both in its form and existence because of changes in materials, methods of production, design etc. This lack of stability is accentuated in transferred terminology, i.e. terminology created by secondary term formation from concepts borrowed from another linguistic community. The co-existence of several methods of secondary interlingual term formation, e.g. direct borrowing, loan translation, paraphrase, parallel formation/constituent recreation, adaptation, complete new creation, which may be used simultaneously or sequentially, provides the occasion for several alternative or competing new terms and it may therefore be several years before a terminology stabilises.

3.2.3.1. *Trends in secondary term formation*

While in principle the practical problems of secondary term formation are the same all over the world, it is in effect useful to draw distinctions between industrially highly developed and less developed linguistic communities and between Indo-European and other linguistic communities.

One position is exemplified by the European language situation. European language communities by and large consist of majority language groups who have developed a standard language model which is widely respected and used by the formally educated classes. The language is fully developed in all modes and for all techniques of expression and is therefore capable of hosting new concepts transferred from other linguistic communities. Since science and technology have been developed steadily in these languages there is in principle no need for other languages. Each language has adequate means to cope with a rapid growth in terminology: teaching and training occurs in this language and though there may from time to time be a heavy influx of foreign language terminology, the situation rectifies itself in a relatively short time through the production of texts for the exclusive use of this linguistic community in the form of manuals, instructions, textbooks etc. There is a new confidence that European languages are strong enough to survive a temporary onslaught of (mainly American) English, that languages are capable of developing resources to create the new terminologies needed and that only small corrective measures need be applied. It has been demonstrated that, after many years of decline, French in Quebec could be restored and revitalised so that it can now maintain itself in opposition to English; equally the relatively strict terminology control in France of the seventies has lost much of its aggressive stance and whatever absurdities it may have produced are now only a folk-memory in the francophobe press. The attitude to secondary term formation in Europe is therefore one of monitored laissez-faire with occasional intervention in the knowledge that the tradition of primary term formation in a given language is capable of finding its own mixture of acceptable borrowing, adaptation, etc.

In other parts of the world the situation is quite different. In developing countries language communities are often divided by political boundaries and grouped into political entities with other language communities. There may be various non-standard varieties of the same language which share modes and techniques of communication. Developing countries may therefore have functional and class languages of different origin, so that there is no clear and obvious candidate for a language of science and technology. Many countries have therefore added to their linguistic complexity by adopting a European language as a lingua franca for science. At the level of technology, however, such lingua francas are less acceptable because fewer technologists in these countries acquire a sufficient command of a lingua franca to manage without interpreters or translators; even if they did they would then need translators and interpreters to communicate with the wide range of workers who are engaged in industrial employment derived from the import of technology. Because of cultural and environmental constraints technological concepts are difficult to represent via a lingua franca and languages of technology are regionally so diversified that a lingua franca cannot hope to provide an adequate vehicle for communication.

With a growing consensus among national governments that language development is either a precondition for, or an inevitable accompaniment to economic and social advancement, the objectives of technological development are currently seen as requiring a language planning dimension. The new objective is therefore to develop the most widely used language to such an extent that it can become a vehicle for scientific and technological communication. In this way language development is the first phase of technology transfer and industrial development. Seen from this aspect, term formation becomes a matter of general education and even of literacy campaigns, as various UN programmes indicate.

In practical terms, it is recognised that both for training and for transfer of technology the subject specialists of developing countries must first learn the language of the exporting country and then transfer this knowledge into their own language. The scientist of the developing country must know the foreign language because of the existing patterns of postgraduate training, the provision of teaching materials, access to international databases, etc. A command of the foreign language permits him to select the information he considers relevant to his own country. He must also develop his own language as a vehicle for scientific communication, so that he can control and steer the dissemination of scientific knowledge in this language and to stimulate the interaction between science and technology. The scientists of developing countries may therefore be little affected in their own work by the absence of an autochthonous terminology.

The terminology problem arises only in the transfer of scientific knowledge to technological applications. In this respect the scientist in developing countries has a special responsibility as conceptual and linguistic mediator between whatever is for him the international lingua franca, e.g. English, Japanese, Russian, and the national language in which the technology is to be expressed and transmitted. Developing countries are creating appropriate channels of communication for the creation of autochthonous terminologies through language agencies, academies of the language and similar institutions.

In theory a language planning agency can re-perform the term formation process systematically and with greater consistency than at the original import stage. It can in principle create in this way a balanced terminology with consistent variations for different levels of discourse. In practice, however, the circumstances of secondary term formation are quite different. Importation of terminology occurs at such a pace that planned assimilation cannot cope. Nor can the circumstances under which it occurs be controlled. The wholesale incorporation of foreign terminology is a fact of life in many communities and a contributory factor to the conflicts between modernisation and indigenous development.

Term formation habits are influenced by perception and observation. When this perception is first-hand and carried out in the observer's first language, he will use the means of that language to designate the concepts he discovers or establishes. Acquiring knowledge in a second language not only influences our term formation habits in the direction of that language, it also inhibits the natural growth of the first language because it is excluded from the cognitive processes which lead to concept naming.

Languages of developing countries therefore also come under the influence of word formation patterns of other languages and may, as a consequence, genuinely widen their means of expression. Little can be said here about the many diverse techniques of term formation since they are as diverse as the languages which evolve new terminologies. They are, however, all exposed to direct borrowing, loan translation, paraphrase etc. and find them more or less acceptable according to common elements between the exporting and importing languages.

Current attitudes to secondary term formation can be broadly divided into purist and permissive and on the whole mirror existing attitudes to any foreign language influence with two possible variants. One is the attitude towards transnational or international terminology where there is greater tolerance; the other is the attitude to whole families of terms which, having entered the language, prove useful and are therefore more readily accepted. While a permissive attitude is generally preferable, since it respects the self-regulatory mechanisms of language, it cannot be defended under circumstances of massive terminology transfer into a linguistic vacuum. Occasional imports (direct borrowings) have to coexist with and come under the influence of established terms in a given subject field. When the entire subject field is new, the importing language has no pattern of absorption to offer and hence needs a general policy.

There is then a rapidly increasing awareness of the importance of a properly monitored development of terminology. Developing countries are setting up language planning agencies, some of which engage in creating their own terminologies and in the process establish their own criteria for influencing term formation.

3.2.3.2. *Attitudes to borrowing*

The mechanisms of borrowing are complex and defy simple systematisation. The theoretically well-meaning injunctions of the past are now being corrected as a result of observation of existing patterns of borrowing and this has led to the more realistic attitude that now seems to guide borrowing patterns.

A nativisation process of borrowings relies on the alteration of phonological, morphological and orthographical forms in conformity with systems in the target language. The semantic import of a term may be unaffected by these changes. The harmonisation of formal structures of loan words is a highly productive means of scientific/technological terminology acquisition because little effort is involved in phonological adaptation. The oral tradition of borrowing is, after all, the oldest and most natural one and has the greatest potential of acceptance by a non-specialist community. Difficulties may arise when a spelling has to be decided, but the very fact of sound adaptation facilitates this adjustment. The proper phonological adaptation of loan words can even be desirable if it enriches the language through exploiting gaps in an existing phonological system.

A second type of adapted borrowing initiates changes on the semantic level. Semantic change may, for example, particularise a polysemous word, borrow from general into special language or indeed shift the original meaning of the borrowed term. It is however increasingly being recognised that while loan words may make orientation in international technical literature easier for a small minority, a modernised word stock, developed through native means, is more instrumental and advantageous in bridging the gap between the higher educated sections of the society and the lower socio-economic groups.

In addition to the direct and adapted borrowing of essentially mono-nucleid words, total and partial translation of phrases and compound terms has been a productive means of lexical expansion. Loan translations may be literal, word-for-word substitution of the lexical components of compounds, and, depending on the lexical rules of the target language, sometimes neces-sitate some syntactic re-ordering of the compound elements in accordance with the target language grammar. Some technical terms typify the conceptual system of a particular society and as a result do not lend themselves to easy translation in a different socio-linguistic environment. Certain countries have also adopted specific policies with regard to loan translation.

Classical Latin and Greek have provided scientists and technologists speaking European languages with basic root forms for a large numbers of terms. The widespread use of these internationalisms facilitates communica-tion by the unambiguous reference to identical concepts of similar conceptual systems. The growing socio-economic interdependence of countries of diverse linguistic backgrounds appears to support the preference for internationalisms over existing or new autochthonous forms. Some of the activities of (European language-dominated) international language planning services have evolved around coining Greek- or Latin-based terms to supersede indigenous alterna-tives. Such a development would effectively deny other languages the possi-bility of exploiting their own semantic system. Developing countries are now fully aware of the relative merits of internationalisms and pursue balanced policies such as accepting only widely used internationalisms based on Greek or Latin derivatives, while encouraging the exploitation of equally prestigious word stocks found in, e.g., classical Arabic or Sanskrit.

In summary, it can be said that linguistic communities which import scientific and technological knowledge tend to prefer the use of autochthonous linguistic resources for the creation of terminology, even if for a short time there is a certain amount of direct borrowing. Loan translation is preferred to direct borrowing, but neither form of term creation is acceptable if it violates the natural word formation techniques of a linguistic community. Transfer of pure scientific knowledge may benefit from the relatively widespread use of Greek and Latin word elements, especially in those fields of knowledge in which terminology has traditionally been regulated by international committees.

3.2.4 *Technical support for term creation*

Terminology creating agencies now have a large number of tools available to guide them in their work. Optimally there are, of course, term banks with complete information on the terminological resources of a language; in practice the theoretical knowledge and the practical know-how are available for a systematic survey of existing linguistic forms which can then guide in the choices to be made. Industrialised countries have large amounts of data in machine-readable form which could be processed so as to supply appropriate information about the term creation patterns of any one discipline; developing countries increasingly have trained terminologists with an understanding of computational techniques for information gathering and exploitation.

Of immediate use are frequency dictionaries, sometimes also containing details of separate wordforms, which exist for the general lexicon of a number of languages but which could be produced for each subject field to yield the fullest benefit. Reverse dictionaries complement the information about prefixes and first elements of compounds already available in alphabetical lists. Of particular interest are various types of permuted indexes, first introduced in the field of information science, which bring together all word forms of complex compounds. Then there are various types of reference works which group words by some type of semantic relationship, as in thesauri, synonym dictionaries, etc. and which can now also be produced automatically from existing databases.

Technical assistance is now available to support the terminological needs of the three phases of the industrial process. This means in particular, the ability to:

(1) collect and disseminate new scientific terminology as it evolves, thus avoiding duplication, distortion and misunderstanding;
(2) plan the systematic collection and dissemination of the terminology of industrial development;
(3) design the terminology required for writing product or service documentation in one or several parallel language versions;
(4) guarantee terminological consistency in documents and their translations.

Language planners and terminologists, even individual translators who have to create terms can now build up their own collections of terms on small computers and so control at least the work they themselves are engaged in.

3.3 Guidelines for the creation of terms

In recent years there has been a growing awareness of the need to create terminologies in all languages in which there is technical instruction, and scientific research and development.

In order to achieve this objective there has been an recognition of the usefulness of language planning in terminology coupled with a greater realism about the possibilities and limitations of influencing term formation. This has lead to the selective establishment of linguistic commissions in those areas in which planning can succeed and to a rejection of the notion that technical and scientific terminology will converge around English. It has further been realised that terminology created as a result of science and technology transfer is unstable and requires considerable time before it adjusts to and stabilises according to the term formation patterns of the respective language.

3.3.1 *International guidelines*

The International Organisation for Standardisation (ISO) has for many years been concerned with providing guidance on the creation of terms. These efforts have usually come up against the difficulties of the diversity of structures and term formation techniques in different languages. Because it is impossible to produce effective guidelines for all languages used by the ISO member countries, such guidelines must remain at a very broad level of generality. It is nevertheless useful to list here the basic postulates expressed by a group of experts, in the, now obsolete, ISO document R 704 (Naming Principles), if only to show their limited scope.

– Terms should be created systematically with respect to their morphological, syntactic, semantic and pragmatic characteristics.
– A term should conform to the morphology, spelling and pronunciation conventions of the language for which it is intended.
– Once a term has gained wide acceptance it should not be changed without compelling reasons and a strong certainty that the new term will become accepted as a full substitute.
– If a new term succeeds only partially in replacing an existing term, the confusion may become worse as this would amount to deliberate synonym creation. In this case it is preferable to introduce a new term.

3.3.2 *Criteria and rules for naming*

At the level of individual subjects or languages, organisations concerned about the uncontrolled proliferation of terminology have also set up rules or guidelines for naming the objects and phenomena they are most concerned with. Others develop guidelines on an ad hoc basis when they are confronted with the task of compiling a glossary of terms and find that they have to order a great number of synonyms. Nevertheless, words and compounds which express scientific and technical concepts must fulfil certain conditions. This is valid for available vocabulary as well as for the formation of new vocabulary.

The following list is an example of a highly idealised requirement which, however, can only be realised in a strictly controlled environment.

1. The term must relate directly to the concept. It must express the concept clearly. A logical construction is advisable.
2. The term must be lexically systematic. It must follow an existing lexical pattern and if the words are of foreign origin, a uniform transcription must be preserved.
3. The term must conform to the general rules of word-formation of the language which will also dictate the word order in compounds and phrases.
4. Term should be capable of providing derivatives.
5. Terms should not be pleonastic (i.e. no redundant repetition, e.g. combining a foreign word with a native word having the same meaning).
6. Without sacrificing precision, terms should be concise and not contain unnecessary information.
7. There should be no synonyms whether absolute, relative or apparent.
8. Terms should not have morphological variants.
9. Terms should not have homonyms.

10. Terms should be monosemic.
11. The content of terms should be precise and not overlap in meaning with other terms.
12. The meaning of the term should be independent of context.

Efforts are also being made to provide guidelines for the highly specialised and relatively rare occurrence of naming internationally agreed concepts. A number of possibilities for such creations can be envisaged:
– creating a new designation through addition to an existing word-family;
– taking over the designation from another language;
– taking over the designation from another language but adjusting its pronunciation, spelling or morphological characteristics;
– producing a loan translation of the term;
– creating a completely new designation.

Direct borrowing can be recommended when the foreign language term can be easily integrated into the phonemic, graphemic and morphological structure of the borrowing language and if it permits derivatives; e.g. the English 'design' has been taken over into German as 'Design' and the derivative 'Designer' is already established.

Adaptation is more likely when the languages involved are cognate, or when an established tradition is being followed, e.g. the use of Greek or Latin word elements. This method produces what in the Western World have been called internationalisms, e.g. 'generieren', 'générer', 'generar', 'generate'; 'Radiographie', 'radiography', 'radiographie', 'radiografia'.

Loan translation is generally used for complex or compound terms and phrases, e.g. 'wood-screw = *Holzschraube*', 'machine-aided translation = *maschinengestützte Übersetzung = traduction assistée par ordinateur* (TAO)'.

The formation of completely new terms can still take into account the existence of widely used prefixes and suffixes which permit the integration of the new term into a system of existing designations.

3.4 Nomenclatural systems

Some scientific disciplines are concerned with the observation and description of large numbers of natural phenomena. This is the case for the biological sciences, geology, including mineralogy and to a lesser extent for chemistry and medicine. The sciences have a fundamental need to order and classify:

individual objects have to be identified, and inherent and consistent features of objects of observation have to be separated from accidental and inessential ones so that individual items can be combined into types and classes of related objects can be established; states and conditions of states have to be determined in order to gain reliable knowledge. Without classifying the great multiplicity of objects, their characteristics, their common features, their use and adaptability to human needs, no meaningful generalisation can be made and no useful and structured knowledge can be gained. It is therefore natural that efforts should be made to reflect this effort of ordering in the naming of the ordered objects.

In their approach to naming, the taxonomic sciences have evolved artificial languages which exploit the systematic nature and the classificatory use of language. By narrowing the functions of language and restricting the use of general language to scientific and technical discourse, they can construct name systems and rules for their implementation which their users will fully understand and use correctly. In the different nomenclatures names are determined by the rule-system of classification adopted. The taxonomic codes cannot, and do not, claim absolute validity for a name but only aim at consistency in any one given classification. Nevertheless, misidentification of concepts occurs, and is very often discovered only much later when the state of knowledge of a subject permits different methods of analysis. Some misdesignations, but by no means all, are later corrected, sometimes involving a sequence of changes in names up and down a hierarchy.

The artificial languages created in this way are variously related to one or several natural languages which have been used in their construction. The degree of dependence on other languages and the area of use of the language decides the influence that natural language can have on the constructed naming system. English medical terminology, for example, is heavily anglicised but in English the difference between Latin and anglicised names is usually so small that no confusion arises; in the applications of biology and chemistry the use of trivial names is also very common. This habit does not invalidate the purpose of nomenclatures, which serve as a fixed point of reference and provide guiding principles for the formation of new terms. The procedures evolved by the nomenclatures can therefore be seen as being more efficient than those usually adopted in standardisation, which can only arbitrate between and regularise existing usage and only rarely succeed in replacing unsystematically formed terms. It must, however, be repeated that nomenclatures are not equally suitable to all fields of knowledge.

3.4.1 *General principles*

According to the nature of the objects observed and according to the purpose
to which this knowledge is put, different sciences have evolved different criteria of classification. In biology the genus–species relationship is employed
for the differentiation of animals and plants. In anatomy, classification is
primarily made on the basis of part–whole relationships, in pathology and
physiology, however, processes and causes, procedures and effects have to
be isolated and related to each other. In chemistry the main objective is to
differentiate elements and components of substances and naturally occurring
compounds, but no less important is the ordering of the products and the
results of the planned interaction of elements.

   Classification can be carried out independently of naming, for example,
by numerical and/or alphabetical codes; this is indeed a common starting
point of naming—vitamins were at one stage identified alphanumerically—
but such a procedure would not obviate the need for naming. Ultimately such
codes would have to be expressed linguistically in definitions, specifications,
test procedures, etc. and this would have required naming of some sort
or another. It has always been felt convenient to use the naming process
for classificatory purposes as far as possible and to supplement it by definitions, since the declaration of special reference is based on observations
first expressed in general language. The classificatory principle, therefore,
becomes the chief motivation in designation and thereby fundamentally distinguishes the special designation process from the arbitrariness of general
language.

   The rule systems of nomenclatures overcome the unpredictability of word
formation and the ambiguity inherent in popular names and general language
naming processes. The names resulting from the application of these rules
can claim to be an international, or at least supranational, instrument of communication. This certainly applies to the written language; in the spoken
forms differences of pronunciation may make understanding more difficult.
For historical reasons Latin and Greek dominate the major nomenclatures in
biology and medicine. Until the 18th century Latin was the scientific lingua
franca of Europe. It was therefore the natural vehicle for medical terminology,
and Latin was the only international language available to Linnaeus when he
devised the principles of biological nomenclature. The growing influence of
national languages can be seen in the chemical nomenclature developed about
one hundred years after the first biological code. The chemical nomenclature
accommodated the principle that the suffixes used in it be consistent with

the natural languages in which the nomenclature was to be used: it is the preeminence of British and French research in chemistry at crucial periods of development which has made the chemical nomenclature used in these countries virtually universal.

The individual stems and affixes used in the nomenclatures derive from a natural language; they are therefore not inherently more systematic than elements of any other language. The systematicity of the nomenclatures resides in the regularity of the processes according to which they are combined with each other and with affixes, so that fixed meanings not available in the original language can be attached to affixes and to patterns of combinations. The stems, usually borrowed from Latin or Greek, are as arbitrary in reference, in letter and sound combination as any other stems; the choice of dead languages, or more specifically, of languages not regularly spoken or written by the new users, however, has the great advantage of stability. The restrictions attached to the borrowed word elements permit the limitation of polysemy and the fixation of reference for the greater clarity expected. Nomenclatures do not recognise the formal distinction between stem and affix, readily converting one into another, and declaring new meanings for new and established affixes according to their classificatory needs. So the ending '-ales' regularly indicates a botanical order and '-acea' a botanical family.

Each classification system determines the types of word-formation processes it needs and the function of each process and element. Chemistry, for example, needs to link together elements and compounds, i.e. it has to coordinate items of equal rank but different internal structure, into new units which themselves can become equal parts of larger units. As in natural languages, however, not all possibilities of rules are exploited. The rules permit an American chemist to say 'potassium sodium tartrate', whereas an English chemist will say 'sodium potassium tartrate' without signifying a different substance. The rules also permit differences in the degree of overt specification, e.g. 'potassium hydrogen sulphate' (BrE) – 'potassium bisulfate' (AmE), 'titanous chloride' (BrE) – 'titanium trichloride' (AmE).

National and international professional and scientific bodies, such as the International Union for Pure and Applied Chemistry (IUPAC), collaborate in the formulation and regular revision of the nomenclature of their discipline and have prescribed procedures for validating new terms and incorporating them into the code.

The rules devised by these bodies which govern the nomenclatures of the sciences are more specific than the general desiderata expressed in section 3.3, but they are based on the same pragmatic principles, i.e.

– existing names should be retained wherever possible; this accounts for such irregular genus names as e.g. 'Palmae' or 'Arcaceae';
– names should be unique, univocal and yet simple and concise;
– existing usage should be the arbiter in the case of choice between alternate designations; e.g. 'Valva mitralis' coexists with the new 'Valva atrioventricularis sinistra';
– rules should not conflict with other rules in different, but related codes;
– rules should be capable of extension with the progress of science;
– trivial names should be replaced by systematic ones wherever possible and the creation of new trivial names should be discouraged, e.g. 'Ductus mesonephricus' not 'Wolffian duct'.
– the rules should be acceptable to different languages and the names which are not Latin or Greek in origin should be adaptable to different languages.

The following sections describe some of the features and rules of some of the nomenclatures.

3.4.2 *Features of medical nomenclature*

In medicine the need is to relate states, conditions or operations to causes or parts of the body or otherwise specify in greater detail. Both composition, e.g. 'appendectomy', and derivation are used for this purpose, e.g. 'angina pectoris', 'delirium tremens', 'scarlatina maligna'. Different areas of medicine such as paediatrics, ophthalmology, neurology and surgery have their individual requirements. Anatomy deals with a finite set of some 5000 concepts, which before the introduction of the Nomina Anatomica were represented by some 50,000 terms; other nomenclatures are open-ended by their nature. Medical nomenclature is more diversified than the other codes because besides actual objects it designates states, conditions, processes and operations, and it is not only subject to expansion, as the other codes are, but to a greater extent subject to revision as knowledge of human physiology, diseases and operations increases, and new methods of diagnosis and treatment are developed.

The anatomical classification is based on topographical principles and on twelve functional systems, e.g. musculo-skeletal, respiratory, nervous, digestive, so that veins, arteries, muscles, nerves, etc. are first identified by their location, e.g. 'Musculi abdominis', 'Nervus lingualis', or by their function, e.g. 'Nervus lacrimalis', 'Musculi ossiculorum auditus'. Differentiating adjectives, preferably forming contrasting pairs, are also frequent, e.g. 'Musculus palmaris longus', 'Musculus palmaris brevis'. Diseases are classified according to their nature and origin into: congenital, traumatic, infective, neoplastic, metabolic, endocrine, allergic, psychiatric, iatrogenic and idiopathic. The causes of diseases are subdivided into thirteen etiological categories, characterised by such suffixes as '-algia', '-iasis', 'ysm', '-itis', '-oma', '-osis', which are added to the name of the organ or the affected part of the body, e.g. aneurysm, thrombosis, cholecystitis, cholelithiasis, cholangitis. Examinations and tests are named according to the instruments or methods involved, e.g. 'auscultation', 'catheterisation', 'angiography'. Operations are also subdivided topographically and according to nine basic procedures, e.g. 'excisio', 'sutura', 'luxatio', which in turn are characterised by such suffixes as '-tomy', '-ectomy', '-stomy', e.g. mastectomy, embolectomy. There is no maximum length specified for terms as in biology; simple terms co-exist with complex terms according to the need for unique, systematic and descriptive identification, e.g. 'Sternum', 'Nervus meatus acustici externi', which is part of the 'Nervus auriculotemporalis'. Long terms can be compressed and shortened as in biology and chemistry.

3.4.3 *Features of biological nomenclature*

The need to express generic relationships between organisms has placed a binomial code at the centre of the biological nomenclature system. Identification of species occurs by firstly attributing it to a genus and secondly by giving it a specific name which may be a noun, e.g. 'Felis leo', an attribute, e.g. 'Passer domesticus', or a proper name, e.g. 'Rosa beatricis'. There are three major codes for bacteriology, botany and zoology based on the same principles but with different degrees of specification at various levels.

A name is not immutable in its form; it can be reduced or expanded according to its type and textual use. When the context is unambiguous, it is possible to abbreviate the generic attribution to species to the initial letter of the genus, e.g. 'Geranium ibericum = G. ibericum'. Names can be supplemented by authority labels such as the author's name and the date of the first valid publication, e.g. 'Galium petiolatum Geddes, (1928)', and the author of the work in which the name is published, e.g. 'Gossypium tomentosum Nutt. ex Seem.'. Double citation can be used to indicate that a species formerly classified under one genus has later been transferred to another genus. The name of the first author then appears in brackets after the name of the species and before the name of the author of the correction, e.g. 'Limonium mouretii

(Pitard) Maire'. The biological codes further provide means for the identification of synonyms, homonyms, misidentifications, ambiguities and even
permit qualifying phrases to indicate a limitation of the reference of the term.
Hybrid plants are identified by a simple x between its two parts, e.g. 'Viburnum
x bodnantense Aberconway' which is a hybrid originating from Viburnum
fragrans Bunge and V. grandiflorum Wallich.

   The following steps are required before a term can be fully accepted into
a biological nomenclature:
1. The name must be constructed according to the rules.
2. Prior names must be considered since the oldest legitimate and properly
   constructed name claims precedence under the 'Law of Priority'.
3. The name must be accompanied by a full description of the new concept
   which lists the attributes and justifies its place in the rank of the taxonomic
   hierarchy.
4. The name must be published in an established journal which regularly presents additions to or modifications of the code.

3.4.4 *Features of chemical nomenclature*

Organic and inorganic chemistry have the same basic principles of naming,
but a great number of special subcodes have been developed for such highly
specialised areas as hydrocarbons, heterocyclic systems and steroids. In addition, in order to provide greater precision in some areas, various separate
nomenclatural notations coexist which permit a more concise and structured
representation.

   Chemical names permit varying types and degrees of specification. There
are:
– parent names, e.g. 'ethane', from which particular names are derived by
  prescribed variation;
– systematic names with or without numerical prefixes, e.g. 'sodium (tetra)
  borate';
– additive names for linking atoms and/or molecules;
– fusion names with the linking vowel '-o-' to indicate that two cyclic systems
  are fused by two or more common atoms, e.g. 'benzofuran';
– radico-functional names in which the name of a radical is placed before the
  name of a functional class, e.g. 'acetyl chloride';
– replacement names which indicate that oxygen is replaced by e.g. 'sulphur'
  as in 'thiopyran';

– substitutive names;
– subtractive names;
– conjunctive names.

In principle, compounds are treated as an assembly of identical units. Given the complexity of some names, simpler trivial names are recommended for use even by the IUPAC rules, e.g. the shorter 'Malonic' is preferred to the systematic 'Propanedioic'. The trivial names of the first four acyclic hydrocarbons 'methane', 'ethane', 'propane', 'butane' and the names of the better known aromatic hydrocarbons, e.g. 'benzene', 'naphthalene', are fully incorporated into systematic nomenclature. The use of trivial names is widespread in applied chemistry, e.g. 'caustic soda = sodium hydroxide', 'laughing gas = nitrous oxide', and even the misnomer 'carbonic acid = carbon dioxide/carbon anhydride'. The most recent international harmonisation of chemical nomenclature has not yet found general acceptance in British English.

Chapter Four

THE COMMUNICATIVE DIMENSION

In this chapter we establish the link between the theoretical conditions and the linguistic possibilities on the one hand and the reality of terminology processing on the other—to be discussed in chapters five to eight of this book. We have to observe how terms, as distinct from words, operate in a model of communication. We also have to analyse how usage affects the nature and use of terminology. It is finally necessary to define the users of terminological services and the uses they make of such services.

Section 2.1.6 introduced the concepts of word, term and standardised term as well as the relationship between knowledge and language. These concepts are now incorporated into a theory of special communication, i.e. purposeful communication between experts on the topic of their discipline, and in particular the way in which the lexicon contributes to the achievement of effective communication.

4.1 A model of communication

In a model of specialist communication we assume the existence of at least two specialists in the same discipline, who are jointly involved in a particular situation where the sender (speaker or writer) is motivated to transmit a linguistic message which concerns the topic of his choice and which he expects a recipient (reader or listener) to receive. We assume that the sender's motivation arises from a need or desire to affect in some way the current state of knowledge of the recipient.

The sender's motivation is translated into an intention which becomes an implicit or explicit part of the message. In its broadest sense, the sender's intention is to transmit information which will have an effect on the current knowledge configuration of the intended recipient. It may be confined to an effect on the store of knowledge itself, i.e. augmentation, confirmation or modification of the existing state of knowledge or it may, in addition, be intended to elicit consequent linguistic or non-linguistic reactions, such as approval, denial or specific behaviour modifications. Basing himself on pre-suppositions about the recipient's knowledge and assumptions about his expectations, the sender decides his own intention, and then selects items from his own store of knowledge, chooses a suitable language, encodes the items into a text and transmits the entire message toward the intended recipient. The message is the totality of intention, assumed expectation, knowledge content and language selected by the sender. The text, which may be written or spoken, is merely its physical manifestation (see figure 4.1).

Figure 4.1. *Presuppositions and assumptions in communication*

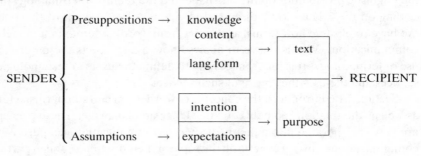

Perfect communication can be said to have occurred when the recipients' state of knowledge after reception of the text corresponds exactly to the sender's intention in originating the message. While the sender has to be aware of, or make presuppositions and assumptions about, the recipient's ability to interpret the message correctly, the recipient, however, has to reconstruct the complete message on the basis of the text and the situation alone (see figure 4.2).

Figure 4.2. *The limitations of coding*

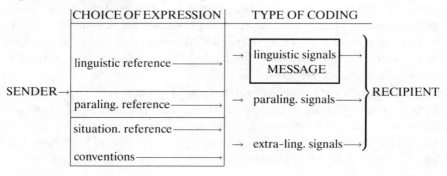

In order to assist communication, the external format of special communication is highly conventionalised and stylised. Society has, for instance, created situations and even places which require certain types of communication— e.g. the lecture theatre, the board room, the confessional. Society and special subject groups have also created text types for the transmission of messages with specific broad intentions well-known to all participants in regular communication in that group. Intention can, therefore, normally be transmitted by non-linguistic means, as, for example, through the text form of instructions, manuals, income tax returns, laboratory reports, application forms, work schedules and so on, where the recipient can concentrate on the content because he already knows how to react to the text. By these techniques of non-linguistic signalling of intention, the participants can more readily concentrate on the transmission and reception of knowledge which is done through the rhetorical structure of a conventional text type.

Inside texts there are also well-established compositional signals, particularly in special subject texts, to signify intention as well as intended modes of reception. This includes such devices as lay-out of text on a page, capitalisation, underlining, paragraph numbering, subtitling, etc. Footnotes and bibliographic references, for instance, do not occur in the main body of a text since they fulfil an additional intention. The organisation of reports takes into account a number of different intentions of reception. The format of dictionaries or cross-references in textbooks is designed for repeated informative reading. A manual may serve both as initial instruction and later confirmation of knowledge.

At the level of the sentence, the most obvious indicator of intention is the choice of one from among the various modalities of assertion, interrogation and direction, reflected in the syntactic form of the utterance. At the semantic level, the existence of ordered knowledge spaces or disciplines and their conventional representation through terms, or by explicit agreement as standards, provides a means for the expression of balanced and graduated knowledge which is only available in conjunction with special reference. The use of undefined terms or standards, or the absence of paraphrases of terms and standards, signals the region of the knowledge structure chosen as the basis of communication. Understanding of undefined terms and standards is taken for granted and serves the purpose of confirmation of knowledge, so that the sender can more clearly signal what he considers to be augmentation and modification of knowledge. If, however, the sender's intention is misinterpreted to the extent that, say, an attempt to confirm the recipient's knowledge is received by the recipient

as augmentation or modification, then communication will not have suc-
ceeded.

The achievement of successful communication is fundamentally dependent on the three choices the sender has to make in formulating his message.
These are discussed in the following three sections.

4.1.1 *The choice of intention*

The sender must choose an intention which is commensurate with the recipient's expectation. For the communication to succeed, the recipient must
capture the sender's intention either from the message or from the situation,
and his interpretation of the intention must be accurate.

Intention is first of all expressed and identified through the text form.
So, a check-list, for example, can only serve to confirm knowledge; equally,
instructions are meant in the first instance to augment knowledge, and can only
on a secondary level serve to confirm knowledge, whereas a manual is designed
to and will serve both functions. Intention is also expressed through the use
of terms, e.g. an undefined term cannot serve to augment knowledge unless
it is assumed that its special reference, possibly in the form of a definition, is
known.

In specialist communication, the intention of the message, derived directly
from the sender's motivation, is most frequently to inform the recipient, in the
restricted sense of augmenting, confirming or modifying his current state of
knowledge. Directive intention, which also occurs in communication between
specialists, can be defined as an attempt to elicit modification of behaviour via
an effect on knowledge. Interrogative intention requires a reversal of roles
so that the sender seeks information from, rather than offers information to
the recipient. Social, aesthetic, emotive and similar potential functions of the
speech act are normally regarded as secondary to the primary intention of
conveying information.

4.1.2 *The selection of knowledge*

In special subject communication it is normally assumed that both sender and
recipient operate within the same subject field or area of knowledge; in order
to affect a recipient's knowledge, a sender must either have prior information
about or make correct presuppositions about the recipient's current state of

knowledge. The area of knowledge referred to is usually signalled by the situation of the speech act and the professional roles of the interlocutors. By using undefined terms or standardised terms the sender signals presupposed knowledge.

In informative speech acts, a sender is normally expected to have greater knowledge of the topic than a recipient, so that there can be an effective transfer, i.e. augmentation or modification of knowledge. Equally, a recipient must recognise a sender as having sufficient authority in the chosen discipline so that he will be willing to accept augmentation, confirmation or modification of his knowledge. The knowledge selection is therefore situation-dependent inasmuch as the situation determines the roles of the participants in the speech act. The situation largely governs the presuppositions which a sender can make about a recipient's knowledge. When the participants are well known to each other, the relative states of knowledge may also be well known to both, and lexical items may then be used and understood which are outside the range of control of the social norm.

In the particular case of communication between specialists in a discipline, the existence of accepted standardised terms and expressions which the sender can assume the recipient to recognise is of considerable utility in ensuring comparability of knowledge, since the standard term presupposes absolute comprehension of its definition. Standardised terms can only serve this particular function, and, indeed, should only be adopted, if the collective state of knowledge in the relevant subject field or subfield is sufficiently stable not to require modification in the foreseeable future. When a sender has no knowledge of the recipient, he can only infer from the situation that he belongs to a general class of individuals—e.g. 'laymen', 'professionals'—and has to rely on the social norm for guidance as to which linguistic realisation of knowledge he should use to formulate his message. A number of locally defined terms are then used to fix the basis of the knowledge space presupposed to be available to the recipient, before reference can be made to the accepted norm.

Because of the evolution of knowledge and the coexistence of various theoretical scientific positions, the conceptual structure of any given area of knowledge is not necessarily uniquely determined at any one time, so that two or more distinct systems of terms, or even of pseudo-standards, may reflect different organisational patterns within the same region. In linguistics, for example, the sequence of terms 'tagmeme-string-frame', indicates a different subdivision of knowledge of the discipline from, 'element-chain-pattern'; the use of one set rather than the other immediately signals the theoretical school of thought reflected by the use of these terms.

4.1.3 *The choice of language*

The sender must choose a language and sublanguage which he assumes the recipient to have command of; the recipient must be able to recognise and understand the linguistic forms chosen in order to analyse the message.

Accurate transmission can be impeded by incompatibility of the sender's or recipient's lexical and knowledge structure, by interference from grammar in the expression of knowledge or intention and finally by distortion during the production or the actual transmission of sound or script. The analytical use of language, i.e. the application of inference rules in the process of comprehension, works only if designations are regularly patterned and if both interlocutors know these rules of designation. The linguistic forms to be used in a message must therefore be planned at every level in such a way that the greatest degree of clarity can be achieved by means of systematic and transparent designations of concepts and by the avoidance of ambiguity at every level of expression.

In communication between specialists we are concerned with special subject languages, normally used by a small, relatively homogeneous group of people, in situations where the topic of discourse is of primary importance. This type of communication has also developed its own linguistic conventions as a result of prior agreement among user of this language about factors of intention and situation and by restricting the potential selection among phonological and syntactic variants. While phonological differences undoubtedly exist between specialists, they are virtually neutralised in the predominant medium of writing. The effect of constraints on syntax can be quite drastic, to the extent that temporal and personal factors are totally removed, as, for example, in laboratory reports and legal contracts.

The use in a text of standardised terms, with their highly specific reference, and, to a lesser extent, the use of terms allow the signalling of a precise area of knowledge intended by the message, provided that both participants share the same subset of language with the same reference values. The role of standardisation is crucial in establishing an agreed system of concepts and their symbolic representation which can be presupposed by potential participants even before communication takes place. It is even possible to standardise the coding mechanisms in such a way that they allow the creation of terms whose reference can be inferred from other known terms. Many such word formation mechanisms exist already in general language, and the general principle of 'transparent' term formation is commonly advocated by terminology-creating bodies such as learned societies and standards institutes.

The practice of naming the concepts in a particular subject field according
to a system which reflects a systematic structure imposed on these concepts
is most clearly evidenced in biological and chemical taxonomies, which are
deliberately constructed as open systems permitting the creation of new terms
for concepts yet to be established.

4.2 The functional efficacy of terms

Special languages have been defined as semi-autonomous, complex semi-
otic systems based on and derived from general language; their effective
use is restricted to people who have received a special education and who
use these languages for communication with their professional peers and
associates in the same or related fields of knowledge.   These languages
differ from general language in that (a) they are constituted of special text
types, e.g. laboratory reports, test certificates, special syntax, and in that
(b) they use terms in addition to words, i.e. linguistic expression forms endowed with special reference as distinct from the general reference of words.
Terms must be learnt separately from words, even if they have, as sometimes occurs, the same expression form.   Only if both interlocutors in a
speech act know the special reference of a term, and, by implication, that
they are using terms rather than words, can special communication succeed.   The conditions which must be fulfilled to achieve successful special
communication are therefore different from the requirements for general
communication.

In special communication terms and standardised terms make a critical
contribution to achieving complete and effective communication. This they do
by making the choice of language, knowledge and intention more systematic
and hence easier. In order to establish criteria for evaluating the effectiveness
of communication in special languages we can postulate three objectives or
properties:

1. The message should be as economical as possible without disturbing the
effective transmission of the intention or knowledge content. Economy is
not simply concerned with strategies for concise transmission, but with all
aspects of the reduction of effort in the transmission of information. These include compactness of substantive realisation, the exploitation of non-linguistic
codes, and the co-ordination of content and intention for ease of coding and
decoding.

Economy of expression and reference can manifest itself easily in a system that has to provide for internal, textual, situational and environmental reference within the social norm governing each sublanguage. The diversity of methods of referring (general, specific, individual) is matched by various means of disambiguation which in some areas of agreed reference can become redundant. Hence, precision and redundancy can be modified within the social norm of each sublanguage to counteract various types of interference created by the requirement of economy.

2. The message should convey the intended content as precisely as possible. Precision is concerned with the association of an expression with a well-defined area of the knowledge space; the more strictly the social norm determines the limits of that area the more precise can be the corresponding term.

Precision is to some extent inherent in the linguistic norm; beyond that it is a teleological criterion operating within the social norm and varying with the extent to which individual reception criteria are adjustable and taken into account by the sender. Non-linguistic codes and artificial languages largely respond to this need for precision combined with economy.

3. The message should be constructed as appropriately as possible so that the sender can optimally affect the state of knowledge of the recipient in the way he intends. Appropriateness of reference is closely allied to intention. An appropriate message should enable the recipient to localise accurately the area of knowledge which is the subject of the discourse, as well as achieving the intention in as effective a manner as possible.

Appropriateness is a purely pragmatic criterion entirely dependent on the social norm. Its rules are largely conditioned by the text type and form; greater flexibility exists in spoken variants. The conventions derived from frequently repeated special speech acts circumscribe the norm for appropriate word formation, syntactic expression and text type selection. Despite its elusive nature appropriateness is the most frequently used criterion in the evaluation of special communication; not only is it used to arbitrate between the sometimes conflicting demands of economy and precision, but it is also used to measure the highly specific and situation-conditioned messages of special speech acts.

These three objectives are interdependent: to achieve maximum efficacy of communication the requirements of one have to be weighed against the requirements of each and both of the others, according to the circumstances of the situation of the message.

These objectives are already inherent in the linguistic norm which maintains the stability of the system and thus ensures the equilibrium required for the maximum efficiency of the system as a whole. Any breach of the limits of efficacy is a move away from the natural language controlled by the linguistic norm and a move towards artificial languages, which are limited in function, and in speech communities, and, as deliberate constructs, are governed only by social norms. The linguistic norm does, however, permit variation in its minimal requirements in sublanguages with restricted functions.

4.2.1 *Lexical expression of economy*

In special communication economy is based on the assumption that in confined subject areas a relatively small group of users can reach agreement on the relationship between language and text, i.e. the form and meaning of frequently occurring messages and lexical items.

Economy has two dimensions: the economy of initial naming of terms and economy of regular speech acts.

In word or term formation there is a potential economy in the use of existing words, rather than newly created ones, i.e. neologisms, which have to be learnt separately. The simple juxtaposition of expression forms into long terms, e.g. 'console printer-keyboard channel attachment', is economical as far as the total stock of words required for multiple combination is concerned. While there is no direct correlation between the complexity of a concept and the length of a term it would appear reasonable to expect that a complex set of relationships be reflected in a complex term. What in general reference has to be expressed in qualifying phrases and other attributes, and gradually developed through the context, must be expressible as a single term in special languages. This is not to say that complex relationships cannot be expressed in words, nor that a greater cognitive effort is involved in understanding special reference items expressed in words, which is the common practice in teaching situations and in popular science. The potential for economy of terms and standards is, however, vastly superior to that of words because of the pragmatic situations in which they are used. Since the use of very complex terms is, however, uneconomical in a speech act, such long terms are usually shortened to two or three elements, sufficient to give the specialist a short label to refer to a well-defined term.

In special speech acts economy is the result of a division of labour: the learning of definitions, which serves for many subsequent speech acts, and the actual use of the term, which is then more economical. Complex concepts can only be expressed by simple terms, sometimes even identical to words, because the term is acknowledged to be a substitute label for the full definition. Accuracy and economy of expression can only be assured if we accept that a text containing terms presupposes the participants' prior familiarity with the appropriate definitions of the concepts. For the same reason it would be uneconomical in popular science writing to introduce terms not likely to be used regularly. If terms are given in popular science they are intended for general information as identifiers.

The concentration of complex relationships into short expression forms increases our cognitive capacity; from psycholinguistic experiments we know that the capacity of short term memory, the scope of distinction of absolute judgement, and the span of attention, oscillate at about seven items. Economy in the vocabulary is achieved by compression, through such procedures as acronymy, blending, derivation and compounding, especially when the compound represents the concentration of a whole phrase or even clause. The use of acronyms, symbols and other abbreviations is the most obvious example of economy. According to the aspect and level of the text, abbreviations are assumed to be known or they are introduced in brackets after the first mention of a name. The efforts of professional organisations such as standardising bodies in reducing information into more concentrated units seems therefore to be fully justified, e.g.

> motor car ⇒ car
> tubular box spanner ⇒ tubular spanner
> spanner key for hexagonal socket screws ⇒ hex (socket screw) key

The reduction of 'the ratio of the circumference of a circle to its radius' to a single Greek letter represents an extreme case of economy, which is, incidentally, also more precise than its numerical representation.

The great diversity of text types is largely due to requirements of economy. Lists, reports, essays and their varieties and subtypes are often highly subject-, situation- and intention-specific so that communication can be very economical. Prior understanding of the purpose of a text makes the overt statement of intention superfluous in such forms as invoices, prescriptions, production memoranda, etc. In many cases these forms dispense even with syntactic links and merely give independent items of information which the recipient interprets correctly as informative, evaluative or directive.

Because of their limited functions and clear specification of intention special languages can develop a high degree of syntactic economy. The various types of memos, reports and schedules which constitute the vast majority of all written communication permit simple listing after colons, the use of brackets to contain explanatory detail, the expression of clauses by simple apposition between dashes, and the use of abbreviations such as 'cr.', 'viz', 'i.e.', 'q.v.', 'etc.' to express syntactic links, all of which increase syntactic economy.

A highly economical means of representing complex relationships among terms exists in the rules of nomenclatures for fixing the meaning of word order and patterns of affixation and compounding. The binomial code of biology, for example, provides a means of identifying uniquely thousands of species, subspecies, and even varieties of physical entities. It can be enlarged to indicate sources of designation, erroneous designations and their correction by the use of capital letters, abbreviation, brackets and other punctuation signs. The various rules for shortening the names of chemical compounds, e.g. the radico-functional names, the replacement names, which use numbers, and the acceptance of trivial names represent systematic efforts at economy (see also section 3.4). Even standardised terms permit optional omission of elements of long compounds in order to increase effectiveness of communication.

4.2.1 *Precision of expression*

Precision is a universal requirement of communication. It is a measure of the accuracy with which knowledge and intention are represented in a text. In special communication the finer differentiation which characterises the internal knowledge structure of a discipline must be reflected as precisely as possible in the language.

The scientific methods aim at precision of statements. Observations are made in the first instance by means of specific or even individual reference. Generalisations are supported by experimental and statistical evidence and logical argument. The formulation of statements claiming general validity in special languages is fully supported by unambiguous reference to measurements or definitions and strengthened, in science by formulae, and in social science by linguistic precedent. Any remaining uncertainty of interpretation can be resolved only by reference to axioms in science or higher human authority in society. In the special language of law, for example, special institutions have been established to interpret language.

In special communication terms are considered substitute labels for definitions because only a full and precise definition is the proper linguistic representation of a concept. A text like a glossary, consisting of a series of definitions which only use terms precisely defined elsewhere is undoubtedly precise, but it is normally only utilised as a 'presupposed' text on the basis of which other special speech acts can develop. Precision in definitions normally conflicts with economy in that a full definition tends to be lengthy. One of the main functions of terms and standards is to allow users of special reference to replace long definitions with a more economical but equally precise expression. Terms and standardised terms are not intrinsically precise, since a term can only be precise if its definition is both itself precise and universally understood and accepted by its potential users. When terms are used that are standardised as parts of other definitions the precision of reference is maximised. Standardisation, which presupposes or imposes general acceptance of the meaning of terms, is an important guarantee of precision of reference (see also section 4.3.5).

Precision is not absolute but gradable and dependent on the intention and knowledge conditions of each speech act. Special reference, i.e. precise delimitation of the region of knowledge referred to, is consequently only established when required.

Precision operates on two planes: precision of reference and precision of syntactic relationships between referents. Criteria frequently associated with precision such as completeness, exhaustiveness and accuracy describe appropriateness rather than precision. The precision required of the substance of expression in correct spelling and phonemic pronunciation is fundamental to all language varieties and general language.

Written forms are considered to be more precise than spoken forms, the syntax of which is frequently more ambiguous, especially when interpreted after the situation in which they have occurred. An exception is the precision required of, and attached to, spoken language in legal proceedings, oaths, etc., where participants are often made to read out a text in order to avoid a dubious interpretation later. A number of types of schedules depend for their validity on precision, and some serve for verification of precision of reference or expression, e.g. defining glossaries of standardising bodies.

The precision of expression of syntactic relationships is highly developed in special languages. In legal language, for example, the requirements are so stringent that pronouns are avoided altogether or are only used when their reference is totally unambiguous. The need for precision is increased by the density and complexity of the information which results from economy. For this reason, precision makes special English appear more formal than general English.

In lexical items precision can take various forms: they can be precise in reference because they designate unique objects; they can be precise in expression form because they may not have developed their polysemic potential, or they have no synonyms with overlapping meaning or they have no homonyms. It is generally accepted that standardised terms are more precise than terms, and terms are more precise than words.

An alternative method of achieving precision of reference resides in the use of nomenclatures. They effectively systematise long-established observation terms, e.g. in biology and anatomy, supported by definitions, and their reference is ultimately confirmable through visual evidence. Nomenclatures are less effective in chemistry and mineralogy because of the various alternate systems of notation and the complexity of proving distinctiveness. They are least effective in the property and process terms of medicine.

Precision can be increased by more complex designations, or reduced by such devices as compression of forms. For example, 'ratio of a pair of gears' is more precise than 'gear ratio' but for most practical purposes the latter form is preferred. Derivation can produce precise terms only when the affix has been given a unique designative function such as -'ance' in electronics seems to be acquiring, or -'osis' and -'iasis' in medicine. Terms formed from prefixed verbs are often preferred to verb + preposition, because they can be matched with nominal equivalents, and because such verbs can be further modified by a single preposition. For example, 'perform' creates 'performance' and is preferred to 'carry out'. Equally, 'absorb (absorption)' instead of 'take in', etc.

The same principle of concentration can be seen in such terms as 'off-print' and 'throughput' which are verbal nouns first and infinitives of verbs second. Precision can also be seen in the use of prepositions. For example, the distinction between 'from', which in 'made from' indicates a basic material which may be further processed, 'by', which indicates indirect means and 'through', which indicates direct transfer, e.g. 'the engine is driven by steam through a piston'. Double prepositions are yet another means of expressing greater precision, e.g. 'downstream of', 'inboard of', 'onto', 'prior to', 'rearward of'.

4.2.3 *Appropriateness of expression*

Appropriateness arbitrates between precision and economy and is the measure of the effectiveness of the intention as it is expressed and understood in a message. Appropriateness of expression results from a proper appreciation of the cognitive effort required of the recipient. It starts therefore with the correct presuppositions that the sender makes. Equally, appropriateness regulates the explicitness of expression of the psychological intention and is therefore based on the correct assessment of the assumptions that can be made about the correct interpretation of the sender's intention.

The intention to augment, modify or confirm the recipient's knowledge is dependent on the situational factors of inequality of knowledge. Confirmation of knowledge, for instance, permits a higher degree of special reference than addition to knowledge and incidentally, therefore, greater economy; the use of undefined terms is a clear signal of presupposed knowledge, but which definitions can be presupposed can only be decided on the basis of appropriateness for a group or an individual. Any such presupposition endows the relevant text item with the intention of confirming knowledge. Modification of knowledge requires a questioning of presuppositions and possibly redefinitions of items of knowledge which render the speech act less economical but more precise. Appropriateness also decides the degree of general and special reference required in the individual speech act and therefore regulates the relative frequency of occurrence of words, terms and standardised terms. Appropriateness is, finally, the measure of the level of specialism aimed at so that the reader of a well-formulated text can distinguish between known and new references. Appropriateness therefore also controls the necessity of creating standards, with respect to both the knowledge structure and its linguistic representation. According to the fixation achieved in the knowledge structure and the range and type of users, appropriateness, for instance, determines the permissibility and admissibility of synonyms, the limitations of their use in particular sublanguages, or their elimination within a special field.

Global appropriateness of texts is in the first instance a property of text types which is established on conventional assumptions about certain groups of people with specified degrees of knowledge and functions within the special subject community. Modes of appropriateness are therefore specified in the pragmatic requirements of text forms.

At the level of the text appropriateness manifests itself through the diversification of forms. This diversification permits a high degree of precision in the conventions attached to each text form, and economy is achieved by not having to express intention linguistically in each case. This leaves the linguistic message free for signalling particular emphasis on intention, or small variations in the intention from the pattern established by the convention. For example, the difference between informative and descriptive abstracts, between an index and a checklist, an introduction and a preface are the result of choices in appropriateness. The various possible patterns of sections of reports and the choice of subtypes of memos in the manufacturing process are also the result of choices which can be assessed only by the criterion of appropriateness.

Text forms are, finally, more or less appropriate according to the extent that assumptions about correct interpretation of informative, evaluative or directive intention are expressed by the conventions accompanying a text form or by the linguistic message itself.

Syntactic appropriateness manifests itself in sentence and segment cohesion, in the density of information and in the degree of compression, which are adjusted within the broad conventions of each text form to the presuppositions and assumptions made about the recipient of a message.

Lexical appropriateness

In general language communication, appropriateness of the expression form, especially polysemic ones, is a matter for individual interpretation. Appropriateness is the criterion for choosing general language designations to become part of the terminological system of a particular discipline. The notion of 'work' in physics, for example, is clearly associated with 'distance' but in general reference is it understood as 'force', or as 'effort'.

The creation of word and term families from basic stems, by means of affixes and compounding, contributes to terminological unity and thus to a greater appropriateness of designation. The consistent use of affixes and compounding patterns creates patterns of recognition which can be applied to the interpretation of new information and even to the systematic designation of new concepts. The nomenclatures have perfected the appropriateness of designations as far as possible, but even in such a stable science as biological taxonomy, misdesignations have been made and are being perpetuated because of the necessary and inevitable rigidity of the system. It is arguable whether other, different sciences and technologies which constantly re-assess and modify their knowledge structure can effectively adopt or introduce the constraints imposed by rules of nomenclature. The introduction of rules for the formation of new terms is dependent upon the predictability of the nature of the new concept to be designated. Adherence to rules is possible in the taxonomic sciences like biology, chemistry and medicine but not in physics in which only well-established concepts lend themselves to regularisation.

4.3 Standardisation

A terminology, i.e. a coherent, structured collection of terms, is a representation of an equally coherent, but possibly differently structured system of concepts. Conceptual innovation logically and chronologically precedes term creation, and conceptual innovation can only manifest itself by means of speech acts which are by definition innovatory. New terms are regularly introduced into the language either to fill a gap created by the introduction of a new concept or to replace an existing, less efficient term. The speech acts which introduce new terms are by their nature also innovatory. This description applies in particular to the metalinguistic text type 'definition' which fixes the reference of a new concept or inversely explains the reference of a new term. Prior to definition, which is normally seen as confirming an act of term creation, innovatory speech acts of a special type may be required; when, for example, the concepts involved may be known to both participants—both sender and recipient may have the same state of knowledge—but the recipient does not necessarily have the same vocabulary of a special language available as the sender of the message. In such a case the sender would, in the first instance, create a new term from existing lexical resources—which may be created from terms or words or their parts—or provide a paraphrase. In this circumstance precision and appropriateness of expression take precedence over economy, since it is important that the recipient should interpret correctly the concept that the sender intends to convey. If the recipient has neither the lexical nor the conceptual resources, then the need for precision and appropriateness, even at the expense of economy, is all the stronger and a full definition is required.

Provided the validity of a new concept is generally acknowledged, it will become established within the specialist community. Usually the specialists will also agree on an suitable expression form. This stage can be called regularisation of usage and sets of definitions in textbooks, glossaries or manuals are the outward manifestation of this process of promulgation of agreed usage.

Standardisation is a separate process and consists of users reaching 'public' agreement to adopt a given term for use in specific circumstances. The motivation for standardisation may come from all manner of commercial reasons or be the result of security and safety considerations. The need for standardisation may be considered stronger or more urgent if competing terms coexist, perhaps because the associated concept was expressed contemporaneously by different individuals in different terms or because the originally proposed term was not favoured by a substantial number of important users.

Besides fixation of meaning standardisation usually involves a choice from among competing terms. The communicative usefulness of a term is determined by its accessibility within a given language or sublanguage, the precision of its relationship to the corresponding concept and the appropriateness of the concept to the topic of discourse.

Standardisation can be introduced for several reasons:

1. in the interest of economy, if one of the competing terms is noticeably more cumbersome than the other;
2. in the interest of precision, if one term offers markedly greater clarity of reference or less inherent ambiguity than the other;
3. in the interest of appropriateness, if one term has, for example, disturbing connotations not possessed by the other.

4.3.1 *Principles of standardisation*

There is a fundamental temporal conflict between the need for naming and the desire to standardise names. Naming occurs as soon as a new concept, object, process etc. is established, which inevitably leads to infelicities in naming and the multiplication of names. Standardisation is introduced at a later stage, when there is felt to be a need for it, e.g. when a conflict has arisen about names; in such a case, a choice has to be made between two or more alternative designations for the same concept, process, etc. When developments of new ideas or objects occur in more than one place it is not easy to determine whether one is dealing with the same or with different concepts, objects, etc., nor can the development of new objects be considered complete until they have been fully evolved, which in practice means that they are commercially designed, tried, tested and sometimes even marketed. By that time names have usually become established and it is difficult to change them. Only when there has been full standardisation of certain significant features of objects which appear to justify a different name, can there be any hope that alternatives will disappear. Standardisation is therefore a retrospective activity which follows naming after an indeterminate length of time. The hope that standardisation will solve the problems caused by alternate designations is therefore not likely to be fulfilled very frequently. In many cases alternate names continue to exist indefinitely and it is such extraneous influences as market dominance of one product or the disappearance of older technologies which decide on the life or death of terms.

4.3.2 *Instruments of standardisation*

Dictionaries and term banks, unless they have a language planning function with appropriate powers, have no influence on the standardisation of terms. Indirectly, however, term banks may exercise a strong harmonising influence on usage in special subject fields by the simple fact that a single term bank may become the preferred terminological reference work for a particular subject and thereby establish a virtual standard. Because of their leading position and role in some countries or international organisations, term banks can and do, however, contribute to national and international discussions on the standardisation of the methods used in terminology preparation for standardised glossaries. While this work is in the first instance intended for the organisations which sponsor it, there is the general expectation, sometimes unjustified, that it will also benefit terminology processing in general.

The role of nomenclature commissions in the efforts of standardisation is long-established in their particular subject fields. This work is extremely valuable in the areas where it can be applied, such as the classification of diseases, viruses, minerals, chemical compounds, plants, animals and a few other taxonomies. Because of the use of Greek and Latin word elements such names can be considered truly international and in most cases they are internationally accepted regardless of the co-existence of any popular alternative names. But the scope for such unified naming and definition with reference to clearly recognisable objects or phenomena and without the involvement of competing alternative industrial processes is virtually exhausted and any other national and international harmonisation of designations is much more complex.

Nomenclature commissions have issued detailed descriptions of the procedures to be adopted in naming a new entity and making this name known; there are no such rules about compiling glossaries in other fields or even for maintaining existing nomenclatures. In the industrial sector, where national standardisation bodies are active, there is little if any guidance about naming and even less about compiling glossaries. It is an amazing fact that national standardisation bodies regularly issue glossaries of terms in standards, but very few have firm guidelines for the selection, definition and publication of terminology. There is consequently great diversity in the visible end product of this labour which permits conclusions about the lack of uniformity of methods of compilation. In this respect work in the Federal Republic of Germany is exceptional as it demonstrates a high degree of awareness of the desirability of harmonisation of principles and methods of terminology creation and processing. Whereas in the United Kingdom there is one standard in this field, i.e. BS 3669:1963, dating from 1963, DIN, the Federal German standardisation body, has several separate standards in force or in preparation for concepts, concept systems, international harmonisation of concepts and names, specialised dictionaries and the preparation and presentation of publications containing harmonised terminology.

DIN, together with ON, the Austrian standards institute, has also been the main driving force behind parallel efforts made by the International Organisation for Standardisation (ISO), which issued a number of basic recommendations between 1963 and 1970. Most of these have lapsed with time but some have since been converted into standards and others are in the process of being revised or re-drafted. Unfortunately few of these documents take account of modern information technology practices and hence they are of very limited value for automated terminology processing.

The biggest obstacle to international agreement on cooperation is not so much the language barrier as the varying importance given to this endeavour. Where there is no perceived need for terminology development, there are no funds for this work, and where there are no funds there can be no activity. In such cases it is only possible to develop theoretical positions. However, in the absence of testing grounds, these cannot then be developed into practical guidelines and methodologies. The work of ISO on principles of and guidelines for terminology has been hampered by this divergence of interest and this difference between the practical experience of the participant countries. In addition, as this work is dominated by industrialised countries with Indo-european languages, any linguistically-based principles and methods have had little if any relevance to countries with a strong need for importing technology and to languages with other structural characteristics and word formation techniques.

The language barrier also manifests itself in other ways. International agreements are usually formulated in very few languages (English and French and Russian for ISO and even fewer in other organisations). But because the participants in such agreements are not necessarily only speakers of these languages, these agreements have to be translated into the languages of any other countries wanting to accept them. In this process a great deal of re-interpretation takes place to fit the circumstances and languages of the society in question and the strength of the agreement may become weakened. International agreements written in French or English also have to be made acceptable to each English or French-speaking country in turn; in this process they may undergo substantial changes which also undermine the strength of the agreement. When such agreements deal with linguistic issues, an area in which there is no established metalanguage, the enterprise of reaching international agreement on methods of terminology is seen to be fraught with complications and difficulties.

4.3.3 *Objectives of standardisation of terminology*

The written form of so-called 'educated' speech is a standardised system. This function is usually carried out through the respective ministries of education which prescribe the accepted spelling, punctuation and some other grammatical rules and which enforce the use of standardised forms through school examination and inspectors. Such standards may also be enshrined in guide books for writing by governmental institutions and are further enforced through the hierarchical system of approval of official documents. On the referential level, general language is regularised, i.e. rule-governed but not usually standardised, i.e. the system permits variation according to a variety of rules. Standardisation of reference is not part of language as a system but occurs in groups of speech acts, i.e. manifestations of 'parole', as a result of agreements between individuals or groups of language users. It can be applied to proper names, words or terms, regardless whether they refer to everyday objects, concrete or abstract notions, to individuals or to types.

It is possible to standardise references to objects or notions without standardising the objects or notions themselves. This is, in fact, the underlying principle of documentation thesauri. Inversely, it is pointless to standardise objects without at the same time standardising their designations, because, without being able to make appropriate linguistic reference to the objects, the fact that standardisation has taken place would not be noticed. It is equally unthinkable to standardise concepts without simultaneously standardising designations.

In order to understand the motivation of standardisation, it is convenient to analyse the principles established by the International Organisation for Standardisation which are concerned primarily with the standardisation of objects. They are here reinterpreted with application to language.

1st Principle. The standardisation of terms always occurs subsequent to the standardisation of objects.

Standardisation of terminology is essentially an act of simplification of expression forms resulting from a deliberate effort made by society. This effort requires a reduction in the number of certain objects, in the case of terminology, of designations, which immediately results in a reduction of the existing complexity and variety of designations and for the future aims at avoiding any superfluous complexity. While a retrospective reduction of objects or designations may be desirable, it is difficult to predict what may be superfluous in future.

2nd Principle. Standardisation of terminology is a social and economic activity and its achievement must be the outcome of collaboration of all interested parties. A standard must be based on general consensus. General consensus can be interpreted as applying to a single special language at a time, i.e. the same expression may exist in general language and in more than one special language with different reference, e.g. 'nut', 'bolt', 'spring'.

3rd Principle. The publication of a standard has little value in itself; its application is all-important. This principle obviously applies to terminology with the same force. Application of commonly agreed terminology will oblige some parties to make changes in their linguistic practices in the interest of the common good.

4th Principle. The establishment of a standard requires firstly a choice of a suitable term and secondly a fixation of this term and its definition. The term chosen for a new concept or a newly unified concept may be any one of the existing terms or a newly coined one. The choice of a term can take into account the possibility of the development of similar objects and be therefore open to derivation and compounding.

5th Principle. Standards must be re-examined at regular intervals and revised when it proves necessary to do so. The intervals between revision normally depend on new concepts or new terms emerging to disturb the existing patterns.

6th Principle. When the conditions of use and other characteristics of a product have been specified, it is necessary to determine test methods in order to verify whether the object conforms to the specifications. When a gradation is to be introduced, it is desirable to specify the method to be followed and, if necessary, the size and frequency of the grades. Verification of object standards is a regular repeated process of measurement and gradation. Verification of terminological standards, on the other hand, is a single and separate operation applied to a group of terms which can be carried out by the users themselves.

7th Principle. The necessity to legally enforce a standard must be studied with regards the nature of the standard, the level of industrialisation and the laws and conditions which predominate in the society for which the standard has been prepared. The legal enforcement of terminological standards is a matter of convenience and economy and must be mindful of the regional, social and subject groupings of language usage.

4.3.4 *Methods of standardisation*

When a new concept is identified and named, the user has at his disposal a variety of methods of naming and possible expression forms. The same methods and possibilities are available to standardisation. They are here briefly reviewed with comments on their effectiveness.

1. *Redefinition of words*. Normally redefinition involves a restriction of the range of denotation, as in 'expectation' and 'variance' in statistics, 'real' and 'imaginary' in number theory, or 'filter' in electronics; occasionally the choice of form may be entirely arbitrary or even fanciful, e.g. 'charm' and 'strangeness' in particle physics.

This method is generally economical, provided the original word is economical, but it may lack in precision, because of possible parallel reference in general language, and in appropriateness, because of the residual connotations which might be retained from general language usage. Precision and appropriateness may be improved if the term is subsequently standardised— i.e. afforded fixed reference within a relatively fixed conceptual framework.

2. *Redefinition of existing terms*. In the process of theory building, concepts are frequently re-defined, e.g. the multiple definitions of 'word' or 'sentence' in linguistics. This method is frequently used in relatively new areas of study, like most of the so-called 'social sciences', where the conceptual system itself may be in flux, and terminologising is extensively practised as a surface indicator of scientific rigor.

While this method is economical, precision is impaired by the instability of the underlying conceptual structure, at least until the conceptual system reaches a stable state; standardisation may accelerate this process, although agreement among users may be difficult to impose.

3. *Derivation*. Exploiting the derivational properties of the sublanguage or of the general language, in which the sublanguage is embedded, can produce

highly regular forms. For example, 'de-hydr-ate', 'internal-ise/ize' use the derivational affixes 'de-', '-ate', '-ise/ize' in their general language usage to create terms; while chemical language has taken over the affixes '-ous', 'ic', 'bi-', for example, and now uses them with terminological force in their own right.

This method can be highly economical, precise and also appropriate when the derivational devices used are themselves partial determiners of a particular topic; it is at its most powerful when the concepts involved form a natural conceptual hierarchy, with a small number of basic relationships which may be adequately expressed by a set of derivational affixes, e.g. in chemical and biological taxonomy.

4. *Composition*. By juxtaposition of existing words, special terms and terms borrowed from other languages or sublanguages, complex terms can be formed, such as 'heavy water', 'heavy hydrogen', 'floppy disc', 'split-plot design'; if such complex terms become established, there is then the possibility that a constituent element which was not originally a term becomes one— cf. the extended use of 'heavy' to describe certain isotopes with greater than normal mass.

5. *Borrowing*. Adopting a term/word from a foreign language is really a special case of redefinition. Frequently the term accompanies a concept imported from the other language community, for example, 'input', 'output', 'printer' in Italian and French, 'Gestalt', 'Zeitgeist' in English, etc.; classical Greek and Latin provide a fruitful source of terms, either for concepts, like 'atom', or by supplying a ready stock of parallel referents alongside the general language vocabulary, and so enabling term formation without affecting the general lexical structure. Some languages, e.g. English, French, are much more ready to accept classical borrowings than others—with consequent repercussions for international standardisation.

This method generates terms which are no more and no less economical than the corresponding forms in the language of origin; it generally produces high precision if the term is imported together with a single concept; but it may not always be appropriate if its form contains no external indicators of its place in the conceptual system, particularly when the concept is also imported.

6. *Compression*. The reduction of an existing complex term to a more compact form can be standardised, by creating an acronym or by use of initial letters alone. This method is characteristic of codes whose primary medium is

writing, e.g. 'radar' (= radio detection and ranging), 'quasar' (= quasistellar), 'thermistor' (= thermal resistor), TG, DNA.

This method is highly economical, and as precise as the complex term from which the abbreviation derives, provided the full form is still remembered by the participants in the speech act. It can be highly appropriate, if the abbreviation is restricted to use only in a particular sublanguage.

4.3.5 *The efficacy of standards in terminology*

Standards are economical because they establish prior agreement of reference among the participants and therefore assist in the achievement of effective communication among specialists by speeding up the process of communication. Standards are precise because they eliminate misunderstanding by establishing a clear one-to-one equivalence between terms and the region of the conceptual system referred to. The agreement on and the conscious use of standardised terminology assumes that participants have decided to put aside individual interpretations of terms and knowledge structure. Finally standards are appropriate to certain types of speech acts because they permit the originator of a message to establish clearly a basis of assumed knowledge upon which the intention can be specified. The recipient of the message can also more readily recognise the intention and therefore adjust his own expectations to the sender's intention.

By measuring the appropriateness of the use of standardised terminology we can demonstrate the limitations of standards as a tool of communication. The degree of agreement on the knowledge structure and its unequivocal linguistic representation upon which appropriate use of standards is based, can only be assumed in specialist communication. When the situational, social and intellectual role differences between participants are minimal a higher proportion of standardised terms can be used. The further apart these differences are, the more it is necessary to use a greater proportion of definitions, paraphrases, circumlocutions, i.e., terms and words rather than standards.

On the negative side we note that, since standardisation fixes the reference of a term, it undermines the natural creativity of language. Most people do not readily accept normative intervention in their language behaviour, and yet more and more standards are published and used annually. The solution to this paradox can be found in two aspects of standardised terms.

Standardised terminology is useful. The formulation of a standard implies that there is prior agreement among its potential users. Users agree to standardise terms because the nature of special reference makes it important for them to achieve compatibility of intention, knowledge and language for the furtherance of their work.

Standardisation only seeks to assist users in achieving a greater than normal degree of economy, precision and appropriateness in their communication, i.e. it only aims at maximising tendencies which are already present in general language. Users themselves assist in the process by agreeing to relax the aesthetic, emotive and other non-informative requirements of language for the purpose of special communication.

Standardisation is, however, not an aim in itself but is merely a device to facilitate the communication of information. It should be seen as part of a process of language development; it artificially exaggerates certain of the natural tendencies of language but nonetheless respects the limitations of language, knowledge and intention imposed by language users. The phenomenon of standardisation can be properly understood and exploited only within this functional framework.

4.3.6 *Limitations of standardisation*

This section raises the question to what extent and under what circumstances terminology can be standardised.

The systematic nature of language requires that its semantic and pragmatic aspects be rule-governed. The communal nature of language identifies these rules with social norms. We associate the application of social norms to language with processes of regularisation and unification of expression form and content. Standardisation must then represent a further narrowing of rules applicable to reference or naming techniques or usage. A first distinction must, therefore be made between standardisation as the most severe restriction of usage on a sliding scale of regularisation–unification–standardisation of language and Standardisation as the product of the work of standardising bodies with respect to language.

Regularisation and even unification are successfully applied on the levels of pronunciation, spelling, punctuation, morphology and even to some extent in syntax. The vigour of standardisation does not, however, fit the creativity of general language and is only applied by small groups of language users, e.g. in the restricted morphology of the nomenclatures, or the special syntax of patents and other legal documents. On the semantic level general language is regularised in a process which is documented in dictionaries. But the system always permits variation, as can be seen in the divergence among dictionaries.

Only in the special reference of restricted subject language does unification find scope since this is the area in which fixation of designation is imperative. Furthermore, standardisation can only be applied to codified knowledge. In areas where knowledge is undergoing change temporary fixations of meaning are achieved by means of stipulative definitions which temporarily associate a term to a concept still susceptible to modification. We therefore do not normally think of standardisation as applicable to language but rather consider it an activity in the sphere of the manufacture of goods, quality or safety control of production. Only exceptionally do we see a necessity of standardising language as, e.g. in legal contracts, safety regulations, or similar official documents.

Standardisation in the sense of the work carried out by national and international standardising agencies, is primarily concerned with objects, their properties, measurements, performance and consequently also with specifications and methods for evaluation and measurement. Such national and international agreements which can be reached are expressed and communicated in natural language. People who want to adhere to standards, or to control compliance with standards or simply to know of their existence must go via the medium of language and therefore expect the language of standards to be clear, precise and unambiguous. Hence the motivation to standardise the language contained in standards documents.

The aims of institutionalised standardisation can be summarised as in the British Standards document BS 0: Part 1:1981.

a) "provision of means of communication amongst all interested parties;
b) promotion of economy in human effort, materials and energy in the production and exchange of goods;
c) protection of consumer interests through adequate and consistent quality of goods and services;
d) promotion of the quality of life: safety, health and the protection of the environment;
e) promotion of trade by removal of barriers caused by differences in national practices."

While these aims are first of all achieved by the standardisation of objects and their characteristics and secondly by the standardisation of methods of achieving, guaranteeing and verifying standardisation of objects, there is no doubt that they can also be served by standardised terminology.

The glossaries produced by national and international standardising agencies can be seen as efforts to facilitate 'communication amongst all interested parties' as quoted above. But not all the terms contained in these glossaries actually occur in standards and not all the terms used in standards are listed in standards glossaries. We must therefore distinguish between the terms listed and defined in glossaries and the terms that occur in other standards. Before we can consider their status with respect to standards, a further distinction is then usefully made between all the terms used in standards and those few which are listed and defined at the beginning of a standard.

Agreement on the technical terms used in standards documents is one of the first steps in the long process of drafting a standards document. Unification of terminology is therefore a by-product of the work carried out by the various bodies concerned with the standardisation of objects, processes and measurements. Where there is general agreement the participants in the standardising process do not normally see the need for recording this agreement. Consequently not all standards contain a section with terms and their definitions.

Here is what the British Standards Guide says on this subject:

5.4. TERMINOLOGY: Properly defined, unequivocal terminology is essential. Terminology within a standard should be consistent, so that the same object or concept is always described or expressed by the same term and not by the use of synonyms. There may be particular reasons for using certain terms in a specialised or more limited sense than that defined in a British Standard glossary. Similarly there may be reason for using technical or other terms not defined in a glossary in a special way because of differences in their use in different industries or contexts. Terminology not included in a British Standard glossary and not specifically defined should follow the generally accepted usage amongst the parties concerned. Unusual terminology should always be defined. (BS 0: Part 3:1981).

The document distinguishes between three types of terms,
– terms defined in a Standard glossary;
– terms more narrowly defined than in a Standard glossary;
– terms not included in a Standard glossary and not specifically defined.
The first two may be considered standardised terms, but a further distinction will be necessary. This document also makes the tacit assumption that in object standardisation standard glossaries are available for reference and that specialised usage can be measured in relation to definitions contained in them. This is far from being the case; very few areas of British standardisation are covered by glossaries. What represents "unusual" terminology is not explained but it should in any case not be too frequent in standards whose aim is to present information simply and unambiguously. Nor is the definition clause in British standards very regularly used. What is accepted usage is determined in each case by the members of the standardising committee.

The motivation for the production of Standards glossaries which, according to BS 0: Part 3:1981, 'bring together agreed sets of terms and definitions for reference', is at least two-fold. Glossaries can be written before standardisation of objects, methods or specifications begins; e.g. a major standard may be preceded by a glossary of the main terms of the specific subject area. Or, alternatively glossaries can be compiled subsequently in order to collect the terminology of a field that has been covered by a number of standards; e.g. the major glossary of building terms (BS 6100), started in 1987, which contains some 8000 terms and is based on a smaller, earlier document (BS 3589: 1976 Glossary of general building terms). It is called a coordinated glossary because it attempts to resolve many conflicts between existing BS construction glossaries and definitions in standards.

Both approaches are distinct and require different methods. The first is preparatory to standardisation and must establish the groups of concepts which are relevant to the standard or standards in question before finding, selecting and fixing their designation. Such work must, however, be provisional since the process of standardisation which follows may yet develop new concepts or modify existing ones which then have to be named and fitted into the terminological system.

In the second case it is a matter of collecting, ordering and harmonising already existing terms. The starting point are the terms that occur in standards to which definitions are associated. The product is a definitive list of preferred (and defined), non-preferred and deprecated terms in classified and alphabetical sequence. Standardisation in the sense of 'an activity giving solutions for repetitive application, to problems essentially in the spheres of science, technology and economics, aimed at the achievement of the optimum degree or order in a given context' (BS 0: Part 1:1981) can properly be applied only to the second case. The provisional glossary, which is the product of the first approach, must be considered an interim document which can only be finalised after a number of standards have been developed using the established terminology.

It is well known that standards are validated by their use. In the case of standards glossaries we have a circular situation: glossaries may be needed to prepare effective standards, and effective standards lead to glossaries which can be used as a basis for future standards.

Glossaries do, of course, also fulfil one of the broad aims of standardisation listed earlier, namely the provision of means of communication. In this case, however, we do not necessarily need a glossary of standardised terms. Something less than standardisation will do.

There is yet another type of British Standard glossary. The Glossary of Documentation Terms (BS 5408:1976), for example, collects 300 terms from more than 3000 suggested terms as a 'synthesis which it is hoped represents current practice in the UK.' The 20 or so government departments and scientific, technical and professional associations represented on the committee entrusted with the preparation of this standard were all British. The foreword makes no reference to a particular origin of the terms nor to their intended use. It comments on the selection criteria which make it clear that the glossary pretends to be neither exhaustive nor exclusive, neither prescriptive nor restrictive. It speaks of avoiding excessive specialisation, excluding newer terms, because no agreement could be reached on their inclusion. Terms 'defined adequately elsewhere' are also excluded as are compound terms where the total meaning of the compound does not differ from that of the sum of the constituent elements. Such a glossary is a supplement to existing dictionaries. It has the merit of responding to a proven need and is truly evolved out of a consensus of experts. It is created under optimal conditions and this rather than a spurious claim to standardisation constitutes its superiority over other glossaries.

The same pattern of glossary making applies to the international or rather multilingual situation.

An example is provided by the circumstances of production of an international standards glossary of terms related to terminology (ISO R 1087 under revision). This work had to be considered at best as provisional inasmuch as it was undertaken for standards yet to be drafted. There was therefore no certainty about the number of terms to be included (there are not enough national standards in any language to provide such certainty) and no basis of agreement on definitions (these could only emerge as part of the work on the associated standards). Even when such an ISO glossary is completed it is forced to lead a shadow existence for quite another reason. Unless an international standard written in English is adopted by an English-speaking national standards body, the English of the international document is a metalanguage which is used only for translation into national languages. It may occur that an English-language version of an ISO glossary is only partly acceptable to an English-speaking country. BS 3203:1964 (Glossary of paper, stationary and allied terms) for example, which appears in English and French and largely coincides with various ISO documents, does however also give ISO definitions which are not acceptable to BSI side by side with additional notes on certain definitions considered to be useful to English-speaking readers. Disagreement is, for example, recorded about such basic terms as 'paper', 'board' and 'pulp'.

These observations do not invalidate this work but merely characterise ISO glossaries as fundamentally different from glossaries based on established national standards. The result may be a comprehensive glossary, but it cannot be called a glossary of standardised terms valid for the English language.

Even glossaries based on established standards can only be considered standardised with respect to the usage in the country that has adopted these standards and only to the extent that communication using the terms of the glossary is related to these standards.

We have thus returned to the question of the meaning of standardisation with respect to glossaries. In order to be considered standardised, a term must be closely defined. This excludes from consideration terminology not included in a standard glossary and not specifically defined in a standard. Yet this is the terminology most generally accepted and therefore most widely used and clear in scope of reference. Terms specifically defined in a standard can be considered standardised but their validity may not extend beyond the area of use of the standard. Such a process amounts to no more than a stipulative definition for text-restricted terminology and leaves the term free to have a wider reference outside the scope of the standard.

The terms included in standards glossaries have, as we have seen, many potential origins. They are produced by teams of experts and this collaborative effort guarantees their quality and acceptability. At the monolingual level agreement on concepts, definitions and terms goes hand in hand. At the level of ISO glossaries, without the support of national standards glossaries in the official languages, the effort is restricted to agreement on concepts and definitions; it applies to terms only to the extent that agreement exists on the meaning of the terms used in the definitions. The ISO glossaries lack a full functional status as they live for each country only through their adoption as national standards. An ISO glossary written in English may however not be acceptable as a national standard in any English speaking country and may have to be translated into the national English of any of the countries whose official language is English. The only real function of ISO glossaries is therefore that of a source for translation into national languages. It may, of course, be this very nature which makes ISO glossaries in English, French and Russian unsuitable for full and direct adoption. The notion of standardisation may therefore be applicable to certain standards glossaries issued by national agencies but is irrelevant as far as international standards glossaries are concerned for the proper use of which it may be more appropriate to distinguish between standardisation of concepts and standardisation of terms.

Chapter Five

COMPILATION OF TERMINOLOGY

It is now recognised that the only practical means of processing lexical data is by computer. This awareness of the benefits of using computers in terms of their speed, flexibility and storage capacity has resulted in a growing trend towards the automation of terminological data processing which is evidenced by the existence of terminological data banks, some of which have been in existence since the early 1970s. There are, however, various views about the ways in which computers are seen as tools for achieving this task. Processing systems for lexical and terminological data have been implemented using standard data processing methodologies but the result is normally far from satisfactory. This leads to the recognition that the storage of lexical data cannot simply be regarded as another application of traditional information processing techniques but that new techniques have to be developed for adequately representing the type of information contained in specialised dictionaries. Much progress is being made but further research is required in both conceptual modelling and computational lexicography/linguistics before anything approaching a complete lexical or terminological databank can be constructed.

Nevertheless, terminological data banks have been a fact of life in some organisations, e.g. the EC, the language services of the German Federal Republic, Siemens AG, the French Association for Standardisation, AFNOR, the governments of Canada and Quebec, for nearly twenty years and many other organisations have converted or are contemplating converting their terminological holdings to machine-readable form. Even individual translators now have tools at their disposal to allow the computerisation of their own personal glossaries.

The current move towards automation is of such overwhelming import that the techniques and methods in the following three chapters are based on the assumption that now and in future all aspects of terminology compilation, storage and retrieval are being assisted by or directly carried out by a computer.

5.1 Principles of compilation

Since automation fundamentally affects the nature and methods of terminology compilation, it is now becoming imperative to evolve an entirely new set of principles for compilation which differs in almost every respect from the principles established in pre-automation days. The possibilities offered by automatic analysis of text and processing of large quantities of data have modified the very basis of terminology compilation, the view on relevance of data and the degree of human intervention in the process. Terminology compilation now also has a greater communality of principles and methods with lexicography than ever before; but both activities still lack a sound theoretical foundation.

Traditionally there are two separate approaches to terminology compilation according to the motivation of this work. So it is necessary to distinguish between:

(a) specific cases of terminology collection, which may then be linked to primary or secondary term creation—often in response to a particular request for a terminologist's services—and

(b) the systematic compilation of terminology, as for instance for the purpose of building up a term bank or making a technical dictionary.

When a terminologist acts as advisor on a single term which is not available in a term bank or other automated collection, his procedure to obtain an answer to a specific query must, of course, be very much the same as it has always been. He has to search existing literature and consult specialists in order to be able to answer the question. But when a terminologist has at his disposal the services of a term bank, or various forms of automatic text analysis for the purpose of creating or adding to a term bank, he proceeds in a manner appropriate to the tools available.

5.1.1 *Corpus-based compilation*

Systematic terminology compilation is now firmly corpus-based, i.e. terminology is no longer extracted from previous lists or by individual searches but from a corpus of material. A corpus is a representative body of texts of a subject field which in this way is confined in a very concrete way. There are, as yet, no reliable guidelines as to what quantity of text represents a representative corpus; this is a matter for future research. Equally, there is no common agreement on the scope of any one subject field; decisions on subject fields are changing with our perception of what is a discipline and what an interdisciplinary subject and this is likely to remain an unresolved issue in the dynamic fields of knowledge. Besides, there will be an overlap of terms extracted from contiguous corpora and also a certain body of terminology common to a number of subject specific corpora. These common terms may respectively represent the interdisciplinary vocabulary, linking one subject to another, and the general scientific or technological vocabulary, both of which have been postulated theoretically but have not been textually identified so far.

Because text corpora are time- and place-conditioned, they reinforce the principle that terminology compilation is an ongoing and repeated activity. A certain item of information extracted from a particular corpus at a particular time is valid as long as the textual basis maintains its actuality. As soon as this is in question, the information has to be revised. There is no hard and fast rule for the life-span of a terminology. Some basic terms rarely change; subjects go through periods of relative stability with a steady set of terms and stages of rapid evolution with a considerable growth and turnover of terminology. Textual information is the most reliable indicator of change and consequently it provides the only reliable data for the revision of terminological records.

The increased use of Information Retrieval systems containing running-text (of all types) in machine-readable form has significantly affected the motivation and indeed methods of terminology compilation. Since many technical texts are now stored on computers, they can be preserved in or converted into a suitable format for terminological analysis using the techniques developed by computational linguists. This has had two main consequences.

Firstly, texts which are to be processed by translators or other terminology users can, in the first instance, be analysed and compared with current machine-readable terminology holdings and a machine-readable general dictionary in order to produce a listing of items not contained in either. This list will, undoubtedly, contain many spurious items which are of no interest to the terminologist (proper nouns, for example). On the other hand it will also contain a significant number of new terms, which can be researched by the terminologist prior to the translator or other end-user editing, translating or otherwise processing the text in question. This methodology could be adapted to suit other requirements; the text analysis software can, for example, identify terms existing in the term bank which lack equivalents in a foreign language; it could produce corpus-oriented supplements to machine-translation lexicons and so forth. The concept of user-oriented terminology compilation is thus taken a stage further with the terminologist pre-empting the users' requests and ensuring that the majority of queries concerning a particular text are satisfied.

Secondly, running text can be used totally independently of user requirements. Terminology extracted from running text or discourse offers a greater guarantee of thematic completeness and coherence. All relevant textual variants will be covered and suitable contexts which demonstrate the linguistic behaviour of terms can be selected. Running text also dates the term. Terminology compilation is therefore becoming increasingly text-oriented and less governed by the desire to construct separate conceptual systems.

Running text can also assist the terminologist in maintaining the correctness of previously entered terminology. Statistical analyses of large volumes of text can be used to pinpoint changes in the frequency or usage of a term. Changes may signify a movement in the linguistic environment in which the term occurs; more importantly it may reveal a change in the meaning of the lexical item which cannot be detected otherwise. Information about frequency of use in a particular text type corroborates or can even replace usage notes. Similarly, text analysis of large corpora can be used to isolate new terms, and therefore new concepts, to discover the possible obsolescence of terms and their concepts and to highlight other changes in conceptual systems. While the use of machine-readable text for semi-automated control over existing term collections, and indeed for machine-assisted terminology identification and compilation per se, is still in its very early stages it is a feature of terminology compilation which will increase dramatically in importance in the future.

5.1.2 *Databases for terminology and related information*

The second major innovation that affects principles of compilation is the division that is now possible between (1) the raw data as they are found in the corpus, (2) the database which contains all the information that is collected in suitably structured form, and (3) all the various subsets of information which are created for specific purposes and uses. It is now possible to construct a term bank which, for example, not only contains bibliographical references to the sources of its information, but also has direct access to the sources themselves. These sources may contain several defining contexts, examples of usage and also the contexts of foreign language equivalents, and so offer a substantial amount of supporting information to the terminological entry. The user may thus be given the choice of access to (1) the selected information in any one of the subsets of the database, (2) the edited information in the master database and (3) the raw information in the source text database. This three-fold division of information on terminology is represented in diagrammatic form in figure 5.1.

Figure 5.1. *Three types of databases with terminological information*

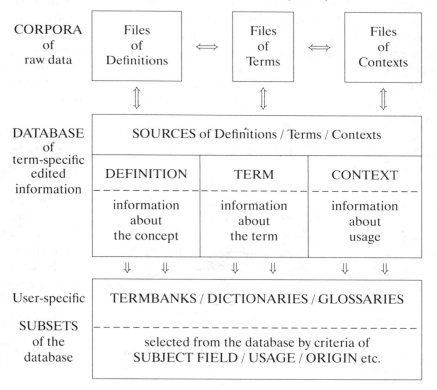

An important side-effect of a database approach is the fact that there is, in principle, no longer a physical restriction on the size of a terminological collection. A term bank can be as large as required, hence contain as much information on any one entry as is desired and have as many entries as necessary for covering the entire range of vocabulary of a subject field. A single large database can then also be subdivided for practical purposes of, e.g. faster access, separate maintenance, printing of subsections etc., and databases may be linked to each other to form even larger units.

The natural conclusion to these observations is that terminological databases can and should serve multiple purposes. This is not only desirable from the point of view of cost and effort; it is in the interest of improved communication that there should be only one major database of terminological information for each language community. A single database, to which all users will refer, exercises a strong unifying influence on terminological usage and thereby facilitates communication across all industrial and institutional barriers. A single database to which all users contribute in the minimal form of providing texts for the corpus or by providing specialist advice on the accuracy of the information would become widely used and thereby act as an informal focus for the unification of terminology. A term bank with which users can identify, because they have contributed to it, acts as an unofficial standard of usage and is therefore much more effective than officially prescribed forms of language.

A single database for terminology can supply the information needed by publishers for the production of all manner of technical dictionaries; it can produce glossaries with or without definitions for very specialised subject areas; it can provide dictionaries for various forms of natural language processing systems such as machine translation or expert systems; it can supply professional organisations with raw information for future development and completion; it can be developed into various forms of term banks for on-line access or for packaging into stand-alone microprocessor-based systems and, it can, of course, be accessed directly by researchers who want to study the large quantity of data collected on terms, definitions and concepts.

To sum up, the corpus and database approach offers the following direct advantages:
- it is possible to produce documentary evidence for most information gathered in a terminological record;
- the fullest set of linguistic information is available;
- the various selections and other decisions a terminologist makes become testable and replicable;
- all information is dated twice, by the date of the corpus and by the date of the terminologist's decision of including the information in the database and can therefore be checked at regular intervals;
- information on terms is collected with a view to providing as full a record as possible; in this way one terminology collection can serve a wide range of diverse users and uses, thus removing the costly duplication of effort which application-driven terminology compilation entails.

A single term bank may therefore serve such diverse purposes as:
- a tool for translators
- a reference tool for standards experts
- a source for NLP lexicons
- a source for printed glossaries and thesauri
- a reference database for industrial and individual users.

5.1.3 *New methods of terminology compilation*

The introduction of new technology into the process of terminology compilation has occasioned a number of fundamental changes in methodology.
Initially 'automated terminology compilation' simply meant the compilation of
terminology using existing methods and techniques and the subsequent input
of that terminology to the computer. An awareness of the potential of the
computer for handling natural language, coupled with developments in Computational Linguistics and Information Processing, has, however, resulted in
a number of new approaches to compilation.

The automation of terminology processing has also had a marked effect
on the motivation for terminology compilation. Theoretically, the regular and
systematic compilation of terminology is mainly undertaken by terminologists
and committees of experts independently of the particular needs of terminology users. This is a time-consuming process which is undertaken some time
after the terminology has been created. Committees in particular often agree
on individual terms only many years after the development or discovery of
the concept which inspired the need for a designation. Users of terminology
are consequently faced with a choice: either they wait for a pronouncement
from a team of experts or they carry out their own terminological research
and use, or coin, a term which may not be officially recognised. The increased
use of computer technology has provided facilities whereby terminology compilation can become user-driven. Whereas in printed dictionaries and closed
collections terminologists have no way of knowing what terms users need and
users have no way of alerting the compilers of terminologies to the absence
of a search term, regularly maintained term banks can provide a monitoring
facility as an integral part of their user-interface. An unsuccessful query by a
user can be automatically logged by the term bank software. A terminologist
can then supply the missing information and store it so that it is available for
a future search. Alternatively it is easy to introduce some sort of mail-box
facility allowing the user to request research on particular terms. In some

terminology processing centres this has resulted in a move away from systematic terminology compilation towards a situation where terminologists add to existing collections as demand arises and spend a large amount of their time researching terms in isolation and entering them into the term bank. This method is, however, only possible if there is already a substantial body of terminology stored in order to attract users in the first place.

Because of the availability of automated procedures, terminology processing can now involve a large number of part-time assistants, i.e. subject specialists who contribute or verify specific items of information. These specialists need easy access to machine-readable information and appropriate methods have to be devised to make their work fully efficient.

Automation reduces the methodological differences between terminological and lexicographical activities. In both fields information is now gathered from corpora of texts in machine-readable form, both accept the principle of a threefold separation of source material, database and separate user products, both can build up the content of their files in any order they want because the computer can take care of the ordering and in both areas is there a trend to reduce the human intervention and interpretation in favour of machine inferences on the basis of existing factual information.

5.1.4 *Qualitative improvements*

The overall effect of automation on terminology compilation can be summarised by saying that the terminologist now has for the first time appropriate tools which lift his work from a craft, with all its association of intuition and inspiration, to that of a scientifically supported activity, which still requires human judgement, but which can now be tested and verified. The greater investment in data verification and documentation of sources which is a second main feature of new developments, can be justified by the greater range of uses to which a terminological product can be put or indeed by the greater demand for such products.

Automatic processing and computer-assisted terminology compilation is therefore qualitatively superior to conventional methods. The terminologist can concentrate on his compilation and directly associated work and does not have to be concerned with the problems arising from the collection and management of large quantities of data. The representation of terminology in the machine need no longer be of relevance to the terminologist since compilation can proceed independently of storage and retrieval requirements.

Freed from such constraints, the terminologist can concentrate on achieving high standards of quality of compilation and he can also rely on the computer to check for completion of records and files and omission of data, thereby introducing an element of automatic quality control. The fast processing capability and the potential for large storage frees the terminologist from the limitations of the past with respect to size of individual records and total quantity of records. His information gathering can now be limited by its value rather than by what can be fitted on a slip of paper. For example, information on the first occurrence of a term and the date of its entry into a collection are important facts which will permit future control of relevance and hence quality of data in a collection. The recording of contexts and their sources permits at a later date the detection of changes of meaning or collocability of terms. Such information was rarely collected in pre-automation days and where it was, it was not in practice usable for manual sorting.

The ease with which data can be re-organised on a computer also reduces the danger of developing inadequate conceptual structures for subsets of terminology. There is, in fact, a significant move away from the compilation of terminology in conceptual systems. Either individual terms are researched according to demand in a production-oriented environment or collections of terminology are produced by analysing corpora of running text. In this way conceptual structures can be built according to perceived necessity and inter-relations can be declared on the basis of fuller information after a substantial amount of data has been collected.

The facility with which terminology can now be compiled even by individual technical writers and translators using commercially available software packages, imposes the necessity of guidance and advice on maintenance of quality. There is a growing trend towards individuals and groups of individuals recording terminological data in machine-readable form according to need. While this has always occurred in the past in manual form, new technology allows the wider dissemination of these private term collections, which in turn increases the danger of poor work being made more widely known.

5.2 The nature and type of terminological information

The information collected for the construction of a terminological record and represented on it is various and subject to change in any of its parts. This has an effect on the nature of the database system chosen for the management of the information. Most information items in the database must be considered independent of each other; mostly they can be entered at separate times and with reference to different sources. It follows that it must be possible to verify and up-date them separately. It should also be a principle to separate the automatically collected factual information from the selective and evaluative information added by the terminologist; in this way factual data are preserved intact and can be used for different purposes by different terminologists or indeed other users. Human interpretation, as it exists in the separation and categorisation of senses or in the declaration of preferred forms, may vary from person to person and with the purpose of a particular dictionary. If the factual evidence which led to a particular interpretation is maintained, it can serve as corroboration of the terminologist's decision and can be re-assessed at a later date.

These observations point to the importance of separately providing full bibliographical information for each item of information as appropriate. A great deal of writing on terminology has in recent years been devoted to 'proper' referencing of sources; less effort has been spent on characterising the types of sources that provide the most suitable information and even less on the criteria for establishing representativeness of sources.

It should be a principle to proceed automatically as far as possible and to limit human manipulation of lexical data to the specific interpretive tasks the computer cannot perform. The machine can increasingly be instructed to draw inferences from the stored information, and end users can be expected to search an automatic dictionary or a term bank at different levels of depth and sophistication.

Other than by definition, a concept is considered to be suitably explained by indication of the linguistic forms of one or several related concepts. This is expressed by listing such obvious related concepts as antonyms, broader and narrower generic terms, broader and narrower partitive terms—classes of relationships that have been taken over from information science.

It is now increasingly considered necessary to exemplify the usage of technical terms by means of example sentences, called contexts, and usage notes, which further specify the appropriate linguistic environment for a term. In addition and as a result of the availability of computer processing and storage, it has become good practice to provide full bibliographic references to the sources from where a term, its definition and context were extracted. This information permits a close control of the usage and possible change of meaning of terms which by their very nature are semantically much more volatile than items of the general lexicon of a language.

In conceptually-based terminological data banks it is customary to give definitions in one language only. This approach reduces terms in a second, non-defining, language to the status of translation equivalents. In this case it is conventionally agreed that the dictionary entry corresponds to a concept and consequently the language of the definition is the source language for the entry term of the terminological record. Since the equivalent term in a second language is not a representation of a matching concept in the culture of this language, this language has the status of a target language. In order to give two terms the same status, two definitions would have to be established and the source and target language definitions would have to be found as being identical in meaning.

Bilingual terminology is therefore usually directional and non-reversible, i.e. translation equivalents cannot be simply converted into entries in their own right with the source language entry becoming a translation equivalent. In many cases a translation equivalent does not in fact refer to an authentic concept in the culture of the target language, because the translated terms effects the introduction of the new concept. For a number of subject fields in natural sciences and for a number of languages of societies enjoying similar states of technological development the strict directional approach is unnecessary because structures of knowledge largely coincide, yet it is difficult to decide where it can safely be abandoned. In cases where terminology is internationally agreed, the reversibility of entries in dictionaries becomes acceptable for the extent of this agreement.

Reversibility of entries is, however, possible and even necessary in dictionaries for bilingual countries or for multilingual regimes of supranational organisations such as the European Communities. In these situations concepts are defined in identical manner in order to permit a multidirectional approach to the entries. This does not apply to the special cases of international standards, which are discussed in section 4.3.6.

5.2.1 *Methodological considerations*

Modern techniques of computational linguistics make it unnecessary for the terminologist to be concerned how the data is stored in the computer. Consequently there are no longer the constraints caused by the necessity to manually sequence and order the entries within the terminology collection and further sequence the individual elements within each entry. The structure of a terminological system can be as complex as necessary—it is not beyond the potential of computers to store a multi-dimensional semantic network. There is also no longer the physical limitation of the size of the record card, slip or other non-magnetic medium. Because computers offer unlimited storage to all intents and purposes, definitions, for example, can be as long as is necessary to properly define the term.

From a practical standpoint, there is less need for rigorous control during the research stage of terminology compilation. The task of checking terminological data can be handled either by the data acquisition software or by the database management system, as appropriate, and takes place either during input to the system or at the level of storage. It is recognised that the task of checking the completeness and consistency of both individual entries, where very complex relational structures are built up, and whole collections of terminological data is beyond the capabilities of a single individual or group of individuals. This task can, however be easily and efficiently performed by a reasonably intelligent piece of software.

This use of computers permits both a physical and temporal distribution of the task of compilation.

Information can be collected and stored in stages. As long as each item of data in the term record satisfies the controls imposed by the term-processing system for that data category, e.g. that a definition has a bibliographic reference or that any related term entered does not invalidate the existing conceptual system, then as much data as available for a term can be entered at any time. This is particularly important where compilation is prompted by a production-type environment. The terminology user does not need to wait for a full record to be recorded but can specify which data elements have a high priority. Indeed, the user may even carry out the initial research and enter a subset of the terminological data which a terminologist would verify and complete at a later date.

Information can be collected on a distributed basis. Work can be distributed among various people and locations without loss of quality. This is particularly important in the case of the compilation of multilingual terminology. Work can be dispersed over several countries or even over several continents such, for example, that all terminology compilation is carried out by native speakers or by subject specialists only.

Terminological data can be collected regardless of the onomasiological or the semasiological approach since ordering of data occurs totally independently of compilation. The dual-linear structure of the conventional dictionary, which forced a distinction between concept- and vocabulary-oriented terminology compilation has thus become irrelevant.

5.2.2 *Quality of data*

The use of a computer for input control and validation has resulted in a trend towards terminology of a higher quality. Because the computer is a far more efficient means of storing and disseminating terminology, the dangers of spreading terminology of low-quality or of a dubious nature are increased unless strict controls are exercised. The inconsistencies in the use of certain data categories can be eradicated, resulting in a more coherent and more reliable terminological collection. This increase in quality is in fact imperative in view of the far-reaching effect which computerised terminology processing will have on terminology dissemination. In order to maintain the higher quality of terminological data, the unchecked integration of existing dictionaries into terminological data banks is not considered sound practice and where this has taken place in the past it has been necessary to spend a great deal of time cleaning up the collection at a later date. It has been known for term banks, actively engaged in both the simultaneous tidying up of their data holdings and the input of new data, to experience a dramatic reduction in the size of their database because the elimination of unsound records proceeded at a faster speed than the input of new records.

The use of existing dictionaries, even those which publishers may have converted to machine-readable form, is fraught with difficulties. This has been a dilemma which computational linguists as well as terminologists have had to face as part of the rapid advance of their knowledge and experience in automation. Existing dictionaries may not prove suitable because of physical limitations, e.g. the data may be stored in a format which, although suitable for type-setting and printing, is unsuitable for useful machine manipulation. More frequently, however, data from printed media which have been compiled without computer assistance are incomplete, out-of-date or unreliable in various other ways.

In order to ensure a high quality of data in multi-lingual terminological collections it has become important to distinguish between original source texts and those which have been translated. Terms extracted from texts in their original language are normally genuine terms of that language and as such have full validity. Terms extracted from translated texts, however, may either be valid terms or only translation equivalents, coined for the particular translation in question. There is, therefore, a trend towards the use of genuine original texts for the extraction both of terms and contexts for a particular entry. Similarly there is a recognition that for many terms no exact match of concepts exists across languages and that the terminologist must offer several possible equivalents along with context and usage information to allow the correct choice to be made by the end user.

5.2.3 *Principles of data collection*

Automation permits the collection and compilation of terminological data in stages and by team work while at the same time making it possible to exercise stricter control over consistency of data than manual methods. These possibilities impose a greater necessity for generally agreed methodologies which should be based on a set of basic principles, such as the following:

1. Terminological data should be collected with a certain consistency of criteria.
2. All terminological information has sources which must be stated with the same accuracy and completeness as bibliographical data.
3. Terminological data have a limited validity in time. Information must therefore be given full temporal identification.
4. The use of existing dictionaries is not considered sound terminological practice.
5. It is important to distinguish between original and translated texts. Terms extracted from translations may be genuine terms of a language or only translation equivalents.
6. Terminology extracted from running text or discourse offers a greater guarantee of thematic completeness and coherence and ensures accurate dating of terms.
7. The linguistic behaviour of terms should be documented by suitable contexts so that all relevant textual variants are covered.

5.3 Compilation

5.3.1 *Terminological information*

The effectiveness of the use of terms is ensured by the 'right' choice of term. The selection of the most effective terms is assisted by reference to terminological information which is conveniently collected in dictionaries, glossaries or term banks. The type and quality of information contained in terminological information tools, of any kind, is therefore the principal determinant of the effectiveness of terminological tools.

There is an international consensus on basic categories which are essential for a sound terminological record. These are:

the entry term(s)
a reference number
a subject field
a definition
an indication of the usage.

In addition to these categories it is now becoming customary to add an indication of the sources of the term(s), of the definition, of the context (if included) and of any foreign language equivalents. This takes the form of a full bibliographic reference and can be considered as a replacement for the previously required 'quality marker'. There is thus a move away from prescriptive terminology as such, leaving the user to decide for himself what is acceptable terminology in each case. It is, therefore, up to the user of terminologies to decide on the appropriateness of particular terms in a given context by making use of the source data, which can be checked if required, in conjunction with the usage note and other pragmatic data.

There is thus fairly wide-spread agreement on what constitutes adequate basic information; divergencies of opinion arise over supplementary information. Differences of opinion at this level and over what constitutes quality of information are heightened by the fact that there is as yet no generally agreed metalanguage for describing the metalanguage that is the information assembled in terminological tools.

5.3.1.1. *Basic data categories*

The information to be included in a multifunctional term record is complex and consists of a number of subsets which can be compiled and processed quite separately. In parallel with the model of the three types of data collections presented in Figure 5.1, it is possible to present a diagram of the structure of a term record. This is attempted in Figure 5.2, which is structured into separate categories:

(1) the source information which links the term record to the raw data files from where the definition, the term and the context and their associated information have been extracted;
(2) the entry term which, according to the approach chosen by the term bank, is either a linguistic item or a label for a concept or both;
(3) the semantic and conceptual specification of the term, consisting of the definition, a subject field attribution, scope notes and, possibly also, a

Figure 5.2: *A model of a Term Record*

CORPORA OF RAW DATA containing definitions, terms and contexts							
⇑		⇑		⇑		⇑	
SOURCE INFORMATION							
origin	type	origin	type	origin	type	origin	type
No.	page	No.	page	No.	page	No.	page
CONCEPTUAL SPECIFICATION		LINGUISTIC SPECIFICATION		PRAGMATIC SPECIFICATION		FL EQUIVALENT SPECIFICATION	
		language		language		language	
definition		term		context		equiv. term	
		grammatical information				grammatical information	
links to other concept		synonyms		usage note or example		synonyms	
scope notes		abbreviation		usage		abbreviation	
subject field		variants		usage		variants	
date	type	date	type	date	type	date	type
record number		pool number		terminologist			
HOUSEKEEPING INFORMATION							

　　set of links to other concepts expressed in the form of terminological relationships;

(4)　the linguistic specification of the term, which can be minimal by giving variants and abbreviations or more complete to include all manner of morphological and syntactic specification required for automatic term recognition and processing or translation;

(5) the pragmatic specification of the term, which consists principally of examples of the context in which the term occurs and usage notes;

(6) the housekeeping or administrative information, which contains the record number, the name of the terminologist and especially the dates of first processing and subsequent up-dating of the record;

(7) the foreign language equivalent in those databases which are translation-oriented or, in fact, the second, third, etc. language term for those databases which work on the basis of a single conceptual system for several languages. There may then also be separate pragmatic information for each language.

These conventional categories are not rigidly exclusive and information entered under one category usually also has a value in another.

The following listing describes a wide range of information categories that can be found in specialised dictionaries, glossaries and term banks. To exemplify existing differences of interpretation and naming alternative names and definitions are listed in some cases. These examples are chosen from the major term banks. English variants and translation equivalents in French and German exemplify the problematic nature of this metalanguage.

ENTRY TERM/term

vedette/entrée principale

Benennung/fachsprachliche Wendung/Grundeintrag/terminologische Einheit

As the entry term is the most common search item, the form of this item must conform closely to user expectations and therefore be based on conventional methods of presentation. The entry term is usually the full form of a term or expression as it occurs and is recognised by subject specialists in reliable running text. It is presented in the grammatically most relevant form as conventionally used in dictionaries, e.g. subject case, singular for nouns, masculine for gender-inflected adjectives, active infinitive for verbs, lower case initials where appropriate. If there is an expanded form, e.g. in schedules or part lists, this can be indicated in a note.

Because the distinction between concept- or term-orientation affects the treatment of homographs and synonyms, it is important to decide whether the entry term represents the concept or is simply the linguistic form of the term. In concept-oriented term banks the definition of the concept is of primary importance and all terms matching the definition are grouped together. This imposes the difficult choice of the order in which terms are to be listed or the selection of one term as the entry term while declaring the others to be synonyms. Exclusive concept orientation, as practised by NORMATERM, is feasible in mono- and bilingual term banks which deal with subject fields of similar conceptual structures. The language-pair orientation of LEXIS also permits strict concept matching. For multilingual term banks explanatory notes are required which indicate in every case the scope and degree of matching of a term with the concept defined in another language.

Three types of entry have to be distinguished:
– simple, compound or complex terms, i.e. fully lexicalised units;
– phrases regardless of lexicalisation;
– sentences.
Most term banks concentrate on terms, and terms make up the bulk of entries in LEXIS, TEAM, TERMDOK, DANTERM and NORMATERM. A number of term banks also admit phrases and sentences, e.g. TEAM, LEXIS and especially EURODICAUTOM, which inputs many whole sentences with marked keywords which can be extracted in context. In bilingual term banks phrases in one language may correspond to lexicalised terms in another.

CONCEPTUAL SPECIFICATION OF THE ENTRY

DEFINITION

The definition is the first item that links the entry term to the concept which it represents. As such it is the bridge between concept and term.

The definition can be in a style specific to the database or term bank; alternatively it can be extracted from an authoritative source. If the entry term permits various definitions, the definition chosen should be adequate for the subject code given and compatible with the source given for the entry term. If a new definition has to be constructed, it is advisable to consult appropriate guidelines, e.g. BS 3669, for English.

Term banks can be classified by the way an entry is identified or explained. There are two major schools of thought, most strikingly represented in the difference between NORMATERM and EURODICAUTOM. The former, dealing with standardised terms, can refer to a definition which is strictly limited in its validity to the range of texts which represent the source material for the term collection. In the latter there is no restricted corpus, and therefore no single valid definition a priori. In such a broadly-based term bank a specialised short definition may not be understood, and may also be too narrow or subject specific in its formulation to be generally applicable to the full extension of the term. A context is therefore considered more useful to a translator in the environment of EURODICAUTOM in which the less clearly defined terminology of the social sciences is quite frequent. The added difficulty for

EURODICAUTOM is the choice of a language for definition. It is clearly impracticable to record nine definitions; besides it may be difficult to find nine definitions for every term which could be considered equivalent.

RELATIONSHIPS
renvoi terminologique
Begriffsbeziehungen/Begriffsumfeld
This is the most controversial and least defined category of information. It may indicate no more than the most obvious broader term, if any, to the entry term and also an indication of the type of relationship that exists between these two terms, e.g. generic, partitive. Full conceptual systems based on the sets of relationships which are found to be the most informative and effective for any one subject field have hitherto been developed only on paper. Complex multidimensional conceptual systems can only be represented and managed by computer; it was therefore impossible until quite recently to have anything other than rather prescriptive and narrow conceptual systems.

The information stored under this label could be a reference to another record in the database, with or without specification of the nature of the link that is being established. Any of the relationships discussed in chapter 2.2.4.1 might be suitable.

SUBJECT FIELD/general field-subfield
classement systematique/domaine d'emploi/sous-domaine
Fachgebietskennung-Teilbestandskennung
Terminology is divided by subject field before it is ordered in any other way. In order to deal effectively with large quantities of terms, it is generally considered advisable to introduce a classification of terms by subject areas. Existing term banks have introduced various classification schemes permitting the attribution of terms to subjects, types of texts or glossaries, but also admit that these schemes are on the whole unsatisfactory, represent a weak point in their data structure and are the greatest single obstacle to effective collaboration and exchange of data. Various subject classification schemes are in use in printed dictionaries with varying depth of classification. A two tier system of broader and narrower subject field is generally accepted.

SCOPE NOTE
domaine d'emploi
Geltungsbereich(skennung)
This note can be considered a further specification of subject or register, and

is intended to indicate a special field of application of the entry term, e.g. a term specific to one particular model of a motor car, or a process which is tied to a particular type of a machine.

LINGUISTIC SPECIFICATION OF THE ENTRY

GRAMMATICAL INFORMATION
This can consist of the conventional information contained in dictionaries such as:

    spelling(s)
    pronunciation(s)
    gender for nouns: m, f, n
    parts of speech: n, v, adj, adv, etc.
    principal parts of verbs: infinitive, past, past participle
    transitivity: tr, i
    special plural or other forms.

In practice, term banks do not record much of this information, though in some languages the gender of nouns is considered important enough to be specially listed.

LANGUAGE/language & country & region code
langue/indicatif de langue/indicatif de pays
Sprache/Sprachraum
This information category which is of little importance for monolingual tools and which is hardly in evidence in print, is vitally important in term banks where it is combined with an indication of the country or region where the term is used. It has been suggested that the two-letter language code of ISO 639 be used, followed, if necessary, by a slash and the country code as in ISO 3166.

Difficulties may arise over the attribution of geographical indicators. A term bank based in France will not mark usage common in France, but will indicate, e.g. Canadian French usage; a Canadian term bank will mark as French usage only those terms not commonly used in Canada, or those which have a different meaning in France.

PARALLEL INFORMATION CATEGORIES TO THE ENTRY TERM
This type of information does not normally have a separate record but is usually listed in an index with a reference to the record of the entry term.

It comprises such information as spelling variants, expanded forms, reduced forms and synonyms which can be considered full substitutes for the entry term in most cases in the same context as specified by the source, usage and scope notes. If required, a usage note should be added. Several overlapping categories exist:

VARIANT
variante (orthographique)
orthographische Variante
In this category alternative spellings are given, sometimes with a note on the range of application of this variant. A variant can also be combined with the entry term.

FULL SYNONYMS
synonyme
Synonym/Suchwort
This category can contain spelling variants, expanded forms, reduced forms and synonyms which can be considered full substitutes for the entry term in most cases in the same context as specified by the source, usage and scope notes. If required a separate note should be added and indicated as such, e.g. by inclusion in brackets.

ABBREVIATED FORM/Abbreviation
sigles/acronym/symbol/formula/terme abregé
Abkürzung/Kurzform
Abbreviations are a special category of synonym which assume a particular importance in some special languages. Dictionaries have generally treated them as a separate category with a special place in the alphabetical order of the printed page. Difficulties arise over the recognition of short or abbreviated forms of terms which are contextually conditioned.

PRAGMATIC SPECIFICATION OF THE ENTRY

CONTEXT
contexte
Anwendungsbeispiele
The exemplification of the usage of the entry term in a segment of running text is generally considered an effective way of showing any peculiarities of

wordform, inflection or collocation. The linguistic environment of the context should be so chosen that it complements the information provided in the definition and the usage note.

USAGE NOTE
note (linguistique ou terminologique)
klärender Zusatz/Gebrauchsangabe
This note should give information about the usage of the entry term in context that cannot be provided in the form of examples of a real context. It may concern collocational restrictions of formal variants or such markers as:

colloquial	i.e. usually spoken language, but also found in documents; obsolete, i.e. no longer in current usage;
slang	i.e. spoken in only very restricted usage of great familiarity and casualness of situation;
mandatory	i.e. prescribed usage for the text type given in the source indication;
firm-specific	i.e. used exclusively by the firm, organisation, etc. and which may therefore have a synonym in general usage;
standardised	i.e. as generally prescribed by a national or international standard or other authoritative body for a particular usage, in which case the authority should be cited;
translation	i.e. coined as a translation equivalent without any claim to general acceptability.

In general language dictionaries there are a much larger number of usage labels, such as 'archaic, informal, taboo, derogatory, offensive, vulgar' which are only rarely found in terminology. Some dictionaries also include geographical usage restrictions under this label by either specifying 'dialect' or indeed giving the region in which the entry is used. Subject or register restrictions of usage are treated under SUBJECT FIELD.

QUALITY LABEL
(cote de) ponderation/fiabilité
Qualitative Bewertung/Gebrauchsstatus/Qualitätsstatus
Term banks variously indicate whether a term is standardised or not and whether a term in a foreign language or borrowed from a foreign language can be considered established usage. For example, TEAM distinguishes between a working designation, i.e. a translation equivalent which is not otherwise documented and therefore not considered reliable, and fully accepted equivalents.

SYNONYMS
synonymes
Synonyme
Synonyms are terms which differ from the entry term by usage, context and sometimes subject field. Synonyms usually are full entry terms in their own right and therefore represent a crossreference in the dictionary or term bank structure.

DEPRECATED FORM
forme fautive
A category with such a label will only be found in a prescriptive database; otherwise we would only speak of a variant, which may, however, be annotated as being obsolete, unusual or not accepted usage.

SOURCE REFERENCE SPECIFICATION OF THE ENTRY

SOURCES
sources
Quellen
Printed dictionaries only rarely give an indication of the source of any of the information represented, though sources are usually kept in the background material. In term banks it is common to record the source of every relevant item of information and to exploit this information in support of the other data categories. Sources are needed for the entry term, the definition, the context, translation equivalents and possibly also for synonyms. Sources can also determine the selection criteria according to which information is collected, which usually guarantees a coherent set of terms around a single subject field or topic.

The source of the entry should be as authoritative as possible. It can consist of the following types of information:

Source origin: This can be either a simple coded reference to a bibliographical database, or a mnemonic code reference to a limited set of commonly used sources, e.g. a reference to a standards authority, government publications, Official Journals or standard reference works. The following sources are frequently cited as reliable sources in the UK:

    BSI   – British Standards Institute,
    CEC – Commission of the European Communities,

HMSO – Her Majesty's Stationery Office,
ISO   – International Organisation for Standardisation,
IEC   – International Electrotechnical Commission,

It is useful to express a well-known and established source in a manner that a user can directly recognise it. Overtly expressed, this information can be of great value because the origin of a term may be its best indication of quality and usage. Detailed reference to the source, for example the year of publication, may be equally informative with respect to the acceptability of a term.

Source type: It is useful to indicate the type of document of the source, because it can reveal areas of application and usage of the term. The following types may be usefully distinguished:

Article in specialist literature;
Contracts and legal usage;
Government circulars to the general public;
Journalistic publications, i.e. general or popular-scientific usage;
Manuals;
Patents;
Publicity material;
Research reports;
Standards;
Dictionary words, i.e. words not otherwise documented. While this type of source should be avoided, it does occur and it is then wise to indicate this clearly, rather that hide it behind an opaque source reference.

The sources of definitions and contexts can be chosen in such a way that they show different areas of usage. For the foreign language equivalent it is advisable to choose a source which matches the source of the entry term so that an equivalence of usage can be demonstrated. If there is no original source available in the foreign language, then it is useful to indicate whether (a) the term has been coined by the translator or terminologist—in which case it can be considered a valid equivalent only with respect to the source of the entry term; (b) whether it is a translation equivalent only documented in a dictionary but not found in text; or (c) whether it is a neologism in general use as translation equivalent.

Source reference code or number: In a large database there is usually a separate source reference file which gives the full bibliographical details for written sources. Where there is a database of raw data, the reference can be directly into the respective file.

HOUSEKEEPING INFORMATION

Every term record also contains a number of data which can be grouped under the general heading of housekeeping information.

RECORD NUMBER
sequentiel de classification
Begriffsnotation/Adresse
This consists of a number for the entry, possibly with some subcategories indicating the general origin of the whole record, e.g. whether it has been obtained by exchange, or whether is has been produced in-house; possible subsets of the database, sometimes called 'pools', can be used to identify a topic, a job, e.g. the terminology of a particular product, manual, congress or set of documents which can cut across subject field divisions. Such pools are frequently the basis for subsets of the database which are then isolated for separate use.

AUTHOR OF RECORD
auteur de la fiche
Verantwortlicher
There must also be information on the author of a record, who can be a terminologist or a committee, so that the work can be checked.

DATE OF RECORD/ Date of update
date de la redaction/mise a jour
Zeitpunkt der Eintragseinrichtung
This information gives the date of the production of the first record, and any subsequent up-dates. In this way the information can be re-assessed and updated, if required, at regular intervals.

5.3.2 *Methods of compilation*

In the absence of a fully acknowledged and tested general methodology, we can here only present a number of key elements which determine the methods to be evolved for fully automated systems.

The principal guideline for modern methods is that terminology compilation must become user-oriented. Only greater attention to user needs will justify the expenditure associated with improved quality and therefore related higher costs. The specific method of terminology compilation adopted in each case depends on the nature of the material available for information extraction and on the ultimate purpose of compilation.

Serious terminology compilation is now firmly corpus-based, i.e. it relies on the analysis of textual evidence which covers the full range of usage of the special language in question. The terminologist works preferentially on textual material from which he selects examples for a source file. In general, he records more contextual information than in pre-automation days. Because automatic assistance in compilation allows the ongoing processing and analysis of texts particular attention can now be devoted to the proper identification of newly coined neologisms and translation equivalents with limited usage.

Compilation can be a discontinuous process as long as certain interrelated items of information are compiled at the same time.

The selective and interpretive function of the terminologist can be both controlled and supported by information technology. Compilation must be seen as an ongoing revision and up-dating process and appropriate techniques for revision should be integrated into the basic methodology and structure. Term Bank softwares should provide a facility for prompting terminologists when building up terminological records. The greater breadth of data required for each entry and the construction of a complex network of conceptual relationships means that some form of expert system is required to control the work of terminologists.

The possibility of machines themselves being end-users of terminological databases demands even greater precision and explicitness of identification in the compilation of data than is currently exercised.

There are two different methodologies for the gathering of terminological information: (1) for the systematic development of terminological files and (2) for advising in particular cases on single aspects of designation, definition, etc. This latter activity is so diverse and on the whole entirely manual—at least until better automated tools are available—that it is not suitable for theoretical description.

The methods to be applied in the regular compilation of terminology depend on the nature of the data available and the purpose of compilation, e.g.
– a relatively complete and consistent monolingual corpus for the development of a separate subject field inside the database provides the classical case of terminological compilation in the interest of systematically enlarging the database;
– monolingual incomplete (textual and dictionary) information may be needed as background for a term harmonisation exercise, for instance, in a set of

standards; such work would take place independently of the large database and would only later be selectively integrated, possibly in a process of updating;

– bi- or multilingual information in various stages of completeness may be required for the production of a multilingual subset of a term bank.

Furthermore the methods change with the degree of automatic support available. At a time of rapid advances in the design of automatic tools, there is therefore no single methodology in existence which could be cited as a model. We can here outline only what seems current and sound practice in most cases.

1. A corpus of text is assembled in machine-readable form according to previously established criteria of representativeness, completeness and relevance.
2. The corpus is fully indexed so as to allow the establishment of accurate source references and the subsequent extraction of contexts and other textual references.
3. Terms are isolated and extracted by semi-automatic methods which will involve some form of parsing, lemmatisation, and other forms of decontextualisation.
4. Terms are sorted automatically and variously grouped so that a first attempt can be made of surveying linguistic forms; a provisional file of terms to be analysed is established; terms are checked against the database to ascertain whether they have been the subject of a record or whether they are referred to in existing records, e.g. synonym, related term.
5. Terms are matched with definitions, which at this stage are purely terminological, i.e. they must satisfy the needs of the terminologist in his effort to survey the completeness of the subject field; a definition is provided for one term and other terms are checked to ascertain whether they match the definition; if they do, they are either variants or the definition is wrong.
6. The provisional file is enlarged and corrected.
7. Terms are placed in relationship to other terms, both in order to check the value of the definition and the validity of synonym attribution and in order to provide a more complex information for cross reference.
8. Terms are attributed to particular subject fields if required.
9. A term record is created which initially contains only the term with its linguistic variants (which arise from stage 5 above), whatever information may be been gathered from stage 4, its terminological definition and relationships and a subject field indication.

The creation of a term record is conveniently carried out on a microprocessor which has access to the relevant cross reference information and which has an input programme which prompts the terminologist in his task.

Creating the term record requires the following steps:

(a) checking the available information: this is usually carried out on the paper slips or record cards on which the information is first assembled.

(b) transferring the information into a computer file: this operation can be monitored and prompted by the computer, thus ensuring control over completeness and accuracy.

(c) completing the remaining datafields: as required by the list of data categories established by the respective database. This usually involves such operations as:
   – recording phonetic, morphological, syntactic information,
   – selecting a suitable context from the machine-readable corpus,
   – providing usage notes, where appropriate,
   – declaring both linguistically and conceptually related terms,
   – providing scope notes, if required,
   – declaring a specific type of relationship and possibly also giving a full definition which may be an existing one or one to be written by the terminologist,
   – providing sources for each of the information categories above as appropriate,
   – giving information on foreign language equivalents of terms,
   – making reference to term records of other languages.

10. The term record is completed with the addition of the house-keeping information (term number, date and identification of terminologist, pointers to other records etc.).

The amount and diversity of data collected in the term record varies according to the range of purposes of the database. There may, for instance, be several definitions, several levels of subject field indications, usage notes etc. so as to supply information for a number of printed dictionaries, or different levels of on-line users.

5.4 New trends in compilation

Beside the application of new computational and data base techniques, the new generation of term banks and associated products aims to incorporate far more terminological theory, which in practice means the representation of terminological relationships in one form or another. The identification and establishment of relationships is already recognised as an essential methodological step in the compilation of terminology; but now computational techniques have made it possible for such relationships to have controlling functions in the storage and maintenance of terminological databases. It has further been ascertained that information about terminological relationships is of value to end users.

5.4.1 *Interrelationships of datafields*

Relatively little attention has hitherto been paid to the interrelation which exists between the data in any one record and consequently in the information that can be extracted from combining information from various data categories. These relationships are based on the datafields highlighted in Figure 5.3 and briefly commented upon.

Interrelationships worth exploring exist both inside the major information categories and between them, as follows:

Definition – Term – Context
This relationship provides for the conceptual and pragmatic identification of the term which only through this link becomes an item of special language discourse. The validity of the definition can be tested through its insertion in the contextual example. The definition itself presents the term in a particular conceptual environment of other terms and this set as well as the other terms occurring in the context together represent a particular terminological environment which may be complementary.

Definition – Subject field – Scope note
The limitations of the applicability of a definition should emerge clearly from the subject field and the scope note. Together these three items of conceptual information should circumscribe the extension and intension of the concept.

Definition – Link to other concepts
The definition itself contains related concepts which together with carefully chosen other concepts, the relationship to which is declared, should provide a sufficient minimal structure for accurately locating the term in its field.

Figure 5.3: *Relationships between data categories*

CORPORA OF RAW DATA containing definitions, terms and contexts							
⇑		⇑		⇑		⇑	
SOURCE INFORMATION							
origin	type	origin	type	origin	type	origin	type
No.	page	No.	page	No.	page	No.	page
CONCEPTUAL SPECIFICATION		LINGUISTIC SPECIFICATION		PRAGMATIC SPECIFICATION		FL EQUIVALENT SPECIFICATION	
		language		language		language	
definition		**term**		**context**		**equiv. term**	
		grammatical information				grammatical information	
links to other concept		**synonyms**		**usage note** or example		synonyms	
scope notes		abbreviation		usage		abbreviation	
subject field		variants		usage		variants	
date	type	date	type	date	type	date	type
record number		pool number		terminologist			
HOUSEKEEPING INFORMATION							

Terms in context – Link to other concepts
There may be complementarity or overlap of information between the terms occurring in these two fields.

Link to other terms – Synonyms
Special attention is required to identify genuine synonyms which, after all, are very special related terms.

Synonym – Usage note
Usage notes should have a special relationship to the various forms of the concept because it is only in these notes that the relationships between the various linguistic realisations of the concept can be made explicit.

Scope note – Subject field
According to the purpose of the scope note, it can either be a further subdivision of the subject field or else simply represent an aspect of looking at the term.

Grammatical information – Term
This relationship is obvious.

Term – Foreign/Second Language equivalent
This relationship is sometimes that of a full synonym and sometimes that of a temporary designation which needs confirming through primary source usage.

Source information – Term – Foreign language equivalent
This relationship is the most directly indicative of the reliability of a term and its usability. If the source origin and types are of authoritative sources the term can be used with confidence. If the first and second language sources have corresponding characteristics, their reliability as translation equivalents becomes obvious.

Relationships between records can, of course, also be explored to great advantage. The collection of terms with identical scope notes, for example, can provide sets of related terms belonging to a particular machine or process. The extraction of similar information in related sets of term records leads, of course, to the creation of subsets of the database.

5.4.2 *Conceptual relationships*

In the discussion of the methodology of compilation (section 5.3.2), it has already been pointed out that the terminologist builds a model of the structure of a subset of the subject field in order to ensure that he has properly and adequately covered his field and defined it. He finishes his work with a model of a structured subject field which is then not normally preserved nor presented in the dictionary or term bank. This work can now be preserved and exploited fully for every stage of terminology processing. We can therefore identify the fact that concepts are represented as elements of accurately constructed conceptual systems as a new feature of modern term bank design.

Computer implementation of terminological relationships overcomes the limitations imposed by the cumbersome processes of cross-referencing on the written page, and permits the automatic construction of multi-dimensional conceptual networks from individually defined relationships. The machine comes to the aid of the terminologist who would not be able to keep track of the growth of such a network. A computer is able to perform this task with ease and can cope with the cases where a concept is declared to be related to several other concepts. Additionally, a computer can explore the complex conceptual environment of a term in as much breadth and depth as required. For example, separately declared relationships during the process of compilation can be verified and connected by a simple computer operation. The isolated statements, made over a period of time by several terminologists,

e.g.   Potentilla belongs to the family of rosaceae,
       Sibbaldia belongs to the group of potentilla
       Fragaria belongs to the family of rosaceae

can be automatically linked and presented as a hierarchical structure, e.g.

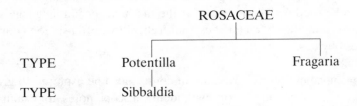

Theoretically a link can be made from any one point in this tree to any other by asking the appropriate question for the next higher, next lower, parallel term etc. Similar connections can be established between the parts of a whole.

The types of relationship which can be declared in a term bank need not, however, be restricted to the generic and partitive types. The incorporation of a wider range of relationships, e.g.

'X is a property of Y'
'A is an end-product of B'

and other non-hierarchical relationships would increase the usefulness of providing related terms at the retrieval stage by complementing the definition and providing helpful guidance for a user whose information need may not have been satisfied by the definition. The more naive user, presented with a set of terms related to his requested term would have at his disposal a valuable cross-referencing facility. He could then consult the related terms provided in order to familiarise himself with concepts within the subject area which are unknown to him.

Such a system can be elaborated further by increasing the types of relationships which may be declared on input; in such a case it is necessary to label the types of relationships that are established, possibly by the use of facets. In order to avoid excessive classification and relating, it is felt desirable to restrict the available relations to a number that can be handled consistently by a group of terminologists. An external control can be introduced by adding a question–answer system to control the relationships chosen by the computer on input. A question–answer system can also be introduced for the retrieval stage where the user could ask for information in natural language such as 'What are the constituent parts of a rotor engine?', or 'What are the members of the Rosaceae family?'

5.4.2.1. *The terminological thesaurus approach in term banks*
Several factors favour the choice of a terminological thesaurus approach for representing conceptual relationships and structuring terminological data in a term bank.

The terminological thesaurus framework provides the most accurate means for building and representing the conceptual structure of a subject field. By basing the research on the concept and its definition, it is possible to represent virtually all other information as being related directly to this central equation. The process of compilation benefits from this approach since the conceptual structure is now the framework inside which all manner of information is collected. As it is collected, every piece of information has already its assigned place and the completeness of the information can be tested by various relational tests. At the same time this approach can supply the end-user with an optimal amount of information. Relational information, systematic ordering and the use of facets in a systematic display have the advantage of helping to pin-point a concept.

There is, however, relatively little experience and research in the field of machine dictionary compilation. The possibilities opened up by applying computer technology to dictionary compilation have not yet been fully explored and it is quite conceivable that further work in this field and in the area of knowledge structures will provide other ways of structuring concepts which will be preferable and more suitable for computer implementation.

Chapter Six

STORAGE OF TERMINOLOGY

This chapter discusses storage with particular reference to term banks. It is assumed that the points raised are equally valid for most other types of terminological data collections.

6.1 A historical perspective

Until the nineteenth century scientific language was used, developed and preserved in written form only by very small communities of scholars in a small number of universities; the technical language required by craftsmen, on the other hand, was passed down mainly in spoken form from generation to generation along with the skills necessary to perform the job. There was therefore no particular need to collect and disseminate terminology as such, and there were consequently very few technical or specialised dictionaries. The development of new technologies which accompanied the industrial revolution, brought about a dramatic increase in the exchange of scientific and technical information. In order to maintain communication over greater distances and among a more diversified group of users, it became necessary to record the terminology of special subject fields so that it could be used by non-experts both for the understanding of specialised texts (e.g. managers in industry, administrators, students of the new science and engineering disciplines) and for the re-interpretation of knowledge in a new form (e.g. by translators, technical writers, teaching personnel, patent lawyers, standardisation experts). So glossaries were compiled for the vocabularies of the many new scientific disciplines and the many areas of technology that became the subject of systematic instruction based on written material. With the advent of the computer many of these glossaries of terminology were integrated into machine-readable dictionaries of technical language. The next and almost simultaneous development was the creation of on-line access facilities to these dictionaries—a development now defined as term banks. This happened principally in large organisations where the transfer of terminology is of vital importance.

In purely physical terms the storage of terminological data in machine-readable form has numerous advantages over the recording of terms in other media. More data can be stored in a smaller space. Many users can access the database simultaneously. Data can be transmitted to the end user in a matter of milli-seconds. Only one master copy for each data entry need be kept, etc. In practice, however, the introduction of computers into the processing of terminology has also caused a number of interesting changes in the form in which terminology is stored.

6.1.1 *The effect of hardware developments on storage*

The printed medium imposed severe restrictions on the size of individual collections of terminology. As hand-held objects, printed dictionaries had a natural limitation on their volume. In large collections this was overcome by multivolume editions but for regular use small compact dictionaries were preferred. Another solution for dealing with a steadily growing vocabulary was to produce separate technical dictionaries and glossaries for each subject field with the inevitable difficulties associated with splitting vocabulary into areas of knowledge. Nowadays the capacity of concurrent data storage devices is such that there need be no constraints on the overall size of a database. Indeed the holdings of some of the major term banks are of one million term entries and more.

Similarly, the restrictions imposed on the breadth of data held in any one entry or for each concept are no longer valid. This has resulted in the storage of a more thorough representation which depicts more closely the true complexity of terminological data.

Furthermore, the introduction of such high-capacity storage devices as CD-ROM allows the representation and retrieval of terminological data in new and interesting ways. Although theoreticians have discussed the use of visual data to enhance textual definitions for many years, the use of printed media precluded the implementation of this on any significant scale. The designers of some recently-established term banks have considered including items of visual data as part of the term record but high quality graphics require a large amount of storage in comparison with other data types. Now that this type of storage is becoming available at a reasonable cost the storage of graphical (and if appropriate aural) data is feasible.

The state of development in hardware also permits the creation of micro-computer-based terminological databases of limited complexity. Disk drives with a capacity of 30 Megabytes and above are now readily available for personal computers and basic, but nevertheless useful terminology processing software packages for micro-computers have appeared on the market.

Another stimulus to the automatic processing and retrieval of terminology has come from the introduction of workstations which can be used either in conjunction with or independently of mini- or mainframe computers. These workstations have windowing capabilities allowing multi-tasking and so facilitate the integration of large-scale term bank access with other types of text processing.

Most existing term bank software fails to make imaginative use of the innovations listed here. Ideally a new generation of terminological data bank software is required to exploit the full potential of currently available hardware.

6.1.2 *The first generation of term banks*

Existing term banks can be classified in many ways. The classification which concerns us here is made on the basis of the software used. In this respect two groups of term banks can be identified which we shall label 'first-generation' and 'second-generation' term banks.

First generation term banks are those which were set up in the early 1970s and have changed little in structure since. They were relatively simple in structure, were mostly built using ad hoc data management software and their data were organised on a lexical rather than a conceptual basis. Initially access to these first term banks was fairly restricted; they were usually only available via intermediaries to in-house staff although some provided intermediaries for dealing with telephone or written requests from external users. In 1980 only 1 out of the 5 term banks made direct on-line access available to their principal target user-group.

Since the 1980s traditional term banks have been pre-occupied with two major improvements to the service they provide. Firstly they have invested a great deal of effort in improving the quality of the data in the system. Secondly they have made attempts to make their (in some cases very large) holdings more easily accessible to existing and to a wider circle of users by various means including on-line access.

Quality control can be planned into a design or it can be allowed to evolve with the growth of a system. In the rapidly changing development of auto-mated terminology the notion of quality of data and their control has itself un-dergone significant shifts of importance as the difference between traditional dictionaries and automated dictionaries became fully appreciated. At their inception term banks were created to satisfy an identified, immediate need and it was deemed necessary that they provide satisfactory responses to the user in a very short period of time. Consequently a large quantity of unvetted data was loaded into the system so that an acceptable response rate was quickly achieved. It was only at a later date, when the law of diminishing returns began to operate, that quality rather than quantity became an overriding factor. Costly tidying-up operations were introduced in which much of the inferior quality data, along with much duplicated data was removed.

In some term banks an additional necessity was the expansion of the lin-guistic coverage to a larger number of languages; this created its own problems because adequate source material was not always available, yet the pressure for creating other foreign language equivalents produced some less reliable terminology.

Access to the majority of the first-generation term banks is now no longer restricted to the original target users. All the traditional term banks now offer on-line access to their in-house staff directly from their own desks. In addition many are now accessible to external users, in some cases via public networks. The problem of orientation, however, still remains; all traditional term banks serve only a very specific clientele and although they perform this task very well, they encounter structural difficulties in adapting to the requirements of the many new user groups who have emerged since then.

6.1.3 *The second generation of term banks*

Since the 1980s there has been much innovation in the design of terminological data banks. Many smaller term banks have been set up and these have been developed independently of large organisations with their narrowly de-fined requirements. Consequently the designers of these 'second generation' term banks have had more freedom to experiment and have attempted to remedy the limitations inherent in earlier systems. Because of the tech-nical innovations of recent years they have been able, and in many cases obliged by necessity, to strive for flexibility rather than the satisfaction of the requirements of one user-group. Examples of 'second-generation' systems are TERMDOK, the term bank of TNC (Tekniska Nomenclaturcentralen) in Sweden, DANTERM, the term bank at the Copenhagen Business School and CEZEAUTERM, a term bank concentrating on the field of Soil Science at the Université de Clermont Ferrand. There are other similar 'second-generation' term banks in existence or in the planning stage in Finland, Norway, the UK and elsewhere. The independence of these new term banks has resulted in their terminological holdings being small as they are severely underfinanced.

6.2 Terminological data banks—a definition

Traditionally the concept of a terminological data bank or term bank has been defined as an automated collection of the vocabularies of a subset of specialised knowledge created to serve a particular user group. This definition implies monofunctional use and was appropriate for those term banks which have been used predominantly as tools for large translation services. The vocabularies collected in this way are in most cases considered as enhanced but still conventional glossaries, thesauri or technical dictionaries transferred to a new medium. Existing term banks were designed to answer the same type of questions one would have consulted a good dictionary for. These questions are perfectly valid, but they are only addressed to and elicit direct responses from the various parts of the conventional dictionary entry, e.g.:

ENTRY PART	QUESTION	ANSWER
gender	What is the gender of 'imprimante'?	– feminine
spelling	What is the spelling of the French word whose English equivalent is 'Woodruff key'?	– clavette Woodruff
equivalent	What is the French for 'laser printer'?	– imprimante laser
definition	What is a 'laser printer'?	– a printer which …
synonym	Can I use 'bit' as synonym for 'binary digit'?	– binary digit – Abbrev.: bit
subject label	Is 'bit' restricted to a subject field?	– Computation
example	Is there an example sentence containing 'bit'?	

While these questions may satisfy existing expectations, they neither exhaust the information available nor do they present all the information that may be useful to a wide range of existing and potential dictionary users. In addition, the answer may or may not satisfy the user and it may be ambiguous. For example, listing a subject field label may mean that a word has a particular meaning in the named subject field, or that its use is restricted to this field.

The questions that a specialist user would address to a conventional term bank are in principle the same as those addressed to a general language dictionary. What difference there is, lies in the frequency with which certain questions are asked and the class of entry that is being consulted. Most existing term banks can provide satisfactory answers to these questions, and according to the specific nature of the term bank, also some other questions regarding sources, date of recording in the term bank and more extensive usage notes.

The potential information of a lexical database is, however, not exploited by existing automated dictionaries and term banks. This has several reasons:
(a) the information held is not unified in a manner suitable for flexible retrieval;
(b) there is a lack of coherent structure and formal representation of data;
(c) existing systems fail to exploit the additional techniques for ordering entries which the machine provides and underutilise or ignore those facilities which allow the storage and representation of terminological data in new and interesting ways.

Modern expectations in both general language lexicography and terminology processing are for flexibility to become the main criterion in designing machine-readable dictionaries. In addition to the type of questions listed above it is now considered desirable that information should be stored in such a way that the following searches and queries become possible:

QUERY	SEARCH OF FIELD
– Compile a glossary of all terms with usage note of 'ICI'.	usage restriction or scope note
– What do you call a machine that performs X?	definition or conceptual links
– What parts make up a Y?	subordinate partitive terms
– Find all terms entered by 'JCS' since 1985	name of the terminologist over a period of time

– Compile a glossary of terms   subject field or a
  related to 'GPSG'.   subdivision

– Print all terms with a   subset of origin of data
  source of CCL.

Much of the data required to answer the above questions is already available in existing term banks but their retrieval requires a cumbersome scan of the whole data-base, i.e. the data is hidden.

These new information possibilities should be reflected in the definition of the modern concept of a term bank, which may, in fact thereby be oriented towards a broader function than that normally associated with dictionaries.

A term bank should therefore be defined as:

'a collection, stored in a computer, of special language vocabularies, including nomenclatures, standardised terms and phrases, together with the information required for their identification, which can be used as a mono- or multilingual dictionary for direct consultation, as a basis for dictionary production, as a control instrument for consistency of usage and term creation and as an ancillary tool in information and documentation.'

A term bank is therefore more than just an automated version of a printed dictionary, designed to meet the needs of a single user group. Using the above definition it should now be possible to specify the design of a term bank so that users with varying degrees of expertise can access the same term bank and retrieve data for a variety of different purposes from a variety of starting points. Indeed, the possibility of using the same term bank to serve both human users and such machine uses as machine-translation, natural language processing and expert systems is well within the reach of possibility, given a flexible and sensitive design and a sophisticated interface both for the input of data and for their retrieval.

6.3 Modern terminological data bank design

NOTE: The model presented in this section was conceived by Richard Candeland as part of the research he carried out at UMIST, and is reproduced here with his kind permission.

At first sight, the design of a terminological data bank presents no problems. The lack of flexibility inherent in traditional term banks can be dismissed on historical grounds. There was no suitable purpose-made software available when the first and second generations of term banks were conceived and consequently they were implemented using custom-built database/file management systems. In order to make them serve all the requirements we now consider essential this software would have had to be completely rewritten to facilitate any significant diversification of use.

An examination of the current term bank facilities and software permits two possible interpretations of the conditions for term bank design:

EITHER: building a term bank is simply a matter of specifying the structure of terminological data using traditional database design techniques and implementing the resultant model by means of an existing database management (DBMS) package;

OR: building a term bank is merely another application of conventional information retrieval (IR) techniques and so can be loaded onto any good IR software package.

Although both methods have been used for the construction of term banks, neither has proved entirely satisfactory, and on closer study it becomes evident that in practice both approaches have their problems.

Concerning the current position of the logical structure of term banks, the following features are still to be found in the majority of well-established term banks:

- There is still strict adherence to the rigid sub-division of the knowledge base into separate areas and a failure to take account of inter-disciplinary and overlapping subject fields. Many identical concepts must consequently either be duplicated or subjectively classified as belonging to a particular discipline. (This inability to satisfactorily represent the relationship subject field:concept can be held to explain the inability of term bank administrators to agree on a subject classification).

- There is a tendency to organise the database linguistically rather than conceptually. In a theoretical model of terminology, terms are subordinate to the concept; in practice, however, the term is the primary, and often the only, entry point into the database and so must be given precedence.

- There is a tendency to ignore conceptual relationships as they are difficult to represent using a network-type database model. Where they have been introduced, only a very restricted subset of the relationships in existence—i.e. those which fit neatly into a hierarchical one:many representation—have been implemented.

- There is a tendency to impose a uniform record structure over the whole database. Subject fields whose terminology is taxonomic in structure share the same logical record format with those whose structure is very loose.

Differences of this kind are often catered for by having a 'put-anything-here-that-does-not-fit-elsewhere' data field but this approach adversely affects the flexibility with which data can be retrieved from the system.

– The inability to represent the relationship 'can be translated in language X by' as a many:many relationship has resulted in the need:
  – to declare each concept as having only one equivalent concept in each foreign language without inferring that the concepts match;
  – to enter foreign-language equivalents only for matching concepts;
  – to store target language equivalents with a limited amount of associated data as part of a monolingual record in the source language database. The full entry is then stored independently as part of a separate logical database.
  – Implementations of network-type data models preclude the dynamic creation of new record types and new relationships.

Consequently it is difficult to change the orientation of existing terminological data banks and adapt them to new and diverse user-groups. Many term banks are therefore unable to meet the requirements of the present information market. Current trends in database management generally favour an approach based on the relational database model. Implementations of this model in the commercial environment began to appear in the early eighties and many powerful data storage and manipulation tools are now available.

6.3.1 *Representation of terminology—a theoretical model*

When applying the computer to any task, it is first necessary to define a theoretical model both of the processing involved and of the data that require processing. A model of the data is devised by defining the entities which are relevant to the application in question and identifying the relationships which hold between them. It is, therefore, a representation of the real world of the application in question and is drafted independently of any of the constraints which will later be imposed by attempts to implement the theoretical model onto a computer architecture using a particular logical data-storage model.

In the majority of existing computerised terminology processing systems the task to be achieved has been very specific. The range of operations to be performed has been limited to those required to satisfy the demands of an ideal user (e.g. a translator of the EC, a standards expert of AFNOR). All theoretical models of terminological data have therefore been heavily biased by the needs of a single user-group and once implemented have resulted in term banks locked into a particular application.

There are a number of very practical reasons which have contributed to the re-assessment of the design requirements of term banks.

1. The demand from new and diverse user-groups for high-quality terminology.
2. The immense cost of terminology compilation.
3. The greater range of expectation of users.

These circumstances have resulted in a call for the pooling of terminological resources in a multifunctional term bank or an even wider-ranging database more properly designated as lexical database. Once a multipurpose tool was envisaged, it also became necessary to re-appraise a theoretical model of terminology processing. In such a situation emphasis must be placed on the definition of a general and exhaustive theoretical model of terminological data, such that all the data models produced by the investigation of individual retrieval requirements can be mapped onto it. Only in this way is it feasible to serve many diverse and disparate user groups from a single central terminological collection.

From a model-theoretic point of view, therefore, the new design objective for optimal terminology processing is the storage of terminological data in an application-independent fashion so that all conceivable purposes can be served equally well. In such a 'new' situation, compilation continues to be governed by the theoretical model of the data but, in contrast, a model of retrieval as such remains undefined. In practice several processing models for terminology retrieval are required. Each will match the specific needs of its target user-group and each will have its own model of terminological data which can be implemented at the logical level as a view of terminological data as a whole, i.e. subsets of the data will be extracted (and converted into an appropriate format) as each application requires.

This notion of user views of data is far from new and has been in use in the world of commercial database management for many years. Only recently, however, has it been recognised as applicable to terminology. We can now define the main types of data that have to be accommodated.

Any contemporary model of terminological data comprises the following broad data categories which are all interdependent:

– Housekeeping/management data (reference/record number, terminologist's name, date of first coding, information about updates);
– Conceptual data (subject, scope, definition, related concepts, related terms and type of relationship);

– Linguistic data (lexical entries, their form and grammatical features);
– Pragmatic data (usage restrictions and special labels, contextual data);
– Bibliographic reference data.

Even though recent developments in modelling terminological data converge on the necessity of creating a multipurpose tool, there are still marked differences in the perception of the data that have to be accommodated in a theoretical model. Different categories are selected as meriting isolation as entities in their own right and there are disagreements about the relationships which hold between entities.

The theoretical model of terminological data which follows is not to be considered a definitive model. It draws on the theoretical models underlying the most recent developments in term bank design as well as models proposed for the application-independent representation of the general-language lexicon.

Figure 6.1. *Theoretical model of terminological data*

Entities in the model

ENTITIES	PROPERTIES
Pool/Collection of terms	Code – number
	Function/purpose
Origin/Update	Originating Centre
	Date
	Originator
Concept	Code – number
	Formal representation
	(language independent)
Conceptual Link	Type of link
	Nature (e.g. reciprocal, arity, ratio, e.g. 1 : N, N : N or 1 : 1, etc)
Language	Language
Definition	Textual definition
Term	Graphemic form
	Phonetic form
	Grammatical features
	(syntactic and morphological)
	Status (preferred, deprecated, abbreviation, equivalent etc.)
Usage	Usage note (stylistic, geographical)

Context	Phrase containing term
Source	Author/organisation
	Title
	Page reference
	Publisher
	Date
	Type of source

Relationships between entities in the model

EXISTS BETWEEN ENTITIES	*TYPE*
Pool – Concept	1 : N
Concept – Origin/Update	1 : N
Concept – Link-Concept(s) (any concept can have any number of links which may be to one or more than one other concepts)	N : N : N (: N :)
Concept – Language – Definition (one textual definition per concept per language)	1 : 1 : 1
Concept – Language – Usage – Term (one concept may have any number of terms in any number of languages, depending on any number of variations in usage. Conversely any term may refer to more than one concept)	N : N : N : N
Term – Context	1 : N
Source – Term Source – Definition Source – Context	1 : N

NOTES:

1. What are traditionally called conceptual relationships have been renamed conceptual links here to avoid any confusion between conceptual relationships and relationships in the data model which exist between any entities.
2. Conceptual links are not enumerated. It is now recognised that hierarchical links are restrictive and are being supplemented by the idea of a network of links. Research into the nature and types of such links continues. In order not to prejudge the results of such research it is necessary to make provisions in the model for the addition of new links and the possibility that such links will not conform to the binary, 1:N nature of traditional hierarchical knowledge representation.

3. As subject fields and scope limitations may themselves be considered as concepts, the membership of particular terms of a conceptual system or subject area (or areas) can be represented as a special type of concept–concept link. This allows the construction of subject domains from the bottom up and may help resolve the controversial question of the sub-division of the knowledge base. The current practice of initially declaring a list of valid subject fields and demanding that all terms are subsequently allocated (normally at the discretion of the terminologist) to a subject field from that list can therefore be replaced by one in which the terminologist enters a concept and describes its environment using conceptual links. The machine itself will then determine to which knowledge domain or domains the term belongs.
4. One further type of specialised concept:term relationship could be used to indicate the nearest term in the language B for a concept in language A where there is no match of conceptual systems across languages. Most current term bank implementations either assume all concepts match or no concepts match and allow no compromise between the two positions. The implementation of a 'nearest equivalent to' relationship would be of particular use when non-standardised terminology was being processed.

6.3.2 *Representation of terminology (logical implementation)*

When implementing the data model with a particular application in mind, using available data-storage models, it is theoretically always possible to adhere to the original definition of the model. In practice, however, the resultant logical database structure is sometimes so cumbersome and unwieldy as to make this unwise. This has been the case with terminological data and has resulted in term bank designers either omitting the more complex structures inherent in the data or simplifying the structure of the model to facilitate an easy implementation.

This problem has been exacerbated by the fact that at the time when most term banks were created research in data storage models was in its early stages and most data storage software was based on the limited hierarchy and network models. Both models support only binary, one:many relationships and as a result attempts have been made to portray terminological data purely in terms of this type of relationship. It has, therefore, been the availability of software and software techniques which have been the driving force behind term bank design rather than a desire to achieve a true logical implementation of the data. As a result logical implementations of terminological data do not reflect many of the trends in the representation theory of terminology outlined above and have consequently failed to make use of the removal of physical restraints which operated on the first and second generation of term banks.

There has been some recent research into the suitability of the relational model for storing terminological data. The CEZEAUTERM term bank, for example, was designed using a relational model of terminological data, although it was not implemented, using a pre-written relational database management package instead. (At that time commercial relational database management packages were not fully developed.) The relational model eliminates some of the problems highlighted earlier. The relatively weak relational structure between the data fields imposed on conventional terminologies by a hierarchical or network approach is replaced by a potentially more powerful set of relationships between all entities, features and values.

The relational model can efficiently and easily represent the many:many relationships, which are so common in terminological data. For example, the representation of synonyms and homonyms in different subject fields is easily achieved. If concept X is signified by terms A and B and concept Y is signified by A and C then the relation concept-term would be represented as follows:

SUBJECT	CONCEPT	TERM
1	X	A
1	X	B
2	Y	A
2	Y	C

Relations in the relational database model are simply represented as two-dimensional tables. For a network database model a link record must be introduced to allow for the representation of the many:many relationships, thus:

Furthermore relationships can be created between more than two entities if required. Thus a particular theoretical model of terminological data may view term W as being the value created by the relationship 'used for concept X in language Y for text-type Z'. A relationship between four entities such as this can be represented using the relational model as one relation. A similar representation using a network or hierarchy model would require the creation of three 'virtual' records which contain no data but merely provide a means of breaking the complex 4-part relationship down into six separate binary relationships. It must also be noted that there is no clear means for deciding the precedence of these binary relationships.

The following sequence of tables shows a comparison of the implementation of a 4-part relationship on the relational and network data models.

Language	Term	Usage	Concept
Y	W	Z	X
Q	A	Z	X
Y	W	P	R
Y	B	T	X

Relational representation of 4-part relationship

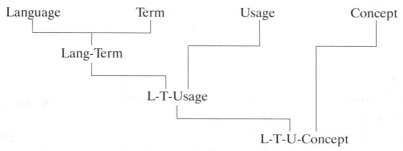

Network representation of 4-part relationship (logical schema)

The relational model too is not without its limitations. Relations impose a uniform structure on the tuples they contain; tuples with a different number of attributes or with attributes containing values from different domains cannot reside in the same relation. This does not however automatically preclude the representation of slightly different data structures for terminological data from diverse subject fields. The relational model contains powerful facilities for dynamically creating relations by cutting and pasting existing relations. Careful design both of the logical representation of the data and the interface to it can reduce this limitation to insignificance.

Despite its name the relational model does not allow the easy retrieval of recursive (e.g. hierarchical) relationships. Traditionally the conceptual foundation of terminology was based precisely on relationships of this nature, i.e. 'is subordinate to' and 'is superordinate of'. The relational model does not preclude the representation of such relationships and indeed the standard operations provided by the model for manipulating data can be used to move up (or down) the hierarchy. Recursion as such, however, is not supported and so before a query can be posed, the questioner must know how many levels of the tree are to be accessed.

The following diagrams give a representation of a hierarchical system of concepts, as it would be implemented in a relation database.

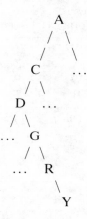

It will be noted that in this structure of a systems of concepts some branches of the hierarchy are longer than others.

Source Concept	Narrower Concept
A	C
C	D
D	G
G	R
R	Y

The Relationship: NARROW TERMS
(Source Concept to Narrower Concept)

It is possible to make a relational representation of the relationship 'is a subordinate concept to' using the above system of concepts. To retrieve all narrower terms for 'A' is impossible unless the questioner knows the depth of the hierarchy; even then the query is very cumbersome, as the example below based on QUEL, the query language to the INGRES relational database, shows. This will retrieve narrower terms 'C', 'D' and 'G' and any other concepts at the same horizontal level in the tree.

Possible Query:

range of t is NARROW TERMS
range of t1 is NARROW TERMS
range of t2 is NARROW TERMS
retrieve t2.narrower concept where
    (t2.source concept = 'A')
    or ((t2.source concept = t1.narrower concept) and
      ((t1.source concept = 'A')
      or ((t1.source concept = t.narrower concept)
        and (t.source concept = 'A'))))

Research into the relational database model as a vehicle for the storage of terminological data is still in progress and as yet no conclusive results have been obtained. From a purely practical point of view, the majority of current research in database technology is oriented towards the relational model and the techniques for applying the model to commercial applications of all types are being continuously improved. It is, therefore, too early to assess the suitability of relational technology for the storage of terminology.

6.4 Storage of terminology—practical considerations

The particular nature and the considerable volume of data to be stored in terminological data banks determines the type of software tools needed for the physical organisation of data on disk, the logical organisation of the structure of the data and the management (security, integrity etc.) and running of the subsequent database. This need is being met in different ways: Some term bank designers have opted to use commercially available systems, where the choice is between database management software and commercial information retrieval software. Others have decided that none of the available software matches their particular requirements and have constructed a termbank software from scratch. All three approaches have their advantages and disadvantages.

Commercial database management systems and information and documentation systems are based on particular models, the relative theoretical merits and failings of which were discussed in the previous section. Both types of system are thoroughly tested before they are released and are consequently reliable and robust. They possess all the facilities which are appropriate to their intended task and allow a wide range of applications to be built onto them. From a practical point of view, however, there are a number of other considerations which affect their usefulness as models for term bank software.

6.4.1 *Database management systems*

In order to build a term bank from scratch it is necessary to first build a data management software; this will without doubt incorporate many of the features already provided in commercial packages. The next step is to develop a user-interface, i.e. the specific application, in much the same way as would be required to implement a term bank using existing software. Whereas the simple structure of early term banks, based loosely on the model provided by the format of the printed dictionary, encouraged the development of custom-built software, the move to more complex terminological data models made this task less attractive. The designers of more recent term banks (with one or two exceptions) turned, therefore, to commercial software as the basis on which to construct their systems.

Commercially available database management systems have proved unsuitable for the implementation of a term bank in a number of respects.

(a) Terminological data is of a predominantly textual nature. Much of the data is of variable length and there is no pre-determined maximum for any of the values in question. It is, for example, extremely difficult to prescribe a fixed length for definitions. This is then exacerbated by the fact that the structure of terminological data and the relative importance of particular data items may vary from one subject field to another. Database management systems are not designed to cater for data of this type. They were written to manipulate predominantly numerical data and strictly formatted information. It is, therefore, difficult to implement terminological data neatly onto the majority of commercially available database softwares.

(b) Database management systems are not usually suitable for more that one language, whereas terminological data is, in the majority of cases, multilingual in nature. Because of the compression techniques used by many database management systems to make more efficient use of available storage, the extended character facilities required to represent diacritics or non-Latin characters are not generally available.

(c) Database management systems generally have ordering systems, such as indexes and other access facilities, in which the differences between upper- and lower-case is not fully acknowledged. The distinction may not be supported at all, in which case the user may remain unaware of the graphemic peculiarities of certain terms. Alternatively, it is always significant; in such a case the term 'Boussinesq equation', for example, would not come between 'boulder' and 'coefficient of consolidation' purely because it begins with a capital 'B'. In terminological data processing the upper-/lower-case distinction is partially significant. In the majority of database searches users will wish any differences to be ignored in order to increase the scope of retrieval. On the other hand, when the term is retrieved they will wish to see it in its true graphemic form.

These problems can be overcome to a certain degree by sensitive and clever design but the resultant logical database schema is somewhat contrived and does not easily lend itself to a flexible or efficient user-interface.

6.4.2 *Information retrieval systems (IR)*

Information and document retrieval packages were designed with the specific task of storing textual data and therefore allow true variable-length text entries. Most good IR packages can adequately handle the problems related to multilingual data but the upper-/lower-case distinctions are usually absent. Most IR software exactly mirrors the model traditional printed dictionaries and glossaries are based on. Each entry consists of a heterogeneous collection of unformatted or loosely formatted data which is accessed via a head-word. IR software generally allows for thesauri of varying complexity to be set up which ought to satisfy the needs of terminologists wishing to portray conceptual links in their term banks. It should therefore be a simple task to transfer a conventional glossary onto an IR package without any loss of data or facilities and indeed make some improvements in the process.

IR packages can therefore supply most of the needs of conventional glossary production and consultation; however, current requirements are for a more complex data structure allowing terminological data to be retrieved in new and more interesting ways. The restricted data model offered by most IR systems is consequently inadequate for the following reasons:

(a) Information retrieval database models lack structure. They allow a limited amount of flexibility in the way the information can be internally structured and retrieved but do not allow the database administrator the full range of options for logical database design; nor do they enable him to select the most efficient storage techniques as appropriate to the data being represented. Consequently they discourage the representation of complex relationships between data such as those discussed in the previous sections and work against a true portrayal of the theoretical representation of terminology presented earlier. On a more practical level, when implementing the theoretical model, it is difficult to preserve the distinction between conceptual and linguistic data categories. Information retrieval packages do not have sufficient data structuring facilities to achieve this purpose. They also preclude any more formal representation of the type required to satisfy the diverse user groups listed above, making the goal of a flexibly constructed term bank difficult if not impossible to achieve.

(b) **The range of thesaurus building facilities offered is insufficient for cur-**rent terminology processing requirements. The relationships which can be represented in the system thesauri are generally restricted to those hierarchical relationships which many terminologists are now claiming to be inadequate to truly portray terminological data.

(c) Information retrieval software is designed on the assumption of a database to which documents are added at pre-determined times, e.g. in batches of new accessions. Once on the database, documents remain practically unaltered until they are finally regarded as obsolete and possibly removed to a back-up store or altogether. Terminological data is not of this nature. It is volatile and undergoes change in line with linguistic usage or the structure of knowledge. New terms are coined to signify new concepts, old terms become obsolete but are simply marked as such and not eliminated, existing terms change their meaning and therefore require a change in the record. Many other consequent changes may then occur; e.g. synonyms may cease to be synonyms and abbreviations can be promoted to become the preferred term, the previous preferred term becoming a synonym. The more complex the representation of terminology used, the more likely it is that individual values and features of a record will change. Addition of new records may require changes in records elsewhere to maintain the system of cross references. As the volume of data held increases, so the number of terms needing monitoring, modification and updating will rise. Information retrieval software does not normally possess facilities for coping with large-scale database modification, nor does it have the facilities for large scale verification of the data and the recovery of the system in the event of a failure. For typical information retrieval applications, these facilities are not deemed necessary; for terminology processing on a large scale they are indispensable.

(d) There are intrinsic differences in the information processing being undertaken and the modes of access required. Firstly, the optimum response to a query in a typical IR application is a set of documents; in terminology retrieval the optimum response is normally a single term record. Secondly, the contents of a typical IR database originate elsewhere (as articles, abstracts, texts etc.) and on conversion to machine-readable format they undergo no logical change. Their sole purpose is to satisfy on-line queries from users. Terminological data, however, are built up initially on the machine and may subsequently be converted to a printed or other format for other uses. It must therefore be structured in such a way that a great diversity of subsets of information can be extracted not only on-line but also on micro-fiche, on paper and in a form suitable for use in machine-(assisted) translation systems, spelling and style checkers, automatic abstracting systems and other natural language processing environments.

The natural conclusion to be drawn from the above discussion is that there are no suitable off-the-peg software packages available for the storage of terminological data. Indeed, recent research activity directed towards the automation of general language lexicography has led a number of computational linguists to the same conclusion regarding the data of general language lexicography. This has prompted a call from a number of sources for a database management software based on the unique representational requirements of a dictionary data model. Such demands are also in line with current trends in Information Science where new developments are towards greater abstraction and the definition of application-oriented data types. However, no specific model for lexical data has as yet been agreed amongst lexicographers, nor has computational lexicography reached a sufficient level of maturity for the specific computational requirements of lexical data to be determined. Research will no doubt continue into methods and strategies for storing lexical data, prompted by the realisation amongst many computational linguists and computer scientists that this area of Natural Language Processing has been sadly neglected in recent years.

The renewed interest in the lexicon will have a profound effect on the storage not only of general language vocabulary but also of terminology.

6.5 Semantic networks

Data storage requirements can become more complex if attempts are made to represent terminological relationships. One of these possibilities is representation in the form of semantic networks.

The idea of semantic networks was first developed in artificial intelligence research for the formal representation of knowledge. It was derived from a model of human memory developed in psychology and was adopted by researchers in artificial intelligence for the development of a functional representation for the types of knowledge needed in their systems. Semantic networks are now considered a convenient way of representing knowledge accessible via the linguistic form of concepts in such diverse applications as expert systems, dictionaries, factual databases etc.

From a formal point of view, these networks have no intrinsic meaning—they are basically directed graphs which are given meaning by the designer of the network who declares the function of arcs and nodes and develops the operational procedure to act on the network. Formally semantic networks are a very loose concept which in practice is realised in a great number of different formalisms.

Despite the diversity of their goals and applications semantic networks have a superficial similarity. The semantic entities of such networks are concepts which occupy the nodes of the structure. Nodes are most commonly concepts of concrete or abstract entities but can also be of activities, states, quantities, qualities etc.

Inside the networks nodes are considered to be connected by labelled arcs which represent the conventional relationships established between concepts. The generic relationship, for example, is expressed as 'is a type of', abbreviated to 'isa', and the partitive relationship, expressed as 'is a part of' or 'consists of' can be abbreviated to 'ispart-of' or 'has-part' respectively.

Nodes can be connected left and right to produce sequences, e.g.

ALSATIAN isa DOG isa ANIMAL isa LIVING BEING
RIM ispart-of WHEEL ispart-of BICYCLE

In semantic networks several types of relationships can be represented at once, e.g.

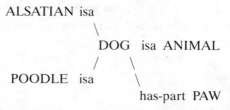

Since the partitive relationship 'has-part' is applicable to all members of the class DOG, we infer that both alsations and poodles have paws.

Sequential links circumscribe the extensions of concepts. For example, by declaring a 'property inheritance link' we can trace common properties up a 'isa' hierarchy. We therefore infer that any facts asserted about higher nodes on the hierarchy can be considered assertions about the lower ones as well, or, as in the above example, we can say that alsations and poodles are classed as animals.

Equally, objects can be linked with their properties, e.g. gas and liquids.

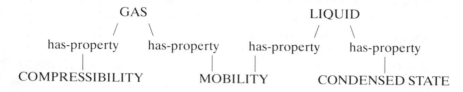

In this way it is possible to capture a wide variety of relationships between concepts.

The semantic network can be considered an equivalent to representation via predicate logic: it can, for instance, note the owner, the object, the start-time and the end-time of ownership. Semantic networks can be built which are closely modelled on predicate logic. Nodes correspond to propositions, connective operators (such as 'and' and 'or'), variables and functions, allowing any logical expression, including quantified ones ('All A are X', 'Some X are Z') in node and arc form. Incorporating predicate logic in a system would refine the information considerably and it would be possible, for example, to represent a quasi-generic relationship using the 'Some A are C' formula.

In order to structure terminological information into semantic networks, it is necessary to define a specific number of relationships, i.e. to provide a limited number of labels to be attached to arcs. It is also necessary to define a coherent internal system of clear procedures, conventions and notation. The system must then only allow a single method of description for each type of relationship and it is therefore likely that networks would have to be subject field-specific.

In order to exploit such a network as fully as possible, it may be useful to incorporate a question-answer facility in the data base, using procedures for making inferences. The end-user could pose questions to the system about the concept in question. The reasoning mechanism used by most semantic networks is based on matching network structures. A network fragment is constructed representing a sought-for concept and is then matched against the network data base. Variable nodes in the fragment are bound in the matching process to the values they must have in order to make the match perfect. This fragment could then be matched against the data base looking for a node that has a particular arc to the concept about which a question is asked. When it is found, the node that the arc points to is bound in the partial match and that is the answer to the question. Had no match been found, the answer would have been 'nothing'. Similarly, questions such as 'Is there a metal with properties X and Y?' may be handled.

Semantic networks have considerable potential for a conceptual and cognitive representation in a term bank. A concept may be linked to a large number of related concepts which in turn are individually linked to many other concepts. As the number of concepts increases, an intricate multi-dimensional model is formed containing much interconceptual information and 'relational paths'.

The success of a semantic network for use in term banks will depend on several factors. The semantics of the network arcs must be carefully defined as well as the operations on them. The system must also be easy to implement and user-friendly. There is a real danger that a designer, attempting to exploit the full range of possible interconceptual descriptions which semantic networks have the potential of capturing, may produce an over-complicated, and unnecessarily detailed system.

In order to control the process of relationship attribution and to assist the dictionary compiler, the generation of relationships could be assisted by an expert system. When a new concept is recorded in the data base, a question–answer system, equipped with 'knowledge' about relational information considered relevant to each subject field and the nature of knowledge structures, could prompt the compiler with carefully formulated questions, the answers to which would enable it to assign the correct relationships. Such a system could bring a high degree of consistency to the process of assigning relationships.

Chapter Seven

RETRIEVAL OF TERMINOLOGY

All users and producers of specialised dictionaries and glossaries are potential users of terminological and lexical databases. They will prefer to use a
database instead of a printed dictionary if it can offer a more reliable and
quicker service than that provided by conventional information media, or if it
can be used to produce dictionaries of a different nature, of higher quality or
lower cost than existing ones. For the user the advantage of the computer-
based data collection over the conventional dictionary lies in the fact that
a single database can now hold information which was conventionally held
in fixed and different formats in a number of separate reference tools. By
bringing such information together in a flexible medium various useful formats
of information can be produced according to specific user needs.

The efficient retrieval of high-quality terminology is the prime objective
of all terminology compilation. In this endeavour human compilation and
machine processing interact. Retrieval is therefore closely dependent upon
compilation and storage techniques. While methods and principles of terminology retrieval are affected by developments in terminological theory
with respect to the material to be collected and the form of its presentation, the practice of terminology retrieval is heavily dependent on current
trends and developments in information and document retrieval systems
generally.

In essence terminological data retrieval is simply a specialised form of information retrieval. Any information retrieval system has two main functions.
Firstly it has a data management function, different aspects of which have
already been discussed. Secondly it has an interface function which allows
users to access and manipulate the information stored. This user-interface
may control not only the retrieval of data but also their creation, modification
and deletion. In this chapter only the retrieval facilities are discussed. In
a commercial environment some information retrieval systems are supplied
as complete systems to which no user code need be added. Others however

Figure 7.1. *Input and output modes of a term bank*

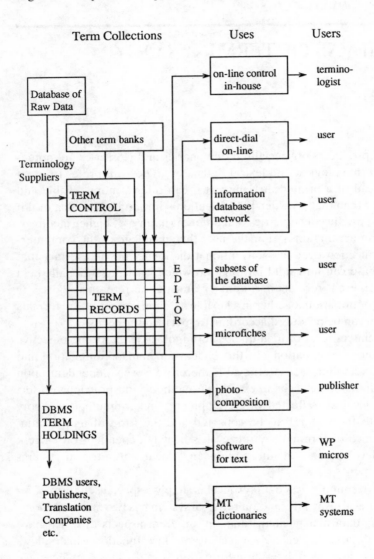

require users to tailor the user-interface to their own particular requirements to a greater or lesser degree.

7.1 Forms of retrieval

A complex multifunctional database of terminological information has multiple points of input and output. This is illustrated in Figure 7.1.

The input is essentially provided by two sources: various suppliers of terminology, who may draw upon a database of texts, and other term banks. According to the mode of operation, the input is usually filtered through a term control mechanism before full integration into the database. Terminology suppliers may, of course also work with other database management systems and supply data for a number of users of terminological information.

The output is either directly from the term bank to on-line use, especially by terminologists who need full information of full records, or it passes through an editor which selects information from the database and recombines it into the forms and units required by a variety of users.

Terminological databases attract users working in different hardware and software environments. Some users may have facilities for temporarily storing subsets of a terminology collection locally and may wish to download data to their machine. Other users may wish to integrate remote term bank access with other locally-based activities (assuming the network allows this) such as word processing. Finally users may require access to a terminological collection while accessing other kinds of information databases. It should, therefore, be possible to create subsets of a terminological database and to allow the possible linking of a terminological database with other databases. Though the provision of these facilities is not beyond the bounds of current hardware and software capabilities, it is in practice impeded by other problems of a more political nature, e.g. questions of copyright, charging etc., which do not concern us here.

The editor has various functions:

- it responds to user's search profiles and selects the items of information requested;
- it creates various subsets of the database for smaller termbanks;
- it prepares various forms of output for the production of microfiches, compact discs or printed dictionaries via phototypesetting.
- it converts data into a form suitable for further machine processing in various text-editing and translation devices.

7.1.1 *Sorting problems in retrieval*

Because of the complexity of terminological units the problem of alphabetically sorting entry terms assumes particular importance. In general lexicography the issue is resolved by various conventions, though even here variation exists, e.g. whether a space between words or a hyphen should be given a value in alphabetical ordering. There is also uncertainty about the place of abbreviations, with some dictionaries listing them in the strict alphabetical order and others treating them as a distinct word category with a separate place before words, or completely separate in an appendix to the dictionary.

In terminology the same problems exist and are even aggravated because of the many letter words, formulae, Greek and numeric characters that occur in particular subjects. Various options are available for sequencing, as shown in the example of the stem 'electr-', below:

STRICT ALPHABETICAL	KEY WORD ALPHABETICAL
electric	electrical
electrical	‾ charge
electrical charge	electric
electric attraction	‾ attraction
electric conduction	‾ conduction
electricity	‾ transducer
electric transducer	electricity
electroballistics	electroballistics
electrochemical equivalent	electrochemical equivalent
electrode	electrodermal reaction
electrode current	electrodynamic
electrodeless discharge	electrodynamic instrument
electrodermal reaction	electrodynamics
electrodynamic	electro-optical effect
electrodynamic instrument	electrode
electrodynamics	‾ current
electrolyte	electrodeless discharge
electrolytic cell	electrolyte
electron	electrolytic cell
electron beam	electron
electronic tuning	‾ beam
electronics	electronic tuning
electro-optical effect	electronics

Greater search efficiency is achieved with a permuted index in which every element in turn is placed in alphabetical order, e.g.

electric	attraction
electron	beam
electrolytic	cell
electrical	charge
electrode	current
electrodeless	discharge
	electric
	electrical
	electrical charge
	.
	.
electro-optical	effect
	electrochemical equivalent
electrochemical	equivalent
	etc.

Automatic sorting techniques make it possible to produce any sequence with a minimum of effort. Many term banks therefore provide an index-browsing facility which permit a user to look for spellings and the existence of terms before asking for fuller information. An alphabetical index of one kind or another is, of course, also required for any conceptually sequenced dictionary. In term banks an alphabetical index can be matched by a conceptually ordered sequence of terms to guide a user into the subject field.

7.2 Retrieval requirements

Most good information retrieval systems have adopted the principle of user-profiles, according to which the user specifies a search profile, an output profile or both. They have also adopted a new principle of user-friendliness which will be discussed separately.

7.2.1 *Search profiles*

The principal difference between the traditional dictionary and the database lies in the way information can be retrieved. The traditional approach offers all available information at once in the sequential order of the dictionary entry.

The dictionary entry may therefore contain too much information for the immediate need. If it contains too little for the user's needs, the information extracted from one dictionary can, of course, be supplemented with information from dictionaries with a different range of content, but in order to get at this information the user has to accept much repetition of information he has already found.

A further difficulty lies in the fact that in the printed, fixed-format dictionary the information is presented in a predetermined and invariable order, regardless of the user's preference of the sequence in which he wants the information. He may therefore have to read the entire article in order to find one synonym or a particular usage example. Since the information provided by lexical databases is, however, divided into data fields the information can be retrieved one field at a time or in any other combination and in any sequence. The amount and order of the information to be extracted is defined for each individual user or for user types through search profiles.

For general purposes there is usually a standard search profile which corresponds to the most common user queries. For specialised users or for particular needs search profiles can be formulated which allow the user to build up a set of search parameters which are utilised for all subsequent interrogations of the database unless they are temporarily overridden. While making enquiries to a term bank, for example, a user may wish all his queries to return only terms from the English language with a usage-note of 'Standardised' for concepts in the field of Nuclear Physics. Users will set search parameters normally once only when they log in to the database system.

The search profile may also be conceived as a procedure which allows the modification of the standard search strategies. On a term bank there may be facilities for the activation/de-activation of less selective search techniques. These possible extensions to searches for terms may include:
– automatic retrieval of all terms containing the search string,
– automatic performance of free text searches on definitions if no separate entry is found,
– removal of upper/lower case distinction when searching,
– removal of significance of diacritics when searching.

7.2.2 *Output Profiles*

Output profiles allow users to define a list of information categories they wish to be displayed for all entries retrieved. Where appropriate users may also define the order in which the results are to appear. Users usually select their preferred output profiles once only on log-in to the system. They normally have the choice of selecting from a range of predefined, system-standard output formats or, if these fail to meet their individual requirements, of defining their own personal format. It is becoming customary to allow users to store search and output profiles for future use, thus eliminating the need to recreate them each time the system is used. It is generally assumed that no user will ever wish to retrieve the complete information although the possibility of doing this is available.

Users normally have the choice of on-line consultation, whether by telephone link or on their own system with independent storage media. There is the further choice of consulting a screen or reading print-out. Alternatively information may be asked for in batch-mode, which is most suitable for substantial and complex searches not needed immediately. More advanced systems may include in their output profile additional facilities which allow the user to obtain a hard copy of all data retrieved and to direct hard copy output to a specific device.

Term banks can also provide a completely new range of services not available via a combination of existing tools. One such service is the text-oriented glossary, a list of terms plus associated information in the order in which they occur in a particular text. A term bank can also be used to produce terminological thesauri, i.e. systematically ordered lists of terms in particular subject fields which express a number of conceptual relationships and facets of the underlying conceptual structure. Such information is of great value to writers and translators but may also be of use to scientists and information brokers.

7.2.3 *User-friendliness*

Once the user has created or has been given a user-profile his interaction with the data base commences. It is imperative that the system is user-friendly, i.e. that it is easy to use and offers a help facility to assist infrequent users. Any information retrieval system will be accessed by users with varying degrees of familiarity not only with the system in question but also with information retrieval in general and computer technology as a whole. The system must allow all users, irrespective of their knowledge of the system, to build up and activate fairly complex search requests. Not only does an unfriendly interface to a database deter potential users from using the service, it can in extreme circumstances result in the user formulating a valid query but not the one which was intended. The user consequently receives either an incomplete or, what is more serious, an incorrect response and may not even be aware that this has occurred.

The concept of user-friendliness has recently been extended to cover not only ease of use but also user-satisfaction with the response given. It is now realised that people have high expectations of information retrieval systems and expect a response of some kind. 'No Find' is no longer acceptable. It is therefore necessary to include very powerful search techniques, as part of an information retrieval system. These may include:
– simple morphological rules which search not only for the search string itself but also for inflected forms;
– some sort of spelling approximation algorithm to retrieve entries spelt similarly to the search string;
– an automatic truncation facility which retrieves all entries containing the search string.

Another aspect of user-friendliness which is important in the majority of information retrieval systems is the ability to perform free-text searches. For most purposes the human organisation of information through key-word indexing yields high responses and user satisfaction. It must, however be recognised that both the selection of keywords and the attribution of texts to keywords and vice versa is unscientific. In some cases therefore the subjectivity upon which this attribution is originally based can lead to a poor response level. Consequently more recent information retrieval systems possess a free-text searching facility which allows users to scan complete texts for particular lexical items. This facility has been further enhanced in many systems to the extent of allowing users to specify particular contexts in which the search string must occur before a particular document is returned to the screen. This more objective method of retrieving documents has greatly increased the accuracy of many information retrieval systems and has important consequences for the retrieval of terminological data where the ability to perform free text searches on definitions, contexts and compound terms to retrieve terminological data by concept rather than lexeme has barely been explored.

7.3   The retrieval of terminological information

Terminology retrieval can be considered as a special application of information retrieval. The trends in information retrieval mentioned in the introduction to this chapter can therefore be regarded as being of relevance to the design of a software to retrieve terminological information. This section investigates those retrieval requirements which are exclusive to terminological data.

Standard information retrieval is based on the premise that the system has only one human user-type, the on-line user. The majority of systems take data which are already in existence in another form (texts, articles, abstracts etc.) and convert them to a new storage medium to allow easier access to and wider dissemination of that data than was possible in their previous printed form. Essentially, the structure of the information remains unchanged. What has altered is the way in which the information can be used.

The situation in terminology information retrieval is the complete reverse. The data is created in the first-place in machine-readable files and then either made available to on-line users or converted to another form (printed dictionary, micro-fiche, microcomputer-based machine-readable glossary). Previous data collections are used as sources but the resultant data structure bears no resemblance to that which existed prior to terminology compilation. Thus in traditional information retrieval applications, information is normally converted from print to machine-readable format and the facilities required for retrieval can be entirely oriented to a narrow range of on-line queries. In terminology retrieval data is created in machine-readable form and may be converted to a printed format to satisfy the requirements of particular user-groups. It must, therefore, be structured in such a way that a great diversity of subsets of information can be extracted not only on-line, but also in formats suitable for effective presentation on other media.

The use of the two types of data also differs. The raw data input to IR systems is textual data which for improved access in retrieval will be analysed and processed in some way. Terminological data could form a particular module within the system assisting in the computational analysis of the text being processed. The form of the output of IR systems is basically of two types: either it is a reference to a text or it is a text. The use of the output is also twofold: either it is used to get hold of a text or it is the end result of the search process, i.e. the information need is satisfied with the provision of the text.

Terminological data output to the end user is of two types: it is either an item selected from a natural language corpus, e.g. a term or a context, or it is information related to an item of natural language, in which case it is entirely the result of human decision-taking and attribution. In most cases the information sought is of a mixed nature, i.e. the end user seeks information in relation to a lexical item of one language and expects a commentary of some sort which relates the lexical item to the user query. The use of the output is more varied than for a IR system. Human uses are discussed in section 7.4., below.

For use in NLP systems it is desirable that terminological information systems be able to produce output in some sort of formal representation. To take this point a step further the output of data in a formal representation is heavily reliant on a similar representation being used internally for the storage of data. This supports the earlier argument for a more structured logical database representation than is possible in most current information retrieval software.

On-line terminology retrieval has several further requirements over and above those provided by standard information retrieval software because of the heterogeneity of the end users. Differences in user requirements can be perceived on a number of distinct planes.

Terminology has many distinct user groups: translators, technical writers, abstractors, teachers etc. These users must be able to retrieve the subsets of data they need; they want also to be able both to commence searching by using any data category and to combine search parameters and data categories in ways which information retrieval software rarely permits. The following access paths, via a powerful non-procedural query language which allows the formulation of any logical query commencing from any point in the database, should be supported as a minimum:

– to the term, e.g.
  via direct query,
  via selection from an index or permuted index,
  via expansion of the search string to retrieve entries containing the term or entries similar in their orthographic or phonetic form.

– to the concept, e.g.
  via direct access using an identification code,
  via conceptual relationships,
  via free text searches on definitions (and possibly contexts).

Terminology databases, like dictionaries, attract users with different levels of subject specialisation. Whereas a scientist will expect a very precise definition of a concept, a translator may prefer a less technical definition and an undergraduate student may be looking for a definition more akin to an encyclopaedia entry. A term bank, if stored in a formal and structured enough manner, should be capable of tailoring output to different levels of technical ability on the part of users as defined in their output profiles.

7.4 User types

Every speaker or writer of a special subject language is a user of terminology and every learner of a special subject, be it in school, college, university or an industrial training course, is a learner of terminology. This very large constituency relies on textbooks, manuals, instructions, regulations, standards etc. for their day-to-day information needs and supports this by the use of reference tools such as encyclopaedias, dictionaries, glossaries and, increasingly, term banks.

Irrespective of the number of languages and other information contained in a term bank, it is possible to identify a number of distinct specialist user groups by the type and combination of information they regularly retrieve.

1. Subject specialists, are assumed to have a full knowledge of the terminology they are using; they can even be expected to create terms. So far they have used existing conventional terminological tools largely as reassurance but could not use them creatively in their work because the information they need most was not available. They need term banks for the occasional reference to ascertain the meaning of an unknown term in their own or in a foreign language, or to check the spelling of a known term. A particular case is the verification of the existence of a term, when, e.g. the user expects the term banks to tell him whether a particular word form is documented in a language and has the meaning the user believes it to have. Other types of potential use are as yet unknown because specialised conventional dictionaries do not provide other information in their printed versions.

2. The largest group consists of professional communication mediators who write technical or scientific texts or convert technical texts into a new format, e.g. by translation into another language, by transferring the text into a less technical language, by summarising or abstracting. They are technical writers, information brokers, journalists as monolingual users, and interpreters and translators as multilingual users. Their use of reference tools is more conditioned by the need to produce specialised texts and less by the need for comprehension than the first user group. The type of information they need is both quantitatively and qualitatively different. It is therefore easy to understand that this group should have initiated the construction of term banks and other automated means of information gathering and description.

This user group demands a high degree of accuracy of description, partly because in the production of texts a user cannot rely on the contextual information which assists in comprehension, and partly because professional communicators usually have a less detailed knowledge and understanding of the subject matter than subject specialists. As communicators they have to range over a wide area of subject fields and this impedes specialisation in any one subject. This observation is particularly true of translators, very few of whom can specialise in a single subject field.

It must also be noted that communicators often have the particularly difficult task of converting specialist texts into more widely acceptable texts for a more general readership which itself may require bridging the vocabularies of several subject fields. In this way they produce or convert linguistic messages on special subjects and so act as intermediaries between specialists of different subjects and languages and between the general reader and the specialist. In this process of popularisation as well as in the process of translation from one language to another these communicators are not infrequently required to paraphrase terms for which there is no name in the new medium, i.e. the popularised text or translation, and to create new designations. To carry out this duty with any degree of effectiveness, communicators need access to a great deal of information not provided in the traditional reference tools, but which can be made available in terminological databases.

Only very few large organisations have recognised the need to support their communication services with adequate terminological information in the form of term banks. In most other cases traditional tools are still the only support available.

3. The next group consists of specialist lexicographers and terminologists who collect and record existing usage. Their special needs are for substantial background information such as citations of terms in context, documentation of usage, alternative definitions and variants to enable them to build up and maintain a reliable information base. Occasionally they also advise on usage or on the coining of new terms or translation equivalents. Being the creators of term banks they can incorporate the information they need and at the same time ensure that retrieval procedures permit them to extract all the information they need for their tasks.

4. Another user group consists of information and documentation specialists such as librarians, information brokers, indexers, who use term banks for the reliable identification and description of specialist documents. The modern practice of using specialist documentation languages for the description of documents creates a particular need for the clear determination of

correspondences between the natural language used by most information users and the artificial language created and used by information scientists and indexers in particular. This work can be described as artificial language planning or rather artificial language creation and maintenance.

5. The last group of homogeneous users is that of language planners. There are on the one hand general language planners, i.e. people charged with maintenance and development of a national language as they are found in language academies or ministries of education; on the other hand there are experts concerned with standardisation of terms and expressions in special subject fields and for limited purposes. None of this work can be carried out without agreed terminology. Both groups therefore need accurate information about all existing designations in order to be able to choose preferred ones, declare deprecated ones, or otherwise regulate usage.

Standardisation organisations collect terminology into glossaries and so provide a useful service for their own committees and incidentally for a wider public. In this sense standardisation organisations find themselves in an exclusive position of being users, collectors and producers of terminological information at the same time and for a potentially very large market. In this sense standardisation organisations are more influential than individual firms because they have access to large sections of industry and in some cases even government departments.

6. In addition there are all manner of language users such as publishers, language teachers, researchers in applied linguistics, etc. whose information needs are quite diverse but who do not normally represent a sufficiently strong and coherent group to command their own lexical tools. The availability of a flexible lexical database can satisfy a large number of their information needs in this direction.

7. Finally there is the general user who occasionally consults a dictionary and who can now be offered a much more pertinent and relevant service at his desktop. Most attention of the planners of term banks must be directed to expanding use among this group for the very practical reasons that only increased consultation will in the long run pay for the cost of creation and maintenance of databases, and that only the general user will be able to define the possible information needs that have yet to be satisfied. Such uses could be, for example,
– an insurance agent dealing with claims in a highly specialised subject field;

– a manufacturer requiring information about the terminology pertaining to a foreign product he wishes to import, compete with or utilise;
– a parliamentarian visiting a foreign country in need of a glossary of expressions so that he can understand a guided tour of a factory;
– a customs official controlling the documentation accompanying imported goods.

The needs of these user groups coincide or overlap sufficiently so that a single database is adequate for all possible enquiries. The considerable information required in any case for the reliable description of a concept can all be made available singly or in combination in response to a query for a single item of information or for a series of related items.

Since users are on the whole only interested in the information they have asked for, it is necessary to restrict the information according to several formats. There is a clear need for user-type specific retrieval packages which contain the information which from experience is normally wanted by a particular user group. At the same time there must be provision for individual user-specific output formats which can be constructed beforehand or modified for a particular occasion. Experience has shown that users initially prefer a ready-made package before they gradually develop their own profiles.

The package technique can be refined for conversational working with the introduction of facilities for the presentation of graduated information. It is also possible to combine several retrieval packages into a single query instruction for simultaneous or sequential presentation. For example, a user may habitually require a term, a foreign language equivalent and a source. In case this information proves inadequate, the next package, e.g. consisting of a definition, may be called up. In this way users can exclude irrelevant information while keeping the option of getting supplementary information for the rare case when it is needed.

The following subsections exemplify the most common types of output formats identified by a user survey. They are divided into preference for on-line and batch retrieval where there is a significant difference in the information so retrieved.

7.4.1 *Translators and other communication mediators*

The following packages seem to satisfy the needs of most translators. When translators consult monolingual information they need the same information, except, of course, the target language (TL) equivalents.

On-line

          term + TL equivalent + source of TL term
     or term + TL equivalent + TL source + TL definition
     or term + TL equivalent + synonym (if available) + quality indicator

If graduated information is requested, the following sequence would correspond to most expectations:

          term + TL equivalent
               + definition
               + context or usage note (if available)
               + quality indicator
               + synonym
               + source
               + subject specification/label or scope note (if available)

Batch retrieval

For this form of retrieval demand is heaviest for alphabetical and systematic mono- or bilingual glossaries consisting of term + definition. The next most important choice is for bilingual text-oriented glossaries, i.e. term + TL equivalent + usage note (if available), in the order of occurrence of the terms in a text. Phraseological glossaries and listings of terms in context are next in demand. There is also a small interest in bilingual indices and relational information.

7.4.2 *Information scientists and other information providers*

The requirements of this group are very similar to those of communication mediators. Their needs for the identification of terms is catered for by the three packages described above. Inter- or intralingual abstractors, though normally attributed to the group of information brokers, have exactly the same requirements as other writers or translators. Specific operations such as indexing, keyword extraction, and thesaurus construction and searching require quite different combinations of terminological data, viz.:

On-line

          term + definition + source
          term + synonym + generic term + specific term
     · term + generic term + specific term + TL equivalent
          term + complete systematic display of relations

In graduated form the following pattern seems to be most widely favoured:

> term + definition + source
> + synonym
> + generic + specific term
> + TL equivalent

In each case the term would have to be understood in its widest acceptation of conceptual synonymy, i.e. including any spelling variants, shortened or long forms, abbreviations and acronyms.

Batch retrieval
This group of users has a regular demand for listings, e.g.

> monolingual alphabetical subject field indices
> alphabetical lists of term + definition
> alphabetical lists of term + key related terms
> systematically ordered lists of subject fields

Terminological thesauri, which are an automatic by-product of sound terminological practice, can be used to provide access to databases or serve as source material for the construction of documentation thesauri. The ROOT Thesaurus, published by the British Standards Institute, is intended to serve a double function as general scientific vocabulary and information storage and retrieval tool.

7.4.3 *Terminologists and other dictionary producers*

Terminologists require on-line services for all their work related to the compilation of terminologies and for their consultancy work in advising on usage. Their most frequent need is for cross references inside the database, in order to verify the many relationships on the conceptual, lexical and pragmatic level. They also need batch output of listings for the verification of the global accuracy of entries.

For the publication of dictionaries from terminological databases large quantities of data have to be handled which is conveniently done in batch mode leading eventually to hard copy. The conventional need is still for alphabetically sorted entries with the usual type of lexicographical information which excludes source references.

7.4.4 *Other users*

The work of standardisation experts and other language planners can be greatly assisted by on-line consultation of comprehensive databases and by off-line produced lists of standardised and non-standardised vocabulary in systematic or alphabetical order. In fact, reliable language planning, supported by linguistic evidence, has only been possible since the advent of the computer for the production of appropriate support tools.

Research and development in theoretical and applied linguistics in general is furthermore assisted by the availability of such additional tools as:
– alphabetical listings of words in texts with reference to a dictionary entry;
– frequency listings of words in texts measured against a standard frequency in a database;
– sequential, text-oriented word lists;
– reverse alphabetical lists;
– lists of terms by date of first appearance in the language;
– lists of preferred, obsolete, or deprecated terms;
– text-type specific sortings of terms.
The production of these lists for their own sake would be very costly; as by-products of regular database house-keeping control they can be readily made available for research and development at very little cost.

7.5 Retrieval from a terminological thesaurus

Terminological databases using the conceptual approach to the structuring of content resemble the form of a thesaurus more than that of the conventional, alphabetically ordered dictionary. It is in fact accepted that the most appropriate form of classifying and presenting terms is via a methodology which owes much to the principles of thesaurus construction.

The advantages and relevance of a thesaural structure to terminology were recognised early by terminologists because it could represent relationships between concepts in as much detail as necessary, in the same way as documentation thesauri do between document descriptors. Wüster's dictionary 'The Machine Tool' (1968) can be seen as a forerunner of the terminological thesaurus in that there is a conceptual organisation of terms, based on the Universal Decimal Classification.

Historically, thesauri have evolved into three specific forms as appropriate to their separate and distinct functions, viz.

– general language thesauri, i.e. dictionaries of synonyms, analogue expressions, ideas suggested by words;
– documentation thesauri for indexing and retrieval of documents;
– terminological thesauri which combine feature of the other two.

The function of a documentation thesaurus is normally perceived as a terminological control device used in translating from the natural language of documents, indexes or users' queries into a restricted language which permits more efficient indexing and retrieval. By form a documentation thesaurus is a controlled and dynamic vocabulary of semantically and generically related terms which covers a specific domain of knowledge. This vocabulary consists of selected terms (known as document descriptors) and declared relationships between them such as 'generic broad term', 'narrow term partitive' or 'related term'. The control is exercised by two references: UF (use for) indicates a preferred term or descriptor, and USE indicates a non-preferred term or non-descriptor.

Thesauri usually have two parts: an alphabetical list and a systematic display.

The alphabetical list may add information on the entries such as scope notes and include a list of related terms up to one hierarchical level (such as 'narrow term' and 'non-preferred term'). Consulting the alphabetical list, the user is led, if need be, to more or less specific terms or possibly more suitable terms of the same level of specificity.

The systematic subject display is the main part of the thesaurus since it provides most of the definitional and relational information in the form of a hierarchical structure. The user may be led to the location of the desired term by an 'address code' given in the alphabetical index. Terms are grouped by subject area and arranged according to their meanings and relationships. Scope notes and reciprocal references to equivalent and related terms may be displayed and relationships to broader and narrower terms are indicated by the position of a term within a hierarchy and its level of indentation. This classification is often refined by using facets in one form or another which serve to indicate the logical basis for subdividing a category.

A terminological thesaurus is more than a simple dictionary, glossary or vocabulary as it aims at a coherent systematic representation of the knowledge structure of a subject field. Such a tool has the advantage of showing the full extension of a term and its place within the broader conceptual environment of the overall knowledge structure it belongs to, thus complementing the definition which can, in this way, concentrate on the intension of concepts. Since the conceptual structure is the basis for any description of the lexicon of special languages, a dictionary or glossary may be created on the basis of the terminological thesaurus, but never vice versa.

Whether or not one can accurately represent the conceptual structure of special subject fields and precisely situate concepts in a terminological thesaurus is a matter of debate. Decisions that have to be made during compilation will often be of a subjective nature and each terminologist may have a different view of the knowledge structure. As yet, there appears to be little in the way of concrete and universally agreed-upon rules and conventions for constructing terminological thesauri and for establishing relationships and hierarchies. This may explain the fact that there are relatively few actual examples of systematically structured dictionaries.

Amongst those glossaries and dictionaries which have adopted some kind of conceptual structure, very few can be described as 'terminological thesaurus' in the full sense of the concept. Many systematic structures consist of groupings and/or hierarchies of terms based on very arbitrary, questionable and often opaque criteria. This applies even to some of the British Standards Institution glossaries, e.g. BS 5408:1976, Glossary of Documentation Terms. This document incorporates a systematic index which, however, lacks consistency and places many concepts in broad, over-generalised categories.

Nevertheless, a dictionary incorporating some indication of interrelationships, provided that this information is neither misleading nor redundant, is a step in the right direction and the terminological thesaurus is, arguably, the most effective means of capturing these relationships usefully.

Chapter Eight

USAGE OF TERMINOLOGY

At the beginning of this chapter, which deals with the applications of terminology as observed through the work of terminologists, it is useful to summarise some of the modern attitudes to current practice.

1.   There is a move towards greater pooling of terminological resources. Small and individual users have begun to share and exchange their specialised term collections, larger centres are making their data available to small and medium-sized user groups while public networks allow remote users to log-in to national and supra-national term banks. In addition the growing availability of term bank holdings in CD-ROM form brings the benefits of very large collections to the attention of the general public.

2.   It is recognised that the process of compilation of terminology should be planned to be descriptive, because any prescriptive function would limit the usefulness of the data base; any influence on usage can only be effected through appropriate use of terminology in relevant text or spoken discourse.

3. A clear distinction is being made between terminology as evidenced from usage in a diversity of pragmatic situations and the idealising tendency which sees a one-to-one correspondence between terminological and conceptual systems. It is now acknowledged that terms have linguistic variants in spoken and written language and within the same text type and it is essential to list these variants in descriptions of terminology.

4. The impact of large terminological databases is likely to be significant for the improvement of precise, economic and appropriate communication. This development imposes responsibilities on terminologists who should construct and store their information in such a way that it can be widely used.

5. Usage changes frequently and therefore it is necessary to plan for regular maintenance of terminological collections.

8.1   The scope and function of terminology processing

As a conscious social activity, terminology, like lexicography, is undertaken for a purpose. Two distinct but interdependent functions can be identified which define the nature of the work and the type of information to be collected.

The primary function is the collection of terminological information which is undertaken in order to improve communication and its economic justification lies in this objective. Consequently all terminological activities can be evaluated with regard to the extent to which improved communication is achieved. This function of improving communication is carried out on two levels:
(1)   by collecting and providing information on concepts and terms, which may imply advising on usage through the type of information provided;
(2)   by explicitly advising on naming of concepts and usage of terms.

The second function is to provide a record of the special subject lexicon of a language, an archive of lexical usage and meanings. This function may be carried out openly and directly by a single national agency, an academy of the language or similar body or it may be carried out piecemeal and incidentally by many terminology processing centres. Every dictionary acquires this function the moment it is superseded by an updated version, or more precisely, every dictionary entry becomes an exhibit in the museum of the lexicon the moment it is superseded by an updated entry.

The collection of terminological information is undertaken in response to two different types of motivation:
(1)   it is carried out in response to specific requests—as in an advisory service for the production of documents, translations etc.;
(2)   it is carried out generally, as in the case of publishers wishing to produce a dictionary of a particular subject field or a term bank expanding its range of coverage.
Both types of activity can be carried out mono-, bi- or multilingually.

A further differentiation of terminological activities is occasioned by the different groups of users making enquiries and by the types of enquiries they make. It is therefore appropriate to consider terminological activities from two points of view:
– the traditional lexicographical/terminological approach which starts from one entity, a concept or a lexical item, and collects appropriate information about it;
– the information service approach which responds to particular user needs.

This second approach eliminates the conventional equation between the head of an entry and the information about this head, and the sequence of the items of information; it incidentally also abolishes the single access route to information via the alphabetically ordered head of the entry, which characterised the ordering for the printed dictionary. Instead, it requires the full articulation and definition both of the head of the entry and the entry itself in order to provide the items of information that will in practice be asked for. Concern about the sequence of information in an entry now gives way to the independent identification of information categories, irrespective of sequence.

The result is a closely structured data record with multiple access points and various sequences or paths through this data record. This data base approach does not deny any of the values of the traditional working methods; on the contrary, it supplements them and brings to the surface a great deal of the information that terminologists have to collect in any case in order to verify the data and to maintain continuous control of the accuracy of the terminological record.

In practice this means adopting a terminological record with clearly defined data fields most of which are addressable singly or in groups while making the information gathered so transparent that the regular user finds it directly readable. A terminological database then becomes a dynamic entity which is regularly undergoing change as records are entered, completed, modified and deleted and from which subsets can be extracted to produce smaller databases or printed glossaries.

8.1.1 *Limitations of terminology processing*

A database approach to terminology also has its problems as there are then no obvious limits to the size and complexity of the collection. Criteria are therefore needed for separating a terminological database from a general language dictionary and for determining the conditions for the continued usefulness of the database. Terminological collections have so far been considered self-renewing entities that are regularly kept up to date. Large databases with virtually unlimited storage capacity have the potential of becoming museums and clear policies are therefore needed about the place of obsolete terminology.

A possible consequence of a heavily user-oriented approach may be a desire to simplify the information so as to guide the user in what is considered to be 'correct' usage. Such a temptation was always strong in terminology and the traditional links terminology had in a number of countries with standardising bodies reinforced it. The development of large term banks for very specific purposes by single firms, government agencies or departments has also strengthened the impression that terminology has a directive rather than merely an advisory function. The storage and processing capabilities of modern databases permit term banks to present sufficient information for the intelligent user to choose sensibly, hopefully reducing the need for advice.

The data gathering and presentation function of terminology should, however, never be confused with its advisory function and modern technology permits the clear separation of the two. Terminologists should advise on the basis of available information and be able to justify their advice by reference to facts, documented theory and methods. The ultimate choice of terms, definitions or usage must, however, rest with the user as it is the user who originally invents or develops and names the concept.

In their advisory function terminologists can be heavily involved in language planning and in particular in establishing new terminologies to accompany the transfer of science and technology to wider user groups in the same or other linguistic communities. This work is carried out in many different ways from the ad hoc translation of manuals and textbooks by unqualified translators without any guidance to the government agency that develops glossaries for an entire programme of technology transfer or the firm which studies the terminological situation of a country as part of a market survey for a new product.

8.2 Attitudes to terminology processing

It is only with the advent of automation that it has become possible to offer a choice of approaches to terminology processing and that the question of alternative methods has become relevant. Since in an applied field of study, theoretical foundations are shaped by the function this discipline serves, it is of interest to examine the impact of modern information technology on terminology processing. The first terminologists' limited perception of this function initially determined the principles and methods of terminology processing; they are today being revised in the light of changed views, different needs and the availability of new tools. It is therefore not surprising to see that there is no single unified theoretical position on the constituents of principles and methods of terminology processing.

8.2.1 *Historical perspective*

There are said to be different schools of thought on terminology and there are certainly different practices in terminology processing as evidenced by different types of dictionaries, glossaries and terminological data banks. These distinctions may be based on different theoretical assumptions but may equally have originated in different objectives and practical circumstances which were later expressed as theoretical principles.

In his *Introduction à la Terminologie*, Guy Rondeau (1980) identified a German-Austrian, a Soviet, a Czechoslovak and a Canadian-Quebec school of terminological theory, and briefly characterised them. The interest in his differentiation lies in the historical circumstances which produced these divergent views since they can explain why differences exist and why their significance diminishes in relevance as new developments occur. His observations may therefore be considered as a contribution to a history of the field.

In Germany and Austria concern with terminological theory was simultaneous with a growth in efforts to standardise German language terminology, itself a problem acutely felt as two standardisation bodies were establishing different linguistic authorities. It is therefore not surprising that a theoretical framework was sought which would justify the harmonisation, unification and lastly the standardisation of terminology and at the same time support principles for its collection and description on a supranational level. In its early phases this work was naively idealistic with a strong belief in the possibilities of international agreement on the question of the simplification of technical communication by such means as Esperanto or sets of term elements of Greek and Latin origin. Though Eugen Wüster—the founder of this school—had applied some of his principles in a model dictionary *The Machine Tool*, this substantial piece of work, written without the aid of a computer, remained an isolated experiment. The methodology proposed proved too complex for human processing; at the same time it was not suited for conversion to automated techniques.

Substantial contributions to theoretical terminology have been made by the Soviet Union of which very little is known in the rest of the world. The historical situation in the early 1930s which prompted this work was one of a need to create Russian technical terms for imported science and technology and to provide equivalents in the many languages of the Soviet Union. From the beginning it was therefore a practical, multilingual and multicultural approach which had to acknowledge the realities of the diversity of technical and scientific language. In the initial stages great stress was put on the need for centrally imposed standardisation, but in later years it has been realised that usage cannot easily be changed through central directives. The German Democratic Republic has in recent years contributed significantly to this tradition.

The work identified by Rondeau as the Czechoslovak school is influenced by the orientation of Functional Linguistics and in practice by the need to create technical terminology in Czech and Slovak.

Canadian concern with terminology is of more recent date and stems from the decision to make French a parallel official language to English. The linguistic requirements of a bilingual government administration, education system, the policy of equality in employment etc. make heavy demands on language planning agencies and can only be met within a national language policy. Canada made selective use of the European experience but in a different situation had to develop theoretical positions of its own. Since this development coincided with the introduction of computers for natural language data processing, this work was from the outset oriented towards term banks and has therefore been able to adjust to changing technology. A great deal of the writing on terminology in Canada is also concerned with the creation of neologisms and the phenomenon of borrowing terminology from other languages.

8.2.2 *Recording of terminological usage*

Earlier terminologists attempted to record only accepted or approved usage, thereby establishing something like a recommended form of a term. It is increasingly being recognised that fixation of usage, e.g. by means of prescription or standardisation, follows established usage and does not precede it. This attitude points to a more realistic appreciation of the uses of language whereby the communicative use is given the primary position before the classificatory and ideational uses which we observe in action during term formation. This fundamental shift in emphasis places considerable stress on the observation and recording of usage which in turn can positively influence term formation.

The recognition of the primacy of usage affects the attitude towards the borrowing of concepts and terms from other language communities. It is now understood that it is difficult to change the linguistic form of terms once they have been created; it is therefore extremely important to create the 'right' form at the outset. Since this is unlikely to occur via terminological commissions, unless these commissions also control the importation of technology, the responsibility of creating the 'right' term lies with the scientists and technologists who are involved in the importation of new concepts and with the translators who work for them. Sound naming principles for new concepts should therefore be taught to all scientists and engineers as well as to technical translators because they are likely to be more immediately involved in term formation than terminologists.

8.2.2.1. *Spoken language*

Until recent times dictionaries and glossaries only recorded written language usage for the simple reason that it was assumed that these reference tools would only be used in conjunction with written documents. At a time of growing importance of the spoken language, through television, video-recording etc., and vigorous research into speech recognition and speech production, it is recognised that research is also needed into the spoken forms of the lexicon. The influence which the spoken language exercises on the written language must be acknowledged as soon as a serious analysis is undertaken of user manuals and instructions, many of which are now accompanied by video cassettes. It may even be possible to stipulate the existence of an intermediate spoken language of instruction in the same way as we accept the almost separate existence of a style and a vocabulary of popular science writing.

8.2.2.2. *Variants and other alternative forms*

Observation of usage permits the identification and categorisation of linguistic variants of terms by text types. It is known that the longest and most complex terms occur in lists and schedules, where their meaning is not supported by context; it is equally known that the greatest degree of concentration or abbreviation occurs in heavily situation-conditioned texts, where the context makes ambiguity impossible. It has been observed that the stylistic variation of terms is motivated by and in direct proportion to the density of terms over a given text segment.

Relatively little serious research exists into these complex processes. The reason for this neglect is easy to state: subject specialists who are capable of distinguishing between a variant and a term are not usually interested or linguistically trained to undertake this work; linguists, on the other hand, rarely have the detailed subject knowledge to produce reliable evidence for determining the regularities underlying these processes of term variation.

Little attention has been paid to the particular case of dynamic use of processes of abbreviation in context. In a recent study of this phenomenon a number of discoveries were made which are summarised in this section (Hope 1984).

There are two possible starting points for studying this technique or communication strategy:

1. Any one term can have a number of context-conditioned synonyms, of which abbreviated forms are a subset. Language users, i.e. specialists know these forms and also their mode of employment.
2. Special language users, just as general language users, know a number of techniques of alternative designation and apply these with a certain degree of freedom to particular text types and communicative situations.

These two assumptions are not mutually exclusive and may, indeed, both be true so that in any one field and for any one term it should be possible to list:

a) the existing and fully acknowledged variants, and
b) the techniques available for variant production either by word-category, word-structure, subject field, or communicative situation (e.g. spoken/written, formal/informal).

Such a distinction would, however, also have an influence on a theory of lexicalisation, i.e. make a contribution to providing an answer to the question: when is a particular designation a properly established lexical item and when is it a permitted alternative which functions anaphorically? The answer to this question can only be provided if we consider that the social norm imposes a special vocabulary and also permits variants.

The questions surrounding the existence and use of variants can be expressed as a number of hypotheses:

1. There is need for lexical/terminological variation and this is variously strongly expressed in different text types. Despite the theoretical claims of univocity of reference, there is, in fact, a considerable variation of designation in special languages.
2. The means of alternate designation do not differ markedly between general and special languages; because of the higher concentration of reference terms, there may, however, be a higher density of alternate forms in special language discourse.
3. The means available for alternate designation are:
   – the use of absolute or true synonyms (probably less in special languages than in general language) of the type 'desire – wish', 'comprehend – understand'.
   – the use of contextual synonyms in the form of the generic for the specific, the whole for the part, etc. In general language the range of alternatives

is wider than in special languages, e.g. cat – animal, spoke – wheel; in general language in a sequence like 'filly-horse-racehorse-animal' any hyperordinate may be chosen, but in special language it is usual to choose the immediate hyperonym only.

4. In either case the synonym may be created by a process of abbreviation. It is then at times difficult, if not impossible, to differentiate between a broader term used synonymously for a narrower term and a shortened form of the narrower term.

5. In compound terms the preferred mode of abbreviation is that of omitting one element.

6. Contextual abbreviation or reduction is pragmatically conditioned. Certain text forms do not permit variation in designation, in others it is accepted practice and therefore expected. Any analysis must be based on text types.

The following examples of compound contraction show a number of variants that have been identified by Hope (1984) in a manual, which by its instructive function would normally be expected to use stylistic variation very sparingly:

Pattern: 1–2–3–4 ⇒ 1–3–4 ⇒ 3–4
dynamo strap clamp bolt ⇒ dynamo clamp bolt ⇒ clamp bolt

Pattern: 1–2–3–4 ⇒ 2–3–4 ⇒ 4
gearbox end cover gasket ⇒ end cover gasket ⇒ gasket
standard air filter unit ⇒ air filter unit ⇒ unit
gearbox final drive sprocket ⇒ final drive sprocket ⇒ sprocket

Pattern: 1–2–3–4 ⇒ 1–3–4 ⇒ 2–3–4 ⇒ 4
non-return ball valve assembly ⇒ non-return valve assembly ⇒
     ball valve assembly ⇒ assembly

Pattern: 1–2–3–4 ⇒ 1–3–4 ⇒ 4
exhaust valve lifter cable ⇒ exhaust lifter cable ⇒ cable

Pattern: 1–2–3–4 ⇒ 3–4 ⇒ 4
timing gear outrigger plate ⇒ outrigger plate ⇒ plate

Pattern: 1–2–3–4 ⇒ 2–3 ⇒ 3
gearbox end cover plate ⇒ end cover ⇒ cover

Pattern: 1–2–3 ⇒ 2–3 ⇒ 3
14mm spark plug ⇒ spark plug ⇒ plug

8.2.3 *The effect of rapid growth, change and innovation in science and technology*

The changes occurring in terminological information due to variation in usage are so rapid that it was not possible to keep reliable records before the availability of computers. We do not know in what areas or in what elements there is the greatest change over the shortest period, nor can we reliably say what effect changes or the neglect to record these changes may have on the quality of a terminological information service. Because of this uncertainty it is important to monitor change carefully and to provide facilities for this monitoring in the construction of a terminological database and its methodology. Once more is known about the rate of change and life-span of terms, it may be possible to reduce this type of information; in the meantime it is advisable to date most items of information and to plan for systematic and regular revisions of the terminological database.

8.2.4 *The dual role of English in terminology*

The evolution of science and technology is occurring at an ever-increasing pace and affects more countries and languages than ever before. Consequently we witness the double phenomenon of the wider spread of English as the dominant medium of scientific and technological communication and the parallel development of terminologies in other languages such that in some areas there is an extended co-existence of terminology in English and another language. At the same time there is continued and growing uncertainty about English language terminology developed in the different parts of the monolingual English speaking world which leads to competing and sometimes conflicting English terminology. It also happens, of course, that there are conflicting and competing English language terminologies in English as an international language. This occurs when, for example, a Japanese innovation is made known outside Japan in English in parallel to a French or German development in the same field which is also made known to the world at large in English. In such cases only time can settle whether all English terms survive independently, whether one becomes a country- or product-conditioned synonym of another or whether only one will eventually outlive the others.

English thus has a dual function, that of a national language to a number of speech communities in Australia, Canada, the United Kingdom, the United States etc. and as an international vehicular language or lingua franca for scientific journals, congresses etc. While this dual role is not exclusive to English—French, German, Russian, Arabic have similar dual roles—the international use of English is so widespread that it affects the coherence of terminology in English, which therefore has to be handled with extreme care.

8.3 Terminology processing centres

Since term banks are changing all the time, it is impossible to give here a satisfactory description which is not out of date within a matter of months. Several descriptions of term banks exist (Sager & McNaught 1981, Rondeau 1982, Bennett et al 1986) and the reader is referred to these and more recent up-dates. The bibliography also gives a comprehensive list of relevant publications.

The term banks used as examples and referred to in previous chapters and here are briefly listed in alphabetical order of their acronyms. No reflection is intended on their relative importance:

BTQ, Banque de terminologie du Québec
OWNER: Office de la language française, Gouvernement du Québec
HOLDINGS: Bilingual (French–English) general language words and specialised terminology

CEZEAUTERM
OWNER: Université de Clermont, France
HOLDINGS: Originally, terminology of soil mechanics, now expanded to cover a wider range

DANTERM
OWNER: Schools of Economics & Languages, Copenhagen
HOLDINGS: Multilingual specialised terminology in Scandinavian languages, English, French, German, Spanish

EURODICAUTOM
OWNER: Commission of the European Communities, Brussels & Luxembourg
HOLDINGS: Multilingual terminology of the nine official EC languages in all areas of concern to the Commission

LEXIS
OWNER: Bundessprachenamt, Huerth, FGR
HOLDINGS: Predominantly bilingual terminology in many language pairs, notably German–English, German–French, German–Italian, German–Spanish, for the translation services of the Government of the Federal Republic of Germany

NORMATERM
OWNER: Institut français de normalisation, Paris
HOLDINGS: The terminology of French standards and of ISO standards documents in French and English

TEAM
OWNER: Siemens AG, München
HOLDINGS: Specialised terminology of relevance to the firm's range of products and services in all the languages required for their business; also terminology of network partners, e.g. the motor industry

TERMIUM
OWNER: Secretary of State, Canada
HOLDINGS: All terminology required for the translation services of this bilingual administration; increasingly also other languages are being added.

The diversity among existing term banks is neither theoretical nor ideological but caused by the different purposes which determined their creation.

Originally, the strongest demand for term banks came from the need of large translation departments in government and industry and it appears that translation needs alone can justify the expenditure that is required for the regular maintenance of term banks. Other term banks are small by comparison and do not seem to get the funding which they would need to grow and avoid obsolescence. But translation needs themselves differ as do the circumstances in which translations are required.

Regular translation from several source languages into a single target language is optimally served by uni-directional dictionaries and consequently by a particular type of term bank, e.g. LEXIS. On the other hand, the regular translation from one source language into several target languages, as, for instance, required by an exporting firm, equally determines the design of a term bank, e.g. TEAM. The third case, that of EURODICAUTOM of the European Communities, requires a service that assists translators to translate from any one official language to any other while at the same time maintaining full parallelism of text since all official languages of the member states of the European Communities have equal status in law. Another special case is that of bilingual countries, e.g. TERMIUM of the Federal Canadian Government.

A second group of term banks is motivated by the needs of language planning, as in the case of the term bank of the Office de la langue française in Québec. In order to maintain French in Québec as an authentic, living language with the ability to expand and regenerate itself in a dominant English-language environment, it is essential to support all human activities involving language with up-to-date vocabularies. These have to be collected from their producers in a continuous effort which can only be sustained by means of a term bank.

Another major development in term banks is under way in standardisation organisations. Here there are a number of simultaneous needs: to keep track of the vocabulary used in standards and especially standards glossaries, to have an index to a complex database and reference to the definitions of the terms, to facilitate the full linguistic control of the regular up-dating required of standards which affect the vocabulary used in other standards, and finally, to assist in international standardisation where agreement on terminology is both the first and last hurdle that has to be overcome.

8.3.1 *The production of terminological collections*

There is no comparative description available of the many different methods used in the production of terminological glossaries, dictionaries and term banks. In fact there is no single published methodology in Europe which can claim to be in regular use as a model for terminology compilation. In Canada a succession of manuals has been published which are based on practical experience and are being used for actual terminology compilation. The same observation applies to lexicography, in which field methods seem to be guarded like craft or guild secrets that can only be acquired in each separate instance through a long apprenticeship. In an area where theory and practice seem to differ quite widely and where commercial interests are very strong, this may not be surprising. It is a theoretical premise that dictionaries are original creations representing one compiler's selection of lexical items, his definitions, his examples etc. and his structure of the dictionary. Pursuing this premise of originality and individuality, there would, of course, be no possibility of a methodology of wider applicability. In practice, dictionary makers heavily rely on each other's work, even to the extent of direct copying.

In terminology, on the other hand, there are some theoretical foundations which are, however, rarely if ever applicable in practice. In the production of terminological collections, theoretically founded methodologies require the exploration of conceptual fields, their delimitation and structuring at the conceptual level before any linguistic material is being considered and processed. This approach is unrealistic and impossible to apply in practice since terminology processing has many different motivations and the starting point is frequently a set of existing terms for which information is to be collected and around which other terms are to be assembled so as to represent a coherent collection. The criteria for cohesion can vary considerably and may indeed be determined by explorations of a conceptual structure but may equally well emerge from the confines of a corpus of texts. It is also well known that entire dictionaries have been copied more or less uncritically into term banks in order to provide an initial working mass in any one subject field.

Nor is there, as yet, a clear profile of the producer of terminological information since the training of practising terminologist is still largely in the hands of the organisations which employ them. Only in Canada can one speak of a body of independently trained professionals who work as terminologists, but their scope of employment and therefore the training structure are still rather limited. In Europe short courses in terminology have been introduced as part of translators training degrees, and a few specialist diploma courses have also been initiated. In most countries and organisations, however, the training occurs on the job and, as in so many new developments, most workers in terminology are converts, from translation, technical writing, language teaching and now also from computer science and computational linguistics. Some organisations feel that the direct contribution made to term bank development by the translator-users has been most beneficial because it has concentrated the work of development on what users need. To involve translators in the making of dictionaries is in fact a development which receives encouragement from new trends in machine-aided translation where translators are required to build up dictionary entries for systems according to very specific rules.

In the absence of a systematically trained profession and clearly documented methodologies the production of terminological information proceeds along different paths as required by each organisation that collects and processes terminology. There is no comparative survey of existing technical dictionaries but several descriptions exist of term banks. Building up these term banks was carried out largely in direct response to user needs so that separate areas of special subject vocabulary were explored in succession and only at a later date were attempts made to round off a subject or complete the search for equivalents for a particular language pair. There is no uniform attitude to the nature of data to be collected or to the degree of selection, annotation and editing required for a complete terminological record. Planners of term banks have certain optimal records in mind when they design their database, but very few can report that they have systematically completed each relevant data field in each of their records. This is a clear indication that term banks can satisfactorily function on much less information than theoretical positions would require.

8.3.2 *Existing collections: common content & exchange*

Terminological data come from two broad types of sources:
– The vast majority comes from existing, original, monolingual texts; in this case the selection criteria for the terminologist are containment and representativeness.
– A fair number of terms, however, are translation equivalents, the occurrence of which in an original monolingual text cannot be proved; they may have been taken from dictionaries or they may have been created for the purpose of translation. This type of term is valid only if there is no second language term in existence with a range of meaning identical to that of the first language term. Even then, such a term may lose its validity if at a later stage another term is created by someone with greater authority than the person who created the first translation equivalent. Such terms must be considered as temporary entries.

There is no point in attempting to produce a survey of existing holdings of term banks since their contents grow very fast and the updating and revision processes regularly change the quantity and quality of contents. Purely quantitative descriptions are meaningless because they cannot give details of the completeness of each record. Qualitative assessments are equally uninformative since quality criteria must vary with user expectations. It has been known for term banks who simultaneously pursue an acquisition and revision process to report overall negative growth of separate records and at the same time an increase in the completeness and therefore the quality of records. There are some partial surveys of terminological holdings in machine readable form and necessarily incomplete descriptions of their content. The value of such reports is strictly limited in time and to the specific purpose which motivated them.

There is a tendency to believe that time and effort can be saved by taking over existing collections. Experience so far seems to indicate that collections are so diverse that little benefit can be derived from large scale data exchanges. This is particularly true for monolingual collections; in bi- or multilingual collections translation equivalents may be of interest but even in this situation, the mode of annotation, for e.g. truncation, or indexing of individual terms, may not permit a direct transfer.

There are several established methods of acquiring data:
– in-house development with or without expert validation,
– exchange with other term banks,
– joint development with others,
– cession from partners or users,
– outside development against payment,
– purchase of existing data in conventional form,
– collaboration with publishers.

8.3.3 *Structural differences between term banks*

Many of the classification criteria for differentiating term banks found in the literature are artificial and more the result of deliberate attempts to find differences than genuine differences in structure and function. The following criteria of differentiation have been used:

– Type of entry: word vs. word and phrase.
There need be no difference between the two techniques as long as phrasal entries are retrievable via key words. With adequate retrieval techniques there is no reason why there should not be substantial collections of frequent collocations which can be of great service to translators. The storage of parallel texts may also be justified in such cases as legislation or regulations which are valid in several languages. Difficulties may arise if in response to a request via a key word a sentence is retrieved which cannot be matched with a sentence in a second language, unless this is a translation. Translated sentence pairs may give too restricted a meaning of a term and do not satisfy the general requirement that each term be documented fully in its source language.

– Concept vs. term-based term banks.
Such a distinction is artificial since the headwords of all entries are terms

which more or less closely or exclusively represent a concept. Homographs can be differentiated by subject codes and this is common practice in term banks; whether synonyms are listed separately is a matter of the function of the term bank. The distinction becomes real in printed dictionaries with a single output format but is irrelevant in term banks which can use varied retrieval techniques.

– Definition vs. context.

There is no real dichotomy between definition and context because they serve quite different functions. A definition can explain the meaning of a term and by limiting its extension indicate its area of usage. Several definitions may be required for different subject fields and are themselves genuine contexts if they are chosen from existing texts. To serve a defining function contexts would have to be much more extensive than they usually are or indeed be chosen among paraphrases of a term. Contexts on the other hand give an indication of the appropriateness of a term in a particular linguistic environment. If there is little guidance on the choice of appropriate definitions, there is even less agreement on permitted or desirable contexts. In bilingual or multilingual term banks parallel contexts are sometimes derived from existing translations or even constructed for the occasion without validation by real textual evidence. Relatively few term banks regularly provide both definitions and context, because they are the most time-consuming data items to create. Most will admit a preference for one or the other, in accordance with the needs of their main users or the data they mainly process.

– Number of languages.

There need be no structural difference between mono- and bilingual or multilingual term banks if second or third language translation equivalents are simply treated as such and constitute a separate data field which is closely related to the corresponding data field of the first language.

– Directionality of language orientation.

This is a genuine distinction since there is a need for term banks with fully reversible entries, e.g. in a bilingual or multilingual context of full equality of all languages and where tools are required to assist translation from any one into any of the other languages. In all other cases term banks are directional in the sense that they have a monolingual database with translation equivalents which may then have pointers to another monolingual database which gives the full range of information on a 'homonymous' term in that language.

It must be recognised that a number of terms may only exist as translation equivalents, e.g. the names of offices and institutions of a particular country, a title, a measurement. On the other hand a term chosen as a translation equivalent may not entirely match the definition of the first language. The degree of matching must then be indicated in a note, as well as the contexts in which the use is appropriate, e.g. the English 'waste' = German 'Müll – Abfall'. Genuine standardisation can overcome some of the difficulties created by translation.

– Method of access.
At one time it was felt that a significant difference existed between term banks consulted in batch-mode and those consulted on-line. Such a difference is only relevant if it is meant to indicate a difference in the flexibility of the information retrieval facilities available. It is now considered common practice to provide for on-line access to term banks, even though for certain types of look-up a batch printout may indeed be considered a useful first approach. Hard copy output produced in batch-mode has the advantage that it can be used to annotate data that a user considers inadequate or incorrect and that such annotations can be used to improve the database.

8.3.4 *Cooperation among term banks and other terminology producers*

Despite regular meetings and good friendly relations between them, there has traditionally been relatively little cooperation among term banks because they were set up for specific functions and accordingly organised in such ways that cooperation was not considered likely. Attempts at data exchange have not been very successful and cooperation in data development is not being actively pursued because of the different nature of their purpose and holdings and because of the difficulties encountered in determining genuine compatibility of data. Incompatibility consists largely in the different definitions of data categories which were established with specific user groups and uses in mind. Data exchanges fail because of the missing common theoretical basis that also prevents sharing of resources in lexicography. Joint data development does not succeed for the same reasons and because of the difficulties involved in the forward planning necessary for this form of cooperation. In practice, term banks know the contents of each others' collections and where appropriate access each others' databases.

In recent years access to the large term banks has been made available to a wider range of users than originally intended and this has produced in

some cases a reassessment of the structure of the information and in others a considerable widening of the content. There are three different approaches:
– copies of the magnetic tape are made available to other users;
– outside users gain on-line access;
– a more complex pattern of sharing of resources is developed whereby subsets of the term bank are made available in return for terminology developed by a partner; in other instances terminology is processed free in return for the term bank's use of the data.

Small term banks currently under development have from the outset stated that they would wish to pursue a policy of joint terminology development and view cooperation in terms of sharing work both by languages and by subject fields. Since their design is for multipurpose use this kind of division of labour is possible. Small term banks have also attempted to describe and define their data capture techniques in such a way that both data exchange and incorporation of data prepared elsewhere is possible. While there are no common data records, file structures nor data-capture procedures, there is enough compatibility to make cooperation a real possibility.

8.3.5 *Other developments*

Beside the large term banks, many smaller term banks have been set up in recent years, but lacking strong financial backing, their development is rather slow and very few can claim a full user service. They are on the whole more flexible in conception, attempt to combine certain theoretical assumptions with practical requirements, and so extend the general usefulness of their work, and also benefit from new hardware and software developments.

In addition, many translation companies, industrial firms and government departments are developing small terminological collections on microcomputers and wordprocessors for personal use or for use by a small circle of users. These collections are usually put together in simple list form only; they lack systematic structure and are probably not usable beyond the very limited sphere of application for which they were intended. Nevertheless, they are indicative of a greater awareness by the general public of the existence of terminological collections, their particular nature and use and the computational means now available to provide access to dictionaries via terminals.

In lexicography there is a trend towards experimentation with existing machine-readable dictionaries. It is assumed that existing work on dictionary compilation, regardless of the degree of computer assistance or control in the production, is of sufficient merit and value for the contents of such dictionaries to be edited for re-use as a dictionary database. The same assumption could then hold for terminological collections, especially since they usually have less scope for more or less arbitrary human decisions in the selection of the content (ranges of vocabulary, number of senses, constructed examples, etc.) and for idiosyncratic editorial decisions (division of senses, sequence of elements, etc.). There is considerable potential for critical exploration of the large terminological collections. Since, unlike lexicography, this type of information has no long tradition, it would be of considerable interest to study the consistency of compilation that can be achieved with the assistance of computers, and the degree of real divergence in information gathered by different term banks.

Lastly, there are dictionary publishers who hold machine-readable terminological data either separately in the form of technical dictionaries or as part of the subject-specifically labelled entries of general dictionaries. Lexicographers have their own theoretical positions as well as their own principles and methods. Specialised lexicography does not automatically identify with theories and principles evolved under the heading of terminology, especially if these have been evolved by national or international standardisation committees. Lexicographers rarely take account of the work carried out by standardising bodies since their philosophy prejudices them against standardisation.

8.4   New uses of terminologies

Historically terminological dictionaries or glossaries have been used by such large organisations as government departments and industrial concerns as a tool for harmonising and controlling the terminology required by their technical writers and translators, either on a monolingual or multilingual basis. It was assumed that the readers of technical literature and the very few subject specialists who wrote scientific and technical articles would possess an adequate knowledge of the special language involved. There was also a certain reservation about sharing terminological information. Terminological collections were considered almost as secret sources of power, not to be shared with competitors. The uses to which collections of terminology could be put were also restricted by the medium on which terminological data were stored: The transfer of terminological data from a two-dimensional storage-medium (paper) to the more versatile and more accessible medium of the computer has made terminology more suitable for other uses. These include the possibility of using terminologies as a teaching aid both in technical subjects and Languages for Special Purposes, the possibility of using a term bank as a reference work (i.e. like a machine-readable encyclopaedia) and the possibility of using terminologies as input to artificial intelligence systems.

This diversification of uses coupled with the ease with which machine-readable data can be manipulated has created the desire to pool terminological data. Since conventional terminological research is a very time-consuming activity, even at the most basic level of a translator searching for a suitable equivalent for a term in a foreign language, there is now a greater will to share, sell and exchange terminologies and the view of terminology as the private property of its compiler is dying out. Large-scale term banks are actively engaged in investigating the means for data exchange and ISO has developed a standard tape format to this end. The exchange of terminological data is one of the most frequently recurring topics at international meetings involving term bank organisers and a major factor in the design of term record formats for new term bank projects is compatibility with existing terminological data banks.

At the individual level, micro-computer technology has been widely introduced into the every-day work of translators in the form of suitable word-processing software. This has created the need for and has led to the development of microcomputer-based glossary-building and terminology-processing software. Translators who previously had private terminology collections in card files are now converting those terminologies into machine-readable form for their own use and also for exchange with colleagues. A need therefore exists for the development of simple software which can be used by translators for building small glossaries. There is no reason why such private collections could not, after suitable vetting and record completion, be integrated into a large-scale term bank for more widespread dissemination. This possibility strengthens the case for versatile and widely compatible software.

The development of computer networks, both public and private, has resulted in the greater availability of many term banks. EURODICAUTOM is available both via EURONET-DIANE and ECHO. In Canada TERMIUM is widely available on-line and a complete CD-ROM version was issued in 1990. CD-ROM held dictionaries and terminologies are coming on the market and will eventually be priced like technical dictionaries and other developments are in progress. At the same time the low cost of magnetic media and higher concentration of storage make it possible to distribute copies of a data base. Copies of subsets of TEAM, for example, are widely distributed to other industrial users in several countries. It is as yet uncertain whether networks or distribution of copies is likely to be the more popular means of gaining access to terminological information.

Because information on scientific and technological innovation is being provided on a wider scale than ever before, through the full range of modern media, the need for a terminological information service for the general reader and new modes of access to such a service are likely to come into being. With the growth of technological education more individuals in society become better educated and there is then a further demand to spread scientific and technical knowledge to a yet wider public. In industry in particular, there is a growing need for personnel at all levels to have access to terminology of a high standard and machine-readable terminology can satisfy this demand.

As a result of the wider spread of scientific and technological information to non-specialists, there will then also be a need for an intermediate scientific and technical vocabulary for use by non-specialists and laymen. Such an intermediate vocabulary should be designed systematically in order to make it easier to understand scientific concepts. The concomitant increase in textbooks, teach-yourself manuals, popular scientific journals etc. will stimulate a demand for popular-scientific terminology information services. Their chief characteristics are likely to be popular encyclopaedic definitions with graphic displays and charts or other diagrams showing terms in relation to other terms. The creation of Teletext-type services makes this feasible. The simultaneous expansion of the home-computer market also has implications for the creation of terminologies oriented towards a mass market.

8.4.1 *Terminology in machines*

At the other extreme, advances in natural language processing (NLP) have meant that the end-user of terminology may not necessarily be a human being. There is a need for high-quality, machine-readable terminological data for input to:
– machine translation/machine-assisted translation systems,
– spelling-checkers and other office-automation tools,
– information retrieval systems,
– natural-language front-ends to databases,
– expert systems and knowledge-based systems,
– Other natural language processing systems.
Currently all these systems require some sort of dictionary or thesaurus which is usually developed specifically and separately for each application. In the

case of machine translation systems this may mean three separate dictionaries for analysis, transfer and synthesis respectively. There is consequently a considerable duplication of effort.

The dictionary requirements of many NLP systems are not intrinsically complex, even though the representation of data is far more formal and hence more detailed and explicit than is necessary for human consumption. Because of the high development cost of dictionaries there is a growing desire amongst the developers of NLP systems to pool lexical resources. Developers of machine translation systems are already planning a rationalisation of dictionaries but their efforts are directed towards system-internal solutions rather than towards using other machine-readable collections. The majority of other NLP systems currently in use or under construction are experimental in nature and therefore cover a very small subset of knowledge; their technical dictionary problems are as yet insignificant but their designers are becoming increasingly aware of these problems. As attempts are made to build more global systems, the decreasing cost of processing power, coupled with the relatively high cost of building up new terminological collections, will motivate the utilisation of existing terminologies for building NLP technical lexicons. Research would therefore be timely into the full range of possible and foreseeable specialised dictionary requirements of NLP systems as a prerequisite for planning a suitably comprehensive record to contain most of the information they need, even though the physical and logical representation might require conversion from application to application.

The trend towards greater natural language involvement in various information technology applications, which would enable a larger number of direct users to access information via the language they most commonly use, puts greater pressure on terminology compilers in two directions: they must cover a wider range of linguistic variants in order to ensure retrieval or response success while at the same time striving towards some form of harmonisation of designations in order not to lose control over an ever-increasing set of terms.

BIBLIOGRAPHY

This bibliography lists all the sources which have contributed to the formulation of the ideas and observations in this book. They are here grouped according to the main aspects of the subject field. The interdisciplinary nature of the field is reflected in the overlap of the divisions, and in the numerical cross-referencing of the works listed. For items contained in a collection, the special reference number (on the right) indicates where full details of the collection would be found.

MAIN DIVISIONS

1. **Concepts and concept systems**: Theories of concepts and concept formation, and the relationship between concepts, linguistic signs and extralinguistic reality. For general writings on semantic theory see Section 7. #[001–034].
2. **Terminography**: The scope of terminology, the methods, types and problems of definition (especially terminological definitions), term identification and delimitation, terminological relationships, and standardization. #[035–101].
3. **Lexicography**: Theoretical issues in lexicography, typology of dictionaries, lexicographic definition and bilingual lexicography. #[102–155].
4. **Lexical data processing**: Dictionary databases, lexical databases, automated processing of dictionary information, computational morphology, analysis and extraction of information from definitions, lexical aspects of NLP. #[156–212].
5. **Termbank design and implementation**: A general section is followed by separate references on individual data banks. #[213–266].
6. **Information Science**: A selective list of titles on document retrieval systems, information retrieval techniques and tools and thesauri of relevance to terminology. #[267–300].
7. **General linguistic aspects**: Communication theory, LSP, semiotics, special subject languages, semantics, synonymy, word- and term-formation. #[301–360].
8. **Dictionaries and standards**: This section contains only dictionaries and standards cited in the book. #[361–390].

1. CONCEPTS AND CONCEPT SYSTEMS

[001] BALDINGER, K. (1957) *Die Semasiologie: Versuch eines Überblicks*. Deutsche Akademie der Wissenschaften zu Berlin. Vorträge und Schriften, Heft 61. Berlin: Akademie-Verlag, 1957.

[002] BALDINGER, K. (1964) 'Sémasiologie et onomasiologie.' In: *Revue de linguistique romane*, juillet–décembre 1964.

[003] BOLTON, N. (1977) *Concept Formation*. Oxford: Pergamon Press.

[004] CARNAP, R. (1956a) 'The methodological character of theoretical concepts.' Reprinted In: ZABEEH et al., *Readings in Semantics*. Urbana, Chicago & London: University of Illinois Press.

[005] CARNAP, R. (1956b) *Meaning and Necessity*. 2nd edition. Chicago.

[006] CHAFE, W. (1970) *Meaning and the Structure of Language*. Chicago: University of Chicago Press.

[007] DAHLBERG, I. (1978) 'A referent-oriented, analytical concept theory of INTERCONCEPT.' In: *International Classification* 5 (1978), No. 3, pp. 142–151.

[008] GIBSON (1966) *The Senses Considered as Perceptual Systems*. Boston: Houghton Mifflin.

[009] GIBSON (1979) *The Ecological Approach to Visual Perception*. Boston: Houghton Mifflin.

[010] GRICE, H.P. (1957) 'Meaning.' In: *Philosophical Review*. Vol. LXVI-1957, 277–388. Ithaka, New York.

[011] HANFMANN, E. & VAKAR, G. (1962) *Thought and Language*. (Abridged & edited translation of Vygotskii's *Myshlenie i rech'*, with introduction by J.S. BRUNER and preface by the translators). Cambridge, Massachusetts: M.I.T. Press.

[012] HEMPEL, C.G. (1952) *Fundamentals of Concept Formation in Empirical Science*. Chicago, 1952, u.o.

[013] HERVEY, S.G.J. (1979) *Axiomatic Semantics*. Edinburgh: Scottish Academic Press.

[014] HORECKÝ, J. (1982) 'Zu Bedeutungsbeziehungen zwischen den terminologischen Benennungen.' In: *Fachsprache* 4/2 (1982), pp. 50–54.

[015] JOHNSON, R.L. & SAGER, J.C. (1980) 'Standardization of terminology in a model of communication.' In: SAGER, J.C. (ed.) (1980:81–104). [089]

[016] KATZ, J.J. & FODOR, J.A. (1963) 'The structure of a semantic theory.' In: *Language* 39, pp. 170–210.

[017] KELLY, G.A. (1955) *The Psychology of Personal Constructs*. (2 volumes). New York: Norton.

[018] KOCH, S. (1941) 'The logical character of the motivation concept.' In: *Psychological Review*, XLVIII (1941).

[019] KUHN, T.S. (1979) 'Metaphor in Science.' In: *Metaphor and Thought*, A. ORTONY (ed.), pp. 409–419. Cambridge: Cambridge University Press.

[020] LAKOFF, G. (1987) 'Cognitive models and prototype theory.' In: NEISSER, U. (ed.) (1987), pp. 63–100. [024]

[021] MEDIN, D.L. & WATTENMAKER, W.D. (1987) 'Category cohesiveness, theories and cognitive archeology.' In: NEISSER, U. (ed.) (1987), pp. 25–62. [024]

[022] MURPHY, G.L. & MEDIN, D.L. (1985) 'The role of theories in conceptual coherence.' In: *Psychological Review* 92, pp. 298–316.

[023] NEISSER, U. (1987) 'From direct perception to conceptual structure.' In: NEISSER, U. (ed.) (1987), pp. 11–24. [024]

[024] NEISSER, U. (ed.) (1987) *Concepts and Conceptual Development: Ecological and Intellectual Factors in Categorization*. Emory Symposia in Cognition 1. Cambridge University Press.

[025] OGDEN, C.K. & RICHARDS, I.A. (1923) *The Meaning of Meaning*. London: Routledge & Kegan Paul.

[026] QUINE, W. (1960) *Word and Object*. Cambridge, Mass.: The M.I.T. Press.

[027] ROSCH, E. & MERVIS, C. (1975) 'Family resemblances: Studies in the internal structure of categories.' In: *Cognitive Psychology* 7, pp. 573–605.

[028] ROSCH, E. (1978) 'Principles of categorization.' In: *Cognition and Categorization*, ROSCH, E. & LLOYD, B.B. (eds.). Hillsdale, NJ: Erlbaum.

[029] ROSCH, E.; MERVIS, C.G.; GRAY, W.D.; JOHNSON, D.M. & BOYES-BRAEM, P. (1976) 'Basic objects in natural categories.' In: *Cognitive Psychology* 8, pp. 382–439.

[030] STRAWSON, P.F. (1950) 'On referring.' In: *Mind* 59, pp. 320–44. Reprinted in PARKINSON, G.H.R. (1968) *The Theory of Meaning*. pp. 86–109. Oxford University Press.

[031] VINACKE, W.E. (1952) *The Psychology of Thinking*. New York: McGraw-Hill.

[032] VYGOTSKY, L.S. (1962) *Thought and Language*. (Edited and translated by E. HANFMANN & G. VAKAR). Cambridge, Massachsetts: M.I.T. Press.

[033] WÜSTER, E. (1959/60) 'Das Worten der Welt, schaubildlich und terminologisch dargestellt.' In: *Sprachforum* 3 (3/4), pp. 183–204.

[034] WÜSTER, E. (1974) 'Die Umkehrung einer Begriffsbeziehung und ihre Kennzeichnung in Wörterbüchern (The inversion of a relation of concepts and its representation in dictionaries).' In: *Nachrichten für Dokumentation* 25 (6), pp. 256–263.

2. TERMINOGRAPHY

[035] AFNOR (1967) *Principes généraux de terminologie*. Règles générales pour l'élaboration des vocabulaires techniques. NF X 03-001.

[036] AILA (Association Internationale de Linguistique Appliquee) (1978) *Table Ronde sur les Problèmes du Découpage du Terme en Terminologie*. 5e Congrès International de Linguistique Appliquée, Montréal 20–26 août 1978, RONDEAU, G. (ed.). Montréal: Office de la Langue Française.

[037] AUGER, P. (1978) 'La syntagmatique terminologique, typologie des syntagmes et limite des modèles en structure complexe.' In: AILA (1978:9–26). [036]

[038] BAAKES, K. (1984) *Theorie und Praxis der Terminologieforschung: Deutsch-Englisch am Beispiel der Umformtechnik in der Metalbearbeitung.* Heidelberg: Julius Groos.

[039] BOULANGER, J.-C. (1978) 'Non-term and term: Commentaire de Jean-Claude BOULANGER.' In: AILA (1978:169–182). [036]

[040] BS 3669 (1963) *Recommendations for the Selection, Formation, and Definition of Technical Terms.* London: British Standards Institution.

[041] CZAP, H. & GALINSKI, C. (eds.) (1987) *Terminology and Knowledge Engineering.* Proceedings. International Congress on Terminology and Knowledge Engineering, 29 Sept.–1 Oct. 1987. University of Trier, FRG. Frankfurt/M.: INDEKS Verlag, 1987.

[042] CZAP, H. & GALINSKI, C. (eds.) (1988) *Terminology and Knowledge Engineering.* Supplement. Proceedings. International Congress on Terminology and Knowledge Engineering, 29 Sept.–1 Oct. 1987. University of Trier, FRG. Frankfurt/M.: INDEKS Verlag, 1988.

[043] DAHLBERG, I. (1979) 'On the structure of definitions.' In: INFOTERM (1981: 568–570). [067]

[044] DAHLBERG, I. (1983) 'Terminological definitions: Characteristics and demands.' In: DUQUET-PICARD, D. (ed.) (1983:15–34). [053]

[045] DAVIDSON, J. (1980) 'Identifying a term or terminology unit.' In: *L'Actualité Terminologique* 13/9 (1980), pp. 1–2.

[046] DIN 820 Pt 1 (1974) *Standardization Procedure: Principles.*

[047] DIN 820 Pt 3 (1975) *Standardization Procedure: Definitions.*

[048] DIN 820 Pt 4 (1974) *Standardization Procedure: Working Procedure.*

[049] DROZD, L. (1978) 'Non-term and term.' In: AILA (1978:117–131). [036]

[050] DUBOIS, J. (1966) 'Les problèmes du vocabulaire technique.' In: *Cahiers de lexicologie* 9 (2), 1966, pp. 103–112. Paris: Didier Larousse.

[051] DUBUC, R. (1978) *Manuel pratique de terminologie.* Montréal: Linguatech.

[052] DUBUC, R. (1978a) 'Découpage de l'unité terminologique.' In: AILA (1978: 53–64). [036]

[053] DUQUET-PICARD, D. (ed.) (1983) *Problèmes de la définition et de la synonymie en terminologie.* Actes du Colloque International de Terminologie. Université Laval, Québec, 23–27 mai 1982. GIRSTERM.

[054] DURAND, A. (1986) 'Vers une nouvelle gestion de la terminologie contrôlée.' In: *TermNet News* 14, Journal of the International Network for Terminology (TermNet), Edition spéciale sur la France, pp. 18–20.

[055] FELBER, H. (1979) 'The Vienna School of Terminology: Fundamentals and its theory.' In: INFOTERM (1981:69–86). [067]

[056] FELBER, H. (1980) 'International standardization of terminology: Theoretical and methodological aspects.' In: SAGER, J.C. (ed.) (1980:65–79). [089]

[057] FELBER, H. (1983) 'The international activities of Infoterm and the TermNet programs.' In: INTERRANTE, C.G. & HEYMANN, F.J. (eds.) (1983:46–55). [069]

[058] FELBER, H. (1984) *Terminology Manual.* Paris: Unesco and Infoterm.

[059] FRAWLEY, W. (1982) 'Aspects of metaphorical definition in the sciences.' In: *Dictionaries* 4. Journal of the Dictionary Society of North America, BAILEY, R.W. (ed.), (1982), pp. 118–150.

[060] FRONTARD, R. (1979) 'Normalisation et terminologie.' In: *Courier de la normalisation* 43 (1976), p.250.

[061] GIRSTERM (1983) *Problèmes de la définition et de la synonymie en terminologie.* Actes du Colloque international de terminologie, Université Laval, mai 1982.

[062] GOFFIN, R. (1976) 'La recherche terminologique: des réalités du métier à son apprentissage.' In: *Terminologies* 76. Colloque internationale. Paris – La Défense, 15–18 juin 1976. AFTERM (Association Française de Terminologie). Paris: La Maison du Dictionnaire.

[063] GOFFIN, R. (1978) 'Le découpage du terme à des fins lexicographiques: Critères formels, sémantiques, quantitatifs et taxinomiques.' In: AILA (1978: 157–168). [036]

[064] GREENFIELD, C.C. & SERAIN, D. (1977) *Machine-Aided Translation: From Terminology Banks to Interactive Translation Systems.* Carnegie Mellon University/ IRIA. August 1977.

[065] GUILBERT, L. (1973) 'La spécificité du terme scientifique et technique.' In: *Langue française* 17, février 1973, pp. 5–17. Paris: Larousse.

[066] IAT (1982) *Termia News Bulletin* 1 (1), 1982, p.4. International Association for Terminology.

[067] INFOTERM (1981) *Theoretical and Methodological Problems of Terminology.* Proceedings of an International Symposium, Moscow 27–30 November 1979. Infoterm Series 6. München: K.G. Saur.

[068] INFOTERM (1986) *Networking in Terminology.* International Co-operation in Terminology Work. Proceedings. Second Infoterm Symposium. Vienna, 14–17 April 1985. Infoterm Series 8. München: K.G. Saur.

[069] INTERRANTE, C.G. & HEYMANN, F.J. (eds.) (1983) *Standardization of Technical Terminology: Principles and Practices.* ASTM STP 806, American Society for Testing and Materials.

[070] IRIS, M.A.; LITOWITZ, B.E. & EVENS, M. (1988) 'Problems of the part–whole relation.' In: EVENS, M.W. (ed.) (1988: 261–288). [312]

[071] ISO (1983) *Magnetic Tape Exchange Format for Terminological/Lexicographical Records (MATER)*, ISO/DIS 6156, April 1983.

[072] ISO 704 (1986) *Principles and Methods of Terminology.* International Organization for Standardization.

[073] ISO/R 1087 (1969) *The Vocabulary of Terminology.* Geneva: International Organization for Standardization.

[074] ISO/R 704 (1968) *Naming Principles.* International Organization for Standardization.

[075] JEFFREY, C. (1977) *Biological Nomenclature*, 2nd edition, London: Edward Arnold.

[076] KOCOUREK R. (1978) 'Commentary on the report "Non-terms and terms" by L. Drozd.' In: AILA (1978: 141–155). [036]

[077] MASSUDI, S. (1985) *The Use and Representation of Conceptual Relationships in a Terminological Data Bank.* Final Year Dissertation. Manchester, CCL/UMIST.

[078] MANUILA, A. & MANUILA, L. (1965) 'Guide de la lexicographie médicale.' In: *CIOMS. Terminologie et lexicographie médicales.* pp. 43–59. Paris: Masson et Cie.

[079] NKWENTI-AZEH, B. (1989) *An Investigation into the Structure of the Terminological Information Contained in Special Language Dictionaries.* PhD Thesis. University of Manchester.

[080] OLF (1979) *Actes du 6ème colloque international de terminologie—Québec (Pointe-au-Pic) du 2 au 6 octobre 1977.* Office de la Langue Française. Editeur Officiel du Québec, 1979.

[081] OPITZ, K. (1983b) 'The terminological/standardised dictionary.' In: HARTMANN, R.R.K. (ed.) (1983:163–180). [127]

[082] PUGH, J.M. (1984) *A Contrastive Conceptual Analysis and Classification of Complex Noun Terms in English, French and Spanish with Special Reference to the Field of Data Processing.* PhD Thesis. University of Manchester.

[083] RONDEAU, G. (1980) 'Terminologie et documentation.' In: *META* 25 (1), pp. 152–170.

[084] RONDEAU, G. (1981) *Introduction à la terminologie.* Montréal: Centre éducatif et culturel.

[085] RONDEAU, G. (ed.) (1979a) *Table ronde sur les problèmes du découpage du terme* (Commission de Terminologie de l'AILA), O.L.F., Montréal.

[086] ROUSSEAU, L.-J. (1978) 'La syntagmatique terminologique.' Commentaire de Louis-Jean ROUSSEAU. In: AILA (1978:27–36). [036]

[087] SAGER, J.C. (1978) 'La syntagmatique terminologique.' Commentary by Prof. J.C. SAGER. In: AILA (1978:37–52). [036]

[088] SAGER, J.C. (1983) 'Terminology and the technical dictionary.' In: HARTMANN, R.R.K. (ed.) (1984:315–326). [128]

[089] SAGER, J.C. (ed.) (1980) *Standardization of Nomenclature.* Special issue of *International Journal of the Sociology of Language* 23. The Hague: Mouton.

[090] SANDERS, T.B.R. (1976) *Objectifs et principes de la normalisation.* Geneva.

[091] SMITH, R. (1981) 'On defining adjectives, Part III.' In: *Dictionaries* 3. Journal of the Dictionary Society of North America, pp. 28–38.

[092] STEARN, W.T. (1983) *Botanical Latin.* 3rd edition revised. London: David Charles.

[093] STOCK, P. (1988) 'The structure and function of definitions.' In: SNELL-HORNBY, M. (ed.) (1988:81–89). [150]

[094] STREHLOW, R.A. (1983) 'Terminology and the well-formed definition.' In: INTERRANTE, C.G. & HEYMANN, F.J. (eds.) (1983:15–25). [069]

[095] TERMINOMETRO (1988) *Boletín Informativo sobre Terminología, Lingüística Automatizada y Edición de Diccionarios.* Publicación trimestral de Unión Latina. Junio 1988, Número 1. Unión Latina.

[096] VINAY, J.-P. (1978) 'Problèmes de découpage du terme.' In: AILA (1978:81–100). [036]

[097] WERSIG, G. (1976) 'Probleme und Verfahren der Terminologiearbeit.' In: *Fachsprachen (Terminologie-Struktur-Normung)*. Berlin: Beuth.

[098] WHITE, J.S. (1988) 'Determination of lexical-semantic relations for multilingual terminology structures.' In: EVENS, M.W. (ed.) (1988:183–198). [312]

[099] WÜSTER, E. (1955) *Bibliography of Monolingual Scientific and Technical Glossaries*. Paris.

[100] WÜSTER, E. (1979) *Einführung in die allgemeine Terminologielehre und terminologische Lexikographie*. Wien: Springer.

[101] WÜSTER, E. (1979a) *Introduction à la théorie générale de la terminologie et à la lexicographie terminologique*. Traduit de *Einführung in die allgemeine Terminologielehre und terminologische Lexikographie*. [Traduction française par le Bureau des traductions du Canada]. Université de Laval, Québec: GIRSTERM.

3. LEXICOGRAPHY

[102] AISENSTADT, E. (1979) 'Collocability restrictions in dictionaries.' In: HARTMANN, R.R.K. (ed.) (1979:71–74). [126]

[103] AL-KASIMI, A.M. (1977) *Linguistics and Bilingual Dictionaries*. Leiden: Brill.

[104] AL-KASIMI, A.M. (1983) 'The interlingual/translation dictionary.' In: HARTMANN, R.R.K. (ed.) (1983:153–162). [127]

[105] ALEKSEEV, P.M. (1973b) 'Haufigkeitswörterbuch der englischen Subsprache der Elektronik.' In: ALEKSEEV et al. (1973:192–205). [106]

[106] ALEKSEEV, P.M.; KALININ, W.M. & PIOTROWSKI, R.G. (eds.) (1973) *Sprachstatistik*. München.

[107] AUSTIN J.L. (1975) *How To Do Things With Words*. 2nd edition. Oxford: Clarendon Press.

[108] AYERS, D.M. (1986) *English Words from Greek and Latin Elements*. 2nd edition. Tucson: University of Arizona Press.

[109] BACHRACH, J.A. (1982) 'Terminological aspects of translation.' In: *Terminology for the Eighties*. Infoterm Series 7, pp. 373–379. München: K.G. Saur.

[110] BIERWISCH, M. & KIEFER, F. (1969) 'Remarks on definitions in natural language.' In: *Studies in Syntax and Semantics*, KIEFER, F. (ed.), pp. 55–79. Dordrecht-Holland: Reidel.

[111] BREWER, A. M. & BROWNE, M. (eds.) (1982) *Dictionaries, Encyclopedia, and other Word-Related Books*. 3rd Edition, in 3 volumes. Vol. 1: English Books; Vol. 2: Multiple languages (with English as one language); Vol. 3: Non-English Books. Detroit, Michigan: Gale Research Company.

[112] COHEN, M. (1962) 'Le fait dictionnaire.' In: *Proceedings of the Ninth International Congress of Linguists*, Cambridge, Mass., pp. 497–503. La Haye: Mouton, 1964.

[113] COLLIGNON, L. & GLATIGNY, M. (1978) *Les Dictionnaires: Initiation à la Lexicographie*. Paris: CEDIC.

[114] COWIE, A.P. (1979) 'The treatment of polysemy in the design of a learner's dictionary.' In: HARTMANN, R.R.K. (ed.) (1979:82–88). [126]

[115] COWIE, A.P. (1986) 'Strategies for dealing with idioms, collocations and routine formulae in dictionaries.' In: *Workshop on Automating the Lexicon.* 15–23 May 1986, Grosseto, Italy.

[116] DEVITT, M. (1981) *Designation.* Columbia University Press/N.Y.

[117] DUBOIS, J. & DUBOIS, C. (1971) *Introduction à la lexicographie—Le dictionnaire.* Paris: Larousse.

[118] DUBS, H.H. (1943) 'Definition and its problems.' In: *Philosophical Review,* LII (1943).

[119] GEERAERTS, D. (1985) 'Les données stéréotypiques, prototypiques et encyclopédiques dans le dictionnaire.' In: *Cahiers de Lexicologie* 46 (1), 1985, pp. 27–43.

[120] GEERAERTS, D. (1987) 'Types of semantic information in dictionaries.' In: ILSON, R. (ed.) (1987:1–10). [134]

[121] GOETSCHALCKX, J. & ROLLING, L. (eds.) (1982) *Lexicography in the Electronic Age.* Proceedings of a Symposium held in Luxembourg, 7–9 July 1981. Amsterdam: North-Holland Publishing Co.

[122] GUILBERT, L. (1969) 'Dictionnaires et linguistique: Essai de typologie des dictionnaires monolingues français contemporains.' In: *Langue française* 2: Le lexique, mai 1969, 4–29. Larousse.

[123] HAAS, M.R. (1960) 'What belongs in a bilingual dictionary.' In: HOUSEHOLDER, F.W. & SAPORTA, S. (eds.) (1975:45–50). [131]

[124] HANKS, P. (1979) 'To what extent do dictionary definitions define?' In: R.R.K. HARTMANN (ed.) (1979:32–38). [126]

[125] HARRELL, R.S. (1960) 'Some notes on bilingual lexicography.' In: HOUSEHOLDER, F.W. & SAPORTA, S. (eds.) (1975:51–61). [131]

[126] HARTMANN, R.R.K. (ed.) (1979) *Dictionaries and Their Users.* Papers from the 1978 B.A.A.L. Seminar on Lexicography. Exeter Linguistic Studies, Volume 4, University of Exeter.

[127] HARTMANN, R.R.K. (ed.) (1983) *Lexicography: Principles and Practice.* London: Academic Press.

[128] HARTMANN, R.R.K. (ed.) (1984) *LEXeter'83 Proceedings.* Papers from the International Conference on Lexicography at Exeter, 9–12 September 1983. LEXICOGRAPHICA Series Maior 1. Tübingen: Max Niemeyer Verlag. 1984.

[129] HAUSMANN, F.-J. (1985) 'Chronique: F.-J. HAUSMANN, O. REICHMANN, H.-E. WIEGAND, L. ZGUSTA: Encyclopédie internationale de Lexicographie.' In: *Cahiers de Lexicologie* 46 (1), 1985, pp. 133–138.

[130] HAUSMANN, F.-J.; REICHMANN, O.; WIEGAND, H.E. & ZGUSTA, L. (1985) *Dictionaries. International Encyclopaedia of Lexicography.* (in English, French, German). Berlin, New York: Walter de Gruyter.

[131] HOUSEHOLDER, F.W. & SAPORTA, S. (eds.) (1975) *Problems in Lexicography.* Indiana University: Bloomington.

[132] IANNUCCI, J.E. (1960) 'Meaning discrimination in bilingual dictionaries.' In: HOUSEHOLDER, F.W. & SAPORTA, S. (eds.) (1975:201–216). [131]

[133] ILSON, R.F. (1987) 'Towards a taxonomy of dictionary definitions.' In: ILSON, R. (ed.) (1987:61–73). [134]

[134] ILSON, R.F. (ed.) (1987) *A Spectrum of Lexicography*. Papers from AILA Brussels 1984. Amsterdam/Philadelphia: John Benjamins Publishing Company.

[135] IMBS, P. (1960) 'Au seuil de la lexicographie.' In: *Cahiers de Lexicologie*, 1960, II, pp. 3–17.

[136] IRIS, M.A.; LITOWITZ, B.E. & EVENS, M. (1988) 'Problems of the part–whole relation.' In: EVENS, M.W. (ed.) (1988:261–288). [312]

[137] KIPFER, B.A. (1982) 'Computer applications in lexicography: A bibliography.' In: *Dictionaries* 4. Journal of the Dictionary Society of North America. BAILEY, R.W. (ed.) (1982), pp. 202–237.

[138] KNOWLES, F.E. (1983) 'Towards the machine dictionary.' In: HARTMANN, R.R.K. (ed.) (1983:181–193). [127]

[139] KNOWLES, F.E. (1984) 'Dictionaries and computers.' In: HARTMANN, R.R.K. (ed.) (1984:301–314). [128]

[140] LANDAU, S.I. (1984) *Dictionaries—The Art and Craft of Lexicography*. New York: The Scribner Press.

[141] LEXETER (1983) *LEXeter '83 Proceedings*. Papers from the International Conference on Lexicography at Exeter, 9–12 September 1983. HARTMANN, R.R.K. (ed.), LEXICOGRAPHICA Series Maior 1. Tübingen: Max Niemeyer Verlag. 1984.

[142] MALKIEL, Y. (1960) 'A typological classification of dictionaries on the basis of distinctive features.' In: HOUSEHOLDER, F.W. & SAPORTA, S. (eds.) (1975: 3–24). [131]

[143] OPITZ, K. (1983a) 'On dictionaries for special registers.' In: HARTMANN, R.R.K. (ed.) (1983:53–64). [127]

[144] REY, A. (1965) 'A propos de la définition lexicographique.' In: *Cahiers de Lexicologie* 6 (1), 1965, pp. 67–80.

[145] REY-DEBOVE, J. (1966) 'La définition lexicographique: Recherches sur l'équation sémique.' In: *Cahiers de Lexicologie* 8 (1), 1966, pp. 71–94.

[146] ROBINSON, R. (1954) *Definition*. Oxford: Clarendon Press.

[147] SCHOLFIELD, P.F. (1979) 'On a non-standard dictionary definition schema.' In: HARTMANN, R.R.K. (ed.) (1979). [126]

[148] SHERMAN, D. (1978) 'Special purpose dictionaries.' In: *Cahiers de Lexicologie* 32 (1), 1978, pp. 82–102.

[149] SNELL-HORNBY, M. (1984) 'The bilingual dictionary—Help or hindrance?' In: HARTMANN, R.R.K. (ed.) (1984:274–281). [128]

[150] SNELL-HORNBY, M. (ed.) (1988) *ZüriLEX '86 Proceedings*. Papers read at the EURALEX International Congress, University of Zürich, 9–14 September 1986. Tübingen: Francke Verlag, 1988.

[151] TOMASZCZYK, J. (1988) 'The bilingual dictionary under review.' In: SNELL-HORNBY, M. (ed.) (1988:289–297). [150]

[152] WEINER, E. (1986) 'Standardization and the New Oxford English Dictionary.' In: LEIDLOFF, V. (ed.) (1986:53–68). [191]

[153] ZGUSTA, L. (1967) 'Multiword lexical units.' In: *Word* 23 (1967), pp. 578–587.

[154] ZGUSTA, L. (1971) *Manual of Lexicography*. Janua Linguarum Series Maior 39, Academia. The Hague: Mouton.

[155] ZGUSTA, L. (1984) 'Translational equivalence in the bilingual dictionary.' In: HARTMANN, R.R.K. (ed.) (1984:147–154). [128]

4. LEXICAL DATA PROCESSING

[156] ACL (1985) *23rd Annual Meeting of the Association for Computational Linguistics*. Proceedings of the Conference, 8–12 July 1985, University of Chicago, Chicago, Illinois. Association for Computational Linguistics.

[157] AHLSWEDE, T. & EVENS, M. (1988) 'Generating a relational lexicon from a machine-readable dictionary.' In: *International Journal of Lexicography*. Special issue edited by FRAWLEY, F. & SMITH, R.

[158] AHLSWEDE, T. & EVENS, M. (1988a) 'A lexicon for a medical expert system.' In: EVENS, M.W. (ed.) (1988:97–111). [312]

[159] AHLSWEDE, T. (1985) 'A tool kit for lexicon building.' In: ACL (1985). [156]

[160] AKKERMAN, E.; MASEREEUW, P. & MEIJS, W. (1985) *Designing a Computerized Lexicon for Linguistic Purposes*. ASCOT [Automatic Scanning system for Corpus-Oriented Tasks] Report No. 1. Amsterdam: Rodopi.

[161] ALSHAWI, H. (1987) 'Processing dictionary definitions with phrasal pattern hierarchies.' In: *Computational Linguistics* 13 (3/4), July–December 1987, pp. 195–202.

[162] ALSHAWI, H. (1989) 'Analysing the dictionary definitions.' In: *Computational Lexicography for Natural Language Processing*, BOGURAEV, B. & BRISCOE, T. (eds.). Longman Group UK Limited.

[163] ALSHAWI, H.; BOGURAEV, B. & BRISCOE, T. (1985) 'Towards a dictionary support for real time parsing.' In: *Proceedings of the 2nd Conference of the European Chapter of the Association for Computational Linguistics*, Geneva, March 1985. pp. 171–178. Association for Computational Linguistics.

[164] AMSLER, R. & WHITE, J. (1979) *Development of a Computational Methodology for Deriving Natural Language Semantic Structures via Analysis of Machine-Readable Dictionaries*. Technical Report TR MCS77-01315, Linguistics Research Center, University of Texas at Austin.

[165] AMSLER, R.A. (1980) *The Structure of the Merriam-Webster Pocket Dictionary*. PhD Dissertation, TR-164, University of Texas at Austin, December 1980.

[166] AMSLER, R.A. (1981) 'A taxonomy for English nouns and verbs.' In: *Proceedings of the 19th Annual Meeting of the Association for Computational Linguistics*. June 29–July 1, 1981, Stanford University, Stanford, California. pp. 133–138. Association for Computational Linguistics.

[167] AMSLER, R.A. (1984) 'Machine-readable dictionaries.' In: *Annual Review of Information Science and Technology (ARIST)* 19 (1984), pp. 161–209.

[168] AMSLER, R.A. (1984a) 'Lexical knowledge bases.' In: COLING (1984:458–459). [183]

[169] ANANIADOU, S. (1988) *Towards a Methodology for Automatic Term Recognition*. PhD Thesis, University of Manchester.

[170] BENNETT, P.A.; JOHNSON, R.L.; MCNAUGHT, J.; PUGH, J.M.; SAGER, J.C. & SOMERS, H.L. (1986) *Multilingual Aspects of Information Technology*. Gower.

[171] BINOT, J.-L. & JENSEN, K. (1987) 'A semantic expert using an online standard dictionary.' In: *IJCAI '87. Proceedings of the 10th International Joint Conference on AI*, Volume II, pp. 709–714.

[172] BOGURAEV, B. & BRISCOE, T. (1987) 'Large lexicons for natural language processing: Utilising the grammar coding system of LDOCE.' In: *Computational Linguistics* 13 (3/4), July–December 1987, pp. 203–218.

[173] BRUSTKERN, J. & HESS, K.D. (1982) 'The Bonnlex lexicon system.' In: GOETSCHALCKX, J. & ROLLING, L. (eds.) (1982:33–40). [121]

[174] BRUSTKERN, J. & SCHULZE, W. (1984) 'The word data base of German.' In: *11th International Conference of the Association for Literary and Linguistic Computing (ALLC)*, Louvain-la-Neuve, 1984.

[175] BYRD, R.; CALZOLARI, N.; CHODOROW, M.; KLAVANS, J.; NEFF, M. & RIZK, O. (1987) 'Tools and methods for computational lexicology.' In: *Computational Linguistics* 13 (3/4), July–December 1987, pp. 219–240.

[176] BYRD, R.J.; KLAVANS, J.L.; ARONOFF, M. & ANSHEN, F. (1986) 'Computer methods for morphological analysis.' In: *Proceedings of the 24th Annual Meeting of the Association for Computational Linguistics*. 10–13 June, Columbia University, New York, New York, USA. pp. 120–127.

[177] CALZOLARI, N. (1984a) 'Machine-readable dictionaries, lexical data bases and the lexical system.' In: COLING (1984:460). [183]

[178] CALZOLARI, N. (1984b) 'Detecting patterns in a lexical data base.' In: COLING (1984:170–173). [183]

[179] CALZOLARI, N. (1988) 'The Dictionary and the thesaurus can be combined.' In: EVENS, M.W. (ed.) (1988:75–96). [312]

[180] CALZOLARI, N.; PECCHIA, L. & ZAMPOLLI, A. (1973) 'Working on the Italian machine dictionary: A semantic approach.' In: ZAMPOLLI, A. & CALZOLARI, N. (eds.) (1980), Vol. II, pp. 49–69. [211]

[181] CHODOROW, M.S.; BYRD, R.J. & HEIDORN, G.E. (1985) 'Extracting semantic hierarchies from a large on-line dictionary.' In: ACL (1985:299–304). [156]

[182] CHURCH, K. (1986) 'Morphological decomposition and stress assignment for speech synthesis.' In: *Proceedings of the 24th Annual Meeting of the Association for Computational Linguistics*. 10–13 June 1986, Columbia University, New York. pp. 156–164. Association for Computational Linguistics.

[183] COLING (1984) *Proceedings*. 10th International Conference on Computational Linguistics. 22nd Annual Meeting of the Association for Computational Linguistics, 2–6 July 1984, Stanford University, California. Association for Computational Linguistics.

[184] EVENS, M.W. (ed.) (1988) *Relational Models of the Lexicon. Representing Knowledge in Semantic Networks*. Cambridge: Cambridge University Press.

[185] FUJIKAWA, M. & ISHIKAWA, T. (1987) 'Topics for "Terminology and Machine Readable Dictionaries in Japan".' In: CZAP, H. & GALINSKI, C. (eds.) (1987: 85–122). [041]

[186] GUCKLER, G. (1983) 'A computer-based monolingual dictionary: A case study.' In: HARTMANN, R.R.K. (ed.) (1983: 198–201). [127]

[187] HANN, M.L. (1978) *The Application of Computers to the Production of Systematic, Multilingual, Specialised Dictionaries and the Accessing of Semantic Information Systems*. CCL/UMIST 78/1, September 1978.

[188] KNOWLES, F.E. (1986a) 'Computational lexicography and lexical databases.' In: *Proceedings of the 13th International ALLC Conference*. April, 1986, Norwich. Association for Literary and Linguistic Computing.

[189] KNOWLES, F.E. (1987) *The Computer in Lexicography*. The text of an article submitted for inclusion in 'Wörterbucher. Dictionaries. Dictionnaires: Ein internationales Handbuch zur Lexikographie, HAUSMANN, F.J.; REICHMANN, O.; WIEGAND, H.E. & ZGUSTA, L. (eds.).

[190] LEHRBERGER, J. (1982) 'Automatic translation and the concept of sublanguage.' In: *Sublanguage: Studies of Language in Restricted Semantic Domains*, KITTREDGE, R. & LEHRBERGER, J. (eds.) (1982: 81–106). Berlin: Walter de Gruyter.

[191] LEIDLOFF, V. (1986) *Standardization in Computerized Lexicography*. Proceedings. ESF/IAI IVth Forum, Information Science and Practice, Saarbrücken 15–17 October 1986.

[192] LENDERS, W. (1986b) 'Problems of machine-readable dictionaries.' In: LEIDLOFF, V. (ed.) (1986: 207–234). [191]

[193] LITOWSKI, K.C. (1978) 'Models of the semantic structure of dictionaries.' In: *American Journal of Computational Linguistics*, 1978.

[194] MARKOWITZ, J.; AHLSWEDE, T. & EVENS, M. (1986) 'Semantically significant patterns in dictionary definitions.' In: *Proceedings of the 24th Annual Meeting of the Association for Computational Linguistics*. 10–13 June 1986, Columbia University, New York. pp. 112–119. Association for Computational Linguistics.

[195] MARTIN, W.J.R.; AL, B.P.F. & VAN STERKENBURG, P.J.G. (1983) 'On the processing of a text corpus.' In: HARTMANN, R.R.K. (ed.) (1983: 77–87). [127]

[196] MCNAUGHT, J. (1980) 'The generation of term definitions from an on-line terminological thesaurus.' In: *Proceedings of the 1st Conference of the European Chapter of the ACL*, 1983, pp. 90–95.

[197] MCNAUGHT, J. (1986) 'Computational lexicography and computational linguistics.' In: *LEXICOGRAPHICA* 4 (1988), pp. 19–33. Special Issue on *Computational Lexicography*. URDANG, L. (ed.).

[198] MICHIELS, A. (1981) Exploiting a Large Dictionary Data Base. PhD Dissertation, University of Liege, Belgium.

[199] MICHIELS, A.; MULLENDER, J. & NOEL, J. (1982) 'The Longman–Liege Project.' In: GOETSCHALCKX, J. & ROLLING, L. (eds.) (1982:201–210). [121]

[200] NAGAO, M.; TSUJII, J.; UEDA, Y. & TAKIYAMA, M. (1982) 'An attempt to computerize dictionary data bases.' In: GOETSCHALCKX, J. & ROLLING, L. (eds.) (1982:51–73). [121]

[201] NEFF, M.S.; BYRD, R.J. & RIZK, O.A. (1988) 'Creating and querying lexical data bases.' In: *Proceedings of the 2nd Conference on Applied NLP*, February 1988, Austin-Texas, pp. 84–92. Association for Computational Linguistics.

[202] OLNEY, J.C. (1968) *To: All Interested in the Merriam-Webster Transcripts and Data Derived from Them.* System Development Corp., 2500 Colorado Ave., Santa Monica, CA 90406: 1968 October 1. (Technical Report L-13579).

[203] PRATT, A.W.; PACAK, M.G.; EPSTEIN, M. & DUNHAM, G. (1973) 'Computers and natural language.' In: *Journal of Clinical Computing* 3 (2), 1973, pp. 85–98.

[204] TEUBERT, W. & WOTHKE, K. (1986) 'The Mannheim lexicographical data base LEDA.' In: LEIDLOFF, V. (ed.) (1986:177–184). [191]

[205] TEUBERT, W. (1984) 'Applications of a lexicographical data base for German.' In: COLING (1984:34–37). [183]

[206] VAN STERKENBURG, P.; MARTIN, W. & AL, B. (1982) 'A new Van Dale project: Bilingual dictionaries on one and the same monolingual basis.' In: GOETSCHALCKX, J. & ROLLING, L. (eds.) (1982:221–237). [121]

[207] WALKER, D.E. & AMSLER, R.A. (eds.) (1983) *Proceedings of the 1st Workshop on Machine-Readable Dictionaries*, April 1983. National Science Foundation, Washington DC.

[208] WALKER, D.E. (1984) 'Machine-readable dictionaries.' In: COLING (1984: 457). [183]

[209] WEBBER, H.R. (1984) 'Machine-readable components in a variety of information-system applications.' In: COLING (1984:463). [183]

[210] YOKOYAMA, S. & OGINO, T. (1984) *Document of Magnetic Tapes of Japanese Language Dictionary.* Bulletin of the Electrotechnical Laboratory [Kango jiten jikitepu no dokyumento. Denshi Gijutsu Sogo Kenkyusho Iho] 48 (8), 1984, pp. 30–35.

[211] ZAMPOLLI, A. & CALZOLARI, N. (eds.) (1980) *Computational and Mathematical Linguistics.* Proceedings of the International Conference on Computational Linguistics, Pisa, 27th August–1st September 1973. (In 2 volumes). Firenze: Leo S. Olschki Editore, 1980.

[212] ZAMPOLLI, A.; CALZOLARI, N. & PICCHI, E. (1986) 'Italian multifunctional data base.' In: LEIDLOFF, V. (ed.) (1986:69–86). [191]

5. TERMBANK DESIGN AND IMPLEMENTATION

5.1 General

[213] AHLSWEDE, T. & EVENS, M. (1988a) 'A lexicon for a medical expert system.' In: EVENS, M.W. (ed.) (1988:97–111). [312]

[214] BAUDOT, J. & CLAS, A. (1984) 'A model for a bilingual terminology mini-bank.' In: *Lebende Sprachen* 2 (1984), pp. 49–54.

[215] DE BESSÉ, B. & MOSLER, A-M. (1986) *Analyse des moyens à mettre en œuvre pour rassembler l'ensemble des terminologies multilingues existant en Europe et pour créer une banque de données accessible à tous.* Etude EUROTERM. Agence Linguistique Européenne.

[216] GOFFIN, R. (1982) 'Linguistic criteria to evaluate terminology banks.' In: GOETSCHALCKX, J. & ROLLING, L. (eds.) (1982:159–169). [121]

[217] HVALKOF, S. (1985) *Etude comparative des données terminologiques des banques de terminologie DANTERM, B.T.Q., EURODICAUTOM, NORMATERM, OFL et Siemens.* København: Handelshojskolen.

[218] MACHOVA, S. (1988) 'Terminological data banks and grammatical information.' In: SNELL-HORNBY, M. (ed.) (1988:325–328). [150]

[219] MCNAUGHT, J. & NKWENTI-AZEH, B. (1983) *European Cooperation in Terminological Data Banks.* Centre for Computational Linguistics Report No. 83/13, UMIST, Manchester.

[220] NEGUS, A.E. (1983) 'Software for term banks.' In: SNELL, B. (ed.) (1983:103–110). [225]

[221] NOMURA, H. (1983) 'Terminology banks and dictionaries in Japan and their computer processing.' In: SNELL, B. (ed.) (1983:72–79). [225]

[222] RAVENTOS DE CASTRO, D. (1986) 'Technology transfer and technical terminology in Venezuela.' In: INFOTERM (1986:238–247). [068]

[223] REICHLING, A. (1982) 'EURODICAUTOM: la banque de données terminologiques de la Commission des Communautés européennes.' In: *TermNet News* 4/5 (1982), pp. 45–68.

[224] SAGER, J.C. & MCNAUGHT, J. (1981b) *Selective Survey of Existing Linguistic Data Banks in Europe.* British Library R.& D. Report No. 5643, CCL/UMIST Report No. 81/9, 1981.

[225] SNELL, B. (ed.) (1983) *Term Banks for Tomorrow's World.* Translating and the Computer 4. London: Aslib.

[226] STELLBRINK, H.–J. (1985) 'Terminology work in the gas industry: A model for international cooperation.' In: *Journées d'études: Coopération en terminologie.* Organisées à Clermont-Ferrand les 4 et 5 mars 1985. Rapport de Laboratoire 1985/1. Université de Clermont-Ferrand II.

[227] THOMAS, P. & JUDGE, A. (1989) 'Knowledge-based integrated terminology system (KITES).' In: LAUREN, C. & NORDMAN, M. (eds.) (1989:411–419). [330]

5.2 The British Term Bank Project

[228] AHMAD, K.; ROGERS, M. & THOMAS, P. (1987) 'Term banks: A case study in knowledge representation and deployment.' In: CZAP, H. & GALINSKI, C. (eds.) (1987:341–355). [041]

[229] CANDELAND, R.C. & SAGER, J.C. (1986) *The British Term Bank Demonstrator Model*. CCL/UMIST, Report Nr. 86/1, 1986.

[230] SAGER, J.C. & MCNAUGHT, J. (1980) *Specifications of a Linguistic Data Bank for the U.K.*, British Library R.& D. Report Nr. 5644, CCL/UMIST Nr. 81/10, 1981.

[231] SAGER, J.C. & MCNAUGHT, J. (1981a) *Feasibility Study of the Establishment of a Terminological Data Bank in the UK*. British Library R.& D. Report Nr. 5642, 1981.

[232] SAGER, J.C. & PRICE, L.E. (1984) *The British Term Bank Project*. CCL/UMIST Report Nr. 83/14, 1984.

[233] THOMAS, P.; AHMAD, K.; BARBOUR, S.; JUDGE, A. & REEVES, N. (1986) *Outline for a British Terminology Data Bank*. Terminologie et Traduction 3 (1986), pp. 45–100. Luxembourg: EEC.

5.3 NORMATERM

[234] AFNOR (ed.) (1973) *Etude de l'enrégistrement et du traitement automatique du vocabulaire normalisé à l'AFNOR*. ISO/INFCO 115.

[235] AFNOR (ed.) (1975) 'La banque automatisée de données terminologiques de l'AFNOR: NORMATERM.' In: *Courrier de la Normalisation* 245, Sept–Oct 1975. Paris: AFNOR.

[236] AFTERM (ed.) (1978) *Etude de faisabilité d'une banque de données terminologiques*. Documents contributifs. Paris: AFTERM.

[237] CLERC, M.-G. (1980) 'Le centre de documentation de l'AFNOR et la diffusion de l'information terminologique normalisée.' In: *META* 25 (1).

[238] LEVY, R. (1978) 'Association française de normalisation.' In: AFTERM (ed.) 1978. [236]

5.4 BTQ

[239] CLAS, A. & BAUDOT, J. (1986) 'BATEM. Une banque de terminologie sur micro-ordinateur.' In: INFOTERM (1986:376–389). [068]

[240] FORTIN, J.-M. (1985) 'BTQ.' In: *Proceedings. National Symposium on Linguistic Services. 'Linguistic Services in Canada: Insight and Outlook'*. Secretary of State, Ottawa, October 9–12, 1984. pp. 201–205. Ministry of Supply and Services Canada.

[241] GLOBENSKY, R. (1983) 'The banque de terminologie du Québec, An instrument of Quebec's program to work in French.' In: INTERRANTE, C.G. & HEYMANN, F.J. (eds.) (1983:111–118). [069]

[242] MOTARD, L. (1982) 'La banque de terminologie du Québec.' In: TermNet News 6 (1982), pp. 25–29.

5.5 Canadian Termbank (TERMIUM)

[243] ADSHEAD, M. (1985) 'A new look for TERMIUM.' In: *TermNet News* 9.
[244] CARDIN, M. (1985) 'TERMIUM.' In: *Proceedings. National Symposium on Linguistic Services. 'Linguistic Services in Canada: Insight and Outlook'*. Secretary of State, Ottawa, October 9–12, 1984. pp. 205–210. Ministry of Supply and Services Canada.
[245] DIRECTION DE L'INFORMATIQUE (1982) *Rapport de faisabilité: Projet: TERMIUM III*. September 1982. Secretary of State, Ottawa.
[246] DUBUC, R. (1972) 'A description of the TERMIUM system of the bank of terminology.' In: *META* 17 (1972). Montréal.
[247] TERMINOLOGY & DOCUMENTATION DIRECTORATE (1977) *The Terminology Bank of Canada: An Overview*. Term. & Doc. Dir., Secretary of State, Ottawa.

5.6 CEZEAUTERM

[248] HENNING, J-M. (1985) 'La banque de terminologie de l'Université de Clermont-Ferrand II.' In: *Journées d'études: Coopération en terminologie*. Organisées à Clermont-Ferrand les 4 et 5 mars 1985. Rapport de Laboratoire 1985/1. Université de Clermont-Ferrand II.
[249] HENNING, J.-M. (1986) 'La banque de terminologie de l'Université de Clermont-Ferrand II.' In: *TermNet News* 14 (1986), pp. 20–22. Edition spéciale sur la France.
[250] MOUSLIM, M.A. (1986) *Conception et réalisation du noyau d'un système de gestion de banques de données terminologiques (Système CEZEAU)*. Thèse présentée à l'Université de Clermont II (UER de Recherche Scientifique et Technique) pour obtenir le titre de Docteur Ingénieur en Informatique., 1986.

5.7 DANTERM

[251] ENGEL, G. & MADSEN, B.N. (1982) 'DANTERM.' In: *Multilingua* 1–4 (1982), pp. 239–243. Amsterdam: Mouton Publishers.
[252] ENGEL, G. & MADSEN, B.N. (1985) 'DANTERM.' In: *TermNet News* 12 (1985), pp. 8–10. Journal of the International Network for Terminology (TermNet). Special Issue on the Nordic Countries, PICHT, H. & DRASKAU, J. (eds.). Wien: Infoterm.
[253] ENGEL, G. (1986) 'DANTERM. A system for terminology banks.' In: INFOTERM (1986:332–342). [068]
[254] HJORTH, E.; MADSEN, B.-N.; NORLING-CHRISTENSEN, O.; JACOBSEN, J. & RUUS, H. (1987) *Descriptive Tools for Electronic Processing of Dictionary*

Data. The DANLEX-Group. Studies in Computational Lexicography. Lexicographica Series Maior 20. Tübingen: Max Niemeyer Verlag.

5.8 EURODICAUTOM

[255] GOETSCHALCKX, J. (1985) 'General characteristics of EURODICAUTOM.' In: *Proceedings. National Symposium on Linguistic Services. 'Linguistic Services in Canada: Insight and Outlook'*. Secretary of State, Ottawa, October 9–12, 1984. pp. 198–201. Ministry of Supply and Services Canada.

[256] REICHLING, A. (1982) 'EURODICAUTOM: la banque de données terminologiques de la Commission des Communautés européennes.' In: *TermNet News* 4–5 (1982), pp. 45–68.

[257] VOLLMER, J. (1981) 'Experience with EURODICAUTOM—the terminology data bank of the European Communities.' In: INFOTERM (1981:447–452). [067]

5.9 LEXIS

[258] BERNER, K.E. (1976) 'Das Lexikographie-Informations-System des sprachendienstes der Bundeswehr.' In: *Sprachmittler* 3 (1976).

[259] HOFFMAN, E. (1983) 'Stages in the life cycle of LEXIS.' In: SNELL, B. (ed.) (1983:186–191). [225]

[260] KROLLMANN, F. (1981) 'Computer aids to translation.' In: *META* 26 (1), March 1981, pp. 85–94.

5.10 TERMDOK

[261] SUNDSTROM, E. (1978a) 'Introducing TNC and the TERMDOK system.' In: *International Classification* 5 (2).

[262] SUNDSTROM, E. (1978b) The *TERMDOK System*. 4th revised edition. Stockholm: TNC.

[263] TNC (ed.) (1980) *TERMDOK in 3RIP—A Term Bank Supported by an Interactive Text Data Base System*. Stockholm: TNC.

5.11 TEAM

[264] BRINKMANN, K.H. (1982) 'The TEAM multilingual terminology bank.' In: *Technical Communication* 29 (4), pp. 6–7.

[265] HOHNHOLD, I. (1984) 'The TEAM terminology data bank system, Language Services Department, Siemens AG, Republic of Germany.' In: *TermNet News* 8 (1984), pp. 19–33.

[266] SCHULZ, J. (1980) 'A terminology data bank for translators (TEAM).' In: *META* 25 (2), Juin 1980, pp. 211–229.

6. INFORMATION SCIENCE

[267] AHLSWEDE, T.; ANDERSON, J.; EVENS, M.; NEISES, J.; PIN-NGERN, S. & MARKOWITZ, J. (1988) 'Automatic construction of a phrasal thesaurus for an information retrieval system from a machine-readable dictionary.' In: *RAIO 88 Program Conference on User-Oriented Content-Based Text and Image Handling*. M.I.T., Cambridge MA., March 21–24, 1988, pp. 597–608.

[268] AITCHISON, J. & GILCHRIST, A. (1972) *Thesaurus Construction. A Practical Manual*. London: Aslib.

[269] BONZI, S. (1984) 'Terminology consistency in abstract and concrete disciplines.' In: *Journal of Documentation* 40 (4), December 1984, pp. 247–263.

[270] BOULANGER, J.-C. (1981a) *Bibliographie linguistique de la néologie: 1960–1980, I*. Etudes linguistiques. Québec: Office de la langue française. (Collection Etudes, recherches et documentation).

[271] BS 5723 (1979) *British Standards Institution—Guidelines for the Establishment and Development of monolingual Thesauri*. BSI.

[272] BSI (1981) *BSI ROOT Thesaurus*. Part 1: Subject display; Part 2: Alphabetical list. British Standards Institution.

[273] BYRD, R.J. & CHODOROW, M.S. (1985) 'Using an on-line dictionary to find rhyming words and pronunciations for unknown words.' In: ACL (1985:277–283). [156]

[274] DAMERAU, F.J. (1970) 'Automatic parsing for content analysis.' In: *Communications of the A.C.M.* 13 (6), June 1970, pp. 356–360.

[275] DAMERAU, F.J. (1976) 'Automated language processing.' In: *Annual Review of Information Science and Technology* 11 (1976), pp. 107–161.

[276] DATTOLA, R.T. (1979) 'FIRST: Flexible information retrieval system for text.' In: *JASIS* 30 (1), January 1979, pp. 9–14.

[277] EVENS, M.; VANDENDORPE, J. & WANG, Y-C. (1985) 'Lexical-semantic relations in information retrieval.' In: *Humans and Machines*, WILLIAMS, S. (ed.), pp. 73–100. Norwood, New Jersey: Ablex.

[278] FOSKETT, A.C. (1977) *A Subject Approach to Information*. London: Clive Bingley.

[279] FOX, E.A.; NUTTER, T.J.; AHLSWEDE, T. & EVENS, M. (1988) 'Building a large thesaurus for information retrieval.' In: *Proceedings of the 2nd Conference on Applied NLP, February 1988*, Austin-Texas, pp. 101–108. Association for Computational Linguistics.

[280] GILCHRIST, A. (1971) *The Thesaurus in Retrieval*. London: Aslib.

[281] GULL, C.D. (1956) 'Posting for the Uniterm system of coordinate indexing.' In: *American Documentation* 7 (1956), pp. 9–21.

[282] HOLM, B.E. & RASMUSSEN, L.E. (1961) 'Development of a technical thesaurus.' In: *American Documentation* 12 (3), July 1961, pp. 184–190.

[283] ISO 2788 (1974) *International Organization for Standardization (ISO)—Documentation: Guidelines for the establishment and development of monolingual thesauri*.

[284] JOHNSON, W. T. (1962) 'A polydimensional scheme for information retrieval.' In: *American Documentation* 13 (1), January 1962, pp. 90–92.

[285] JOYCE, T. & NEEDHAM, R.M. (1958) 'The thesaurus approach to information retrieval.' In: *American Documentation* 9 (1958), pp. 192–197.

[286] KAY, M. (1984) 'The dictionary server.' In: COLING (1984:461). [183]

[287] KIPFER, B.A. (1982) 'Computer applications in lexicography: A bibliography.' In: BAILEY, R.W. (ed.) (1982:202–237). [137]

[288] LANCASTER, F.W. (1968) *Information Retrieval Systems: Characteristics, Testing and Evaluation*. New York: Wiley.

[289] LANCASTER, F.W. (1972) *Vocabulary control for information retrieval*. Washington: Information Resources Press.

[290] MCGREGOR, G.L. & MALONE, J.R. (1983) 'The Fact system—a hardware-oriented approach.' In: *Infotech* (1983), pp. 99–112.

[291] MICHIELS, A. & NOEL, J. (1982) 'Approaches to thesaurus production.' In: *Proceedings of the 9th International Conference on Computational Linguistics*, Prague, Czechoslovakia, 1982. COLING.

[292] MICHIELS, A. (1983) 'Automatic analysis of texts.' In: *Informatics* 7, JONES, K. (ed.). Cambridge, England: Assosiation of Specialized Libraries (ASLIB).

[293] MOOERS, C.M. (1951) 'Zatocoding applied to mechanical organization of knowledge.' In: *American Documentation* 2 (1951), pp. 20–32.

[294] NYAH, P.L. (1987) *Keyboarding Errors in Information Retrieval with Particular Reference to English and French Technical Terms*. M.Phil Thesis, The City University, London.

[295] SAGER, J.C. (1982) 'Terminological thesaurus: A more appropriate designation or a deprecated synonym?' In: *Lebende Sprachen* 27 (2), pp. 59–63.

[296] SAGER, J.C.; SOMERS, H.L. & McNAUGHT, J. (1981) *Guidelines for the Establishment of Comparison and Compatibility Matrices between Thesauri in the Social Sciences*. CCL/UMIST Report No. 81/2, Submitted to the Division for the International Development of Social Sciences, UNESCO, February 1981.

[297] VAN RIJSBERGEN, C.J. (1979) *Information Retrieval*, 2nd ed. London: Butterworths.

[298] VICKERY, B.C. (1970) *Techniques in Information Retrieval*, London: Butterworths.

[299] WÜSTER, E. (1955) *Bibliography of Monolingual Scientific and Technical Glossaries*. Paris.

[300] YARKER, C. (1982) *The Development of a Faceted Classification for a Specialised Computer Dictionary*. Final Year Dissertation. CCL/UMIST.

7. GENERAL LINGUISTIC ASPECTS

[301] ALBER-DEWOLF, R. (1984) *Etude sur la création néonymique: Analyse comparée des procédés morphologiques et morphosyntaxiques de formation des termes du domaine de la spectroscopie en anglais, en allemand, en français et en russe.* Québec: GIRSTERM.

[302] ALEKSEEV, P.M. (1973a) 'Lexikalische und morphologische Statistik der Subsprache der Elektronik (Englisch).' In: ALEKSEEV et al. (1973:157–169). [106]

[303] BALDINGER, K. (1980) *Semantic Theory—Towards a Modern Semantics.* Translated by W.C. BROWN. Oxford: Basil Blackwell.

[304] BAUER, L. (1983) *English Word Formation.* Cambridge Textbooks in Linguistics.

[305] BENVENISTE, E. (1966) 'Formes nouvelles de la composition nominale.' In: *Bulletin de la Société linguistique de Paris* 61 (1966), pp. 82–95.

[306] BOULANGER, J.-C. (1981a) *Bibliographie linguistique de la néologie: 1960–1980, I.* Etudes linguistiques. Québec: Office de la langue française. (Collection Etudes, recherches et documentation).

[307] BUCHHOLZ, E. (1978) 'Zum Wortschatz der englischen Fachsprache der Seewirtschaft.' In: HOFFMANN, L. (ed.) (1978). [321]

[308] BUNGARTEN, T. (ed.) (1986) *Wissenschaftssprache und Gesellschaft.* Aspekte der wissenschaftlichen Kommunikation und des Wissenstransfers in der heutigen Zeit. Hamburg: Edition Akademion.

[309] DIKI-KIDIRI, M.; JOLY, H. & MURCIA, C. (1981) *Guide de la néologie.* Paris: Conseil de la langue française (CILF).

[310] DOWNING, P. (1977) 'On the creation and use of English compound nouns.' In: *Language* 53 (4), 1977, pp. 810–842.

[311] DROZD, L. & SEIBICKE, W. (1973) *Deutsche Fach- und Wissenschaftsprache: Bestandsaufnahme, Theorie, Geschichte.* Wiesbaden: Oscar Brandstetter Verlag.

[312] EVENS, M.; LITOWITZ, B.; MARKOWITZ, J.; SMITH, R. & WERNER, O. (1980) *Lexical-Semantic Relations: A Comparative Survey.* Carbondale, USA and Edmonton, Canada: Linguistic Research, Inc.

[313] FLOOD, W.E. (1960) *Scientific Words—Their Structure and Meaning.* London: Oldbourne.

[314] FRASER, B. (1983) 'The domain of pragmatics.' In: *Language and Communication*, RICHARDS, J.C. & SCHMIDT, R.W. (eds.). Longmans.

[315] GOOSSE, A. (1975) *La néologie française aujourd'hui.* Observations et réflexions. Paris: Conseil International de la Langue Française (CILF).

[316] GRICE, H.P. (1957) 'Meaning.' In: *Philosophical Review* LXVI (1957), pp. 277–388. Ithaka, New York.

[317] GUILBERT, L. (1965) *La formation du vocabulaire de l'aviation (1861–1891).* Paris: Larousse.

[318] GUILBERT, L. (1967) *Le vocabulaire de l'astronautique.* Enquête linguistique à travers la presse d'information à l'occasion de cinq exploits de cosmonautes. Paris: Publications de l'Université de Rouen.

[319] HOFFMANN, L. (1976) *Kommunikationsmittel Fachsprache—Eine Einführung.* Sammlung Akademie-Verlag, 44. Berlin: Akademie-Verlag.

[320] HOFFMANN, L. (1976a) 'Languages for special purposes as a means of communication: An introduction, by L. HOFFMANN.' Compte rendu par R. ALBER-DEWOLF. In: RONDEAU, G. (ed.) (1980:1–38). [344]

[321] HOFFMANN, L. (ed.) (1978) *Sprache in Wissenschaft und Technik.* Leipzig.

[322] HOGBEN, L. (1969) *The Vocabulary of Science.* London: Heinemann.

[323] HOPE, C.F.W. (1984) *Synonymy and Abbreviation in Special-Language Compound Terms.* MSc. Thesis, University of Manchester.

[324] INMAN, M. (1978) 'Lexical analysis of scientific and technical prose.' In: *English for Specific Purposes: Science and Technology,* TODD-TRIMBLE, M. et al. (eds.), pp. 242–256. Oregon State University: English Language Institute.

[325] JONES, S. & SINCLAIR, J.McH. (1974) 'English lexical collocations.' In: *Cahiers de Lexicologie* 24 (1), 1974, pp. 15–61.

[326] JUMPELT, R.W. (1961) *Die Übersetzung naturwissenschaftlicher und technischer Literatur.* Berlin: Langenscheidt.

[327] KITTREDGE, R. (1978) 'Textual cohesion within sublanguages: Implications for automatic analysis and synthesis.' In: *Proceedings of the COLING '78 Conference on Computational Linguistics,* Bergen, Norway.

[328] KITTREDGE, R. (1982) 'Variation and homogeneity of sublanguages.' In: *Sublanguage: Studies of Language in Restricted Semantic Domains,* KITTREDGE, R. & LEHRBERGER, J. (eds.), 1982, pp. 107–137. Berlin: Walter de Gruyter.

[329] KOCOUREK, R. (1982) *La langue française de la technique et de la science.* Wiesbaden: Brandstetter.

[330] LAUREN, C. & NORDMAN, M. (eds.) (1989) *Special Language: From Humans Thinking to Thinking Machines.* Papers presented at the 6th European Symposium on LSP at the University of Vaasa, Aug. 3rd–7th, 1987. Clevedon & Philadelphia: Multilingual Matters Ltd.

[331] LEECH, G. (1981) *Semantics: The Study of Meaning* (2nd Edition). Penguin Books.

[332] LYONS, J. (1977) *Semantics* (in two volumes. Volume 1: 1–371; volume 2: 373–897). Cambridge: Cambridge University Press.

[333] MITTERAND, H. (1963) *Les mots français.* Collection 'Que sais-je'. Paris: PUF.

[334] MORRIS, C.W. (1971) *Writings on the General Theory of Signs.* The Hague: Mouton.

[335] MULDER, J.W.F. & HERVEY, S.G.J. (1972) *Theory of the Linguistic Sign.* The Hague: Janua Linguarum Series Minor, Mouton.

[336] NATANSON, E. (1979) 'Formation des termes par abréviation.' In: *Fachsprache* 1 (3), 1979, pp. 83–91.

[337] NYBAKKEN, O.E. (1959) *Greek and Latin in Scientific Terminology.* Ames, Iowa: Iowa State College Press.

[338] OPITZ, K. (1979) 'How does special purpose in communication result in special language?' In: *Fachsprache* 2 (1), pp. 21–27.

[339] PHAL, A. (1968) 'De la langue quotidienne à la langue des sciences et des techniques.' In: *Le Français dans le monde* 61, décembre 1968, pp. 7–11.

[340] PHAL, A. (1969) 'La recherche en lexicologie au CREDIF—La part du lexique commun dans les vocabulaires scientifiques et techniques.' In: *Langue française* 2, mai 1969, pp. 73–81, Paris: Larousse.

[341] PHAL, A. (1971) *Vocabulaire général d'orientation scientifique (V.G.O.S.)*. Part du lexique commun dans l'expression scientifique. Paris: Credif.

[342] RIGGS, F.W. (1986) 'Lexical lucidity: The intelligibility of technical communications.' In: *Wissenschaftssprache und Gesellschaft: Aspekte der wissenschaftlichen Kommunikation und des Wissentransfers in der heutigen Zeit*, BUNGARTEN, T. (ed.). Hamburg: Edition Akademion.

[343] RONDEAU, G. (1979) 'Les langues de spécialité.' In: *Le Français dans le monde* 145 (1979), pp. 75–78.

[344] RONDEAU, G. (ed.) (1980) *Langues de spécialité* 1, Avril 1980. Université Laval, Québec: GIRSTERM.

[345] ROULET, E. (1975) *F. De Saussure: Cours de linguistique générale*. Paris: Hatier.

[346] SAGER, J.C.; DUNGWORTH, D. & MCDONALD, P.F. (1980) *English Special Languages*. Principles and Practice in Science and Technology. Wiesbaden: Oscar Brandstetter Verlag.

[347] SAGER, N. (1981) *Natural Language Information Processing: A Computer Grammar of English and its Applications*. Advanced Book Program, Reading, Mass.: Addison-Wesley Publishing Company, Inc.

[348] SAUSSURE, F. de. (1916) *Cours de Linguistique Générale*. Paris: Fayot. [English Translation by W. BASKIN: Course in General Linguistics. New York: Philosophical Library (1959).].

[349] SCHREUDER, R.; FLORES d'ARCAIS, G.B. & GLAZENBORG, G. (1985) 'Semantic Decomposition and Word Meaning.' In: *Meaning and the Lexicon*, HOPPENBROUWERS, G.A.J.; SEUREN, P.A.M. & WEIJTERS, A.J.M.M. (eds.), pp. 108–114. Dordrecht-Holland: Foris Publications.

[350] SEARLE, J.R. (1969) *Speech Acts*. London: Cambridge University Press.

[351] SEARS, D.A. (1971) 'The noun adjuncts of modern English.' In: *Linguistics* 72, pp. 31–60.

[352] SEBEOK, T.A. (ed.) (1966) *Current Trends in Linguistics* (Vol. III). The Hague: Mouton.

[353] SHANNON, C. & WEAVER, W. (1949) *The Mathematical Theory of Communication*. Urbana: University of Illinois Press.

[354] SIEPER, G. (1979) 'Die lexikostatistische Beschreibung fachsprachlicher Texte.' In: *Fachsprache*, Sonderheft I, pp. 128–136. Wien.

[355] SOWA, J.F. (1988) 'Using a lexicon of canonical graphs in a semantic interpreter.' In: EVENS, M.W. (ed.) (1988: 113–137). [312]

[356] ULLMANN, S. (1962) *Semantics: An Introduction to the Science of Meaning*. Oxford: Basil Blackwell.

[357] VARANTOLA, K. (1984) *On Noun Phrase Structures in Engineering English*. PhD thesis. Turku University.

[358] WARREN, B. (1978) *Semantic Patterns of Noun–Noun Compounds*. Gothenburg Studies in English 41. Goteborg, Sweden.

[359] WEINREICH, U. (1965) 'Explorations in semantic theory.' In: SEBEOK, T. (ed.) (1966:395–477). [352]

[360] ZÜRILEX (1986) *ZüriLEX '86 Proceedings*. Papers read at the EURALEX International Congress, University of Zürich, 9–14 September 1986, SNELL-HORNBY, M. (ed.). Tübingen: Francke Verlag. 1988.

8. DICTIONARIES AND STANDARDS

[361] AFNOR (1980) *Traitement de l'information*. Vocabulaire international de l'informatique. Norme française Z 61-000. Décembre 1980. Association Française de Normalisation.

[362] BRINKMANN, K.-H. & SCHMIDT, R. (eds.) (1974) *Wörterbuch der Datentechnik, Deutsch-Englisch*. Data Systems Dictionary, English-German. Wiesbaden: Oscar Brandstetter Verlag KG.

[363] BRITISH COMPUTER SOCIETY (1984) *A Glossary of Computing Terms: An Introduction*. (4th Ed.). Cambridge: CUP.

[364] BROWN, P. (1985) *Dictionary of Electrical, Electronic and Computing Abbreviations*. London: Butterworths.

[365] BS 3203 (1964) *Glossary of Paper, Stationery and Allied Terms*.

[366] BS 3527 (1976–80) *Glossary of Data Processing Terms*. 13 Parts. British Standards Institution.

[367] BS 3589 (1976) *Glossary of General Building Terms*.

[368] BS 5408 (1976) *Glossary of Documentation Terms*.

[369] BS 6100 (1984) *Glossary of Building and Civil Engineering Terms*.

[370] BS O (1981) *Part 1: 1981; 2: 1981 A Standard for Standards; 3: 1981*.

[371] BUDIG, P.-K. (ed.) (1985) *Dictionary of Electrical Engineering and Electronics*. (in 2 volumes, English–German, German–English). Elsevier Science Publishers.

[372] CHANDOR, A.; GRAHAM, J. & WILLIAMSON, R. (1985) *The Penguin Dictionary of Computers*. 3rd edition. Penguin Books.

[373] CLASON, W.E. (ed.) (1971) *Elsevier's Dictionary of Computers, Automatic Control and Data Processing (in English/American (with definitions), French, Spanish, Italian, Dutch, German)*. 2nd revised edition.

[374] COLLOCOTT, T.C. & DOBSON, A.B. (eds.) (1974) *Chambers Science and Technology Dictionary*. Chambers.

[375] DICTIONARY OF COMPUTING (1986) *Dictionary of Computing*. Oxford Science Publications: Oxford University Press.

[376] ERNST, R. (1975) *Wörterbuch der Industriellen Technik*. Wiesbaden: Oscar Brandstetter Verlag KG.

[377] HOLMSTROM, J. E.; FICKELSON, M. & JEJCIC, D. (1971) *Trilingual Dictionary for Materials and Structures, English/French/German*. International Union

of Testing and Research Laboratories for Materials and Structures (RILEM). Oxford: Pergamon Press.

[378] ISO 2382 (1974–1980) *Data Processing Vocabulary*. International Organization for Standardization.

[379] LONGMAN (1979) *Longman Dictionary of Scientific Usage*. Burnt Mill, Harlow, Essex: Longman Group Ltd.

[380] MAYNARD, J. (1981) *Dictionary of Data Processing*, 2nd ed. London: Butterworths.

[381] MORRIS, W. (ed.) (1979) *The American Heritage Dictionary of the English Language*. Boston: Houghton Mifflin Co.

[382] ONIONS, C.T. (ed.) (1973) *The Shorter Oxford English Dictionary on Historical Principles*. 3rd edition, in 2 volumes. Oxford: Clarendon Press.

[383] PROCTER, P. (ed.) (1978) *Longman Dictionary of Contemporary English*. London, England: Longman.

[384] QUEMADA, G. (ed.) (1983) *Dictionnaire de termes nouveaux des sciences et des techniques*. Paris: CILF.

[385] SCHLOMANN, A. (ed.) (1920s–30s) *Schlomann-Oldenbourg Illustrated Technical Dictionaries* (in 6 languages, English, German, Russian, French, Italian, Spanish). e.g. Vol. 16, 1925, Spinning. London: Lewenz & Wilkinson Ltd.

[386] SINCLAIR, J. (editor in chief) (1987) *The Collins COBUILD English Language Dictionary*. London & Glasgow: Collins.

[387] VAN DALE, J.H. & KRUYSKAMP, C. (compilers) (1976) *Groot Woordenboek der Nederlandse Taal*. 10th Edition. Den Haag: Nijhoff.

[388] VOLLNHALS, O. (1984) *Elsevier's Dictionary of Personal and Office Computing*. Elsevier Science Publishers.

[389] WITTMANN, A. & KLOS, J. (1984) *Dictionary of Data Processing: Including Applications in Industry, Administration and Business (in English, German, French)*. 4th Rev. Ed. München: R. Oldenbourg Verlag.

[390] WÜSTER, E. (1968) *The Machine Tool—An Interlingual Dictionary of Basic Concepts*. London: Technical Press.

INDEX